LIVES OF THE PSYCHICS

LIVES of the PSYCHICS

THE Shared Worlds OF Science AND Mysticism

FRED M. FROHOCK

THE UNIVERSITY OF CHICAGO PRESS

CHICAGO AND LONDON

FRED M. FROHOCK is professor of political science in the Maxwell School at Syracuse University. He is the author of several books, including *Healing Powers: Alternative Medicine, Spiritual Communities, and the State* and *Public Reason: Mediated Authority in the Liberal State.*

The University of Chicago Press, Chicago 60637
The University of Chicago Press, Ltd., London
© 2000 by The University of Chicago
All rights reserved. Published 2000
Printed in the United States of America
09 08 07 06 05 04 03 02 01 00   1 2 3 4 5

ISBN: 0-226-26586-2 (cloth)

Library of Congress Cataloging-in-Publication Data

Frohock, Fred M.
    Lives of the psychics : the shared worlds of science and mysticism / Fred M. Frohock.
        p.   cm.
    Includes bibliographical references (p.) and index.
    ISBN 0-226-26586-2 (alk. paper)
    1. Psychics.   2. Parapsychology.   I. Title.
BF1031.F73   2000
133.8′092′2—dc21
                                                        99-054663

For my parents,
Marie Antonia Domenech and Fred Clifton Frohock

[Socrates:] Then reflect, Cebes: Of all that has been said is not this the conclusion?—that the soul is in the very likeness of the divine, and immortal, and intelligible, and uniform, and indissoluble, and unchangeable; and the body is in the very likeness of the human, and mortal, and unintelligible, and multiform, and dissoluble, and changeable. Can this, my dear Cebes, be denied?

[Cebes:] No, indeed.

—Plato *Phaedo* (Jowett translation)

((CONTENTS))

((PREFACE))

A number of people have asked me whether I believe in experiences outside the parameters of what we call the natural world. The best answer I can provide begins with the following story. One night in late August 1982, my younger daughter, Christina, started crying in her bedroom. I woke up and went into her room to comfort her. She was then eleven years old and having periodic nightmares (which she outgrew fairly easily). I sat down on her bed and began the routine I had found successful in bringing her through these bad dreams and back to a peaceful sleep. "It's just a nightmare," I told her, rubbing the tears from her face. "Just tell Dad the dream, and it will go away." Then, in words that I remember as if heard this evening, she said, "Oh, Dad, I dreamed I was downstairs watching television, and the news came on that your plane had crashed. I started screaming even though I knew you were coming home later."

The chill that went through my body at that moment was at odds with the warm summer air coming through the window. I had two plane trips ahead of me in the next two weeks. The first was to Denver, Colorado, to present a paper at the national political science meetings. The second, the following Saturday, was to Madrid, Spain, to spend a week evaluating a program that I had organized for my university in 1972. I rubbed my daughter's hair gently until she went back to sleep, and then I went back to rejoin my wife in our bed.

The trip to Denver was uneventful, as was my presentation of a mediocre paper at the meetings. The flight to Spain was on a charter airline used frequently by universities that have study-abroad programs. We flew without incident to Madrid, landing at about 3 A.M. the next day. The academic chair of the program was waiting for me and for the students on the flight, who had enrolled in our program for the fall semester. We immediately boarded a chartered bus, which took us to El Escorial for a three-day orientation. The airplane we had arrived on, after being serviced at the airport, turned around for the trip back to New York on the following day and promptly crashed and burned outside Malaga near the beginning of the return flight. Most of the people on board were killed. When I read about the crash in the Spanish newspaper *ABC* a day later, I realized that my daughter's words described the events with painful accuracy, with the exception that she did not relive the dream in front of our TV screen.

I honestly do not know what to make of these kinds of experiences. To accept them as true often requires abandoning fundamental natural laws and principles (in this case no less than time's arrow). The evidence for them is typically restricted to the case at hand. There are almost no inference rules that can be assigned to support the generalities we expect in good explanations. The experiences also have several possible explanations, and usually a secular and a spiritual approach to experience will fit the events equally well. All of this means that there are no good ways to make conclusive sense of experiences like my daughter's. Yet they occur. In some powerful sense my daughter (who is by no means inclined toward mysticism) dreamed what happened.

This much I do know with reasonable certainty: in yet one more version of the Delphic oracle's declaration, we understand very little about the universe we live in even using our best science. So, yes, I believe in the possibility of realities governed by laws that we do not and cannot understand because I am sure that the human intellect commands a very small place in the universe. By default there must be larger realities than those we perceive and try to explain, meaning that there are worlds outside nature as we comprehend it. Perhaps occasionally these realities can be momentarily and partially glimpsed by the sensing capabilities of human beings, maybe in the altered consciousness of prayers or dreams. This partial seeing may include an imperfect look into the future of ordinary life.

The research path from the event with my daughter to this book has been remarkably free of what critics might call roadkill. Many people have openly shared their skepticism and faith with me as I worked on this book, and many more have listened with real or feigned patience as I told and retold the stories, and reflected on the explanations, that the reader will shortly encounter in the text. It was a congenial research journey with no casualties that I could see. I am grateful that my colleagues in the social sciences and philosophy have more or less accepted a professor who is by conventional standards a mystic in his orientations to experiences. "More or less" is pretty good these days for mystics on secular college campuses.

The reader should note that some of the interviews reported here are somewhat old. They were originally part of the field work for *Healing Powers* that I lifted from the manuscript before sending it off to my editor at the University of Chicago Press, Doug Mitchell. My thought at the time was that the material was good, interesting, but did not have much to do with healing (the subject of that book). These pages were set aside while I worked for several years in traditional areas of political philosophy. I am happy to resume these explorations with a new purpose and pleased to be able to retrieve some of the early texts and integrate them with the more recent ethnographic materials introduced here. One benefit of the passage of time for these subjects is that I have had a chance to measure the predictions of the psychics against the events that have occurred. The second section of the last chapter presents this delicious exercise.

The materials presented in the work are diverse on both method and substance, and thus appropriate for a wide range of psychic experiences: multiple theories, a variety of narratives, interview data, history, critical anecdotes—generally, whatever is necessary to illuminate any set of interesting claims on the supernatural. In this sense the work follows P. W. Bridgman's observation that "the scientist has no other method than doing his damnedest." In all uses here of this eclectic methodology, however, the voices heard in the interviews are integrated into the main text to take the examination of psychic experiences directly into real-world beliefs and practices. The goal is to allow the ethnographic materials to fold into literatures and theories in the areas of the supernatural without either domain losing intellectual integrity. This sets up a kind of creative tension that can be quite productive, since we then have simultaneous access to the stories of participants and the competing theories that attempt to explain what the narratives are rendering intelligible. I have believed for a long time that this is the best way to negotiate the well-known research problems of connecting indigenous beliefs with explanatory theory, providing a meta-language that translates across the vocabularies of scholarly communities and the words of those who tell us their life stories, and, hardest of all, retrieving internal concepts and expressing them in generalizable terms that maintain at least some of the original cultural meanings of the concepts.

The book is controlled by these questions: How are claims for supernatural experiences to be regarded? Are the experiences real in some sense, or reducible to causal factors that "explain away" the phenomena (like those that assimilate the paranormal to hallucinations, perhaps psychoses)? The work, organized loosely as a journey, begins with an examination of recent literatures on consciousness. This opening discussion raises the question of how rival claims on the supernatural can fit within the confines of conscious experiences. Then the book turns to field work, beginning with psychics, and moves on to the heroic attempts of the Rhines to introduce experimental science to the paranormal. A discussion of the limits of controlled experiments takes us to an exploration of the supernatural in terms of a broader view of science, one that allows an examination of spontaneous psychic events in the larger worlds of human experience outside the laboratory. This wider canvas stretches easily to out-of-body, near-death, and mystical experiences. At the end, in the last two chapters, I offer conclusions on the possibility of alternative realities, drawn up from the interviews and reflections that form our journeys into the supernatural and from a theory of limits that I am proposing.

The organizing frame for the book is the opposition between skeptic and believer introduced on the first page of chapter 1. This opposition sets up both the theoretical excursions and the interview material. In chapter 2, for example, the believers are represented by practicing psychics and the dominating (or at least intimidating) skeptic is James Randi. Chapter 3 moves comfortably across the early (whom I call "grand") psychics, the efforts by the Rhines to test *psi* with controlled experiments, and the critical examinations of, for example, Zusne and Jones. The most interesting move (I think) occurs in the opening sections of chapter 4, where I begin enlarging the playing field by moving from the skepticism of Will Provine (a biologist) to the lyrical metaphysics of Stuart Ledwith and Ada (both practitioners of therapeutic touch). I am convinced that the main action on the supernatural occurs in the larger terrains of spontaneous psychic experiences, and at this point I take the discussions into this uncontrolled area, accompanied now by a more robust conception of science. The materials (field work and theory) on out-of-body, near-death, and mystical experiences command a new set of understandings of the self, the boundaries of the real (and so also the meanings of the research questions), and the proper methods to employ in studying claims for supernatural experiences. On all points on the journey of this book, the work is structured to allow the reader to *listen* to the practitioners while being guided by the best research in the areas that the practices represent. The reader will notice that some of the stories told in the interviews dominate the best theoretical materials I could find. This is the way it has been in almost all of my recent work and counts as one more triumph of ethnography over the isolated reflections of pure theory.

I should add that in my research I do all of the interviews (no work for assistants here). I tape the sessions, and I keep the tapes. The only exception I make to taping is when the subject objects and I am faced with a choice between no interview and one where I rely on notes, *and* the interview is worth the exception. The only primary subject who did present such a choice in this work was the last psychic included in the first chapter. In this case I did what I always do after such (rare) situations: I went immediately to a quiet place and wrote down my memories and thoughts on the session before I had a chance to forget anything. All of the other interviews used in this book were taped. So the research record is just about indisputable. For the record, however, I have on four occasions used fictitious names for the interview subjects. I do this whenever a subject asks me for privacy, which I provide with the tender shields of a made-up name and sometimes small changes in the factual circumstances of the interviews. But the stories are all intact, whether the subject's name in the text is real or fictitious. Also, again for the record, on a few very brief occasions this work relies on the same uncertainty assumptions found in the recent book I have written in political philosophy, *Public Reason: Mediated Authority in the Liberal State* (Ithaca: Cornell University Press, 1999), a congruence that represents again for me what I have been trying to tell friends and colleagues for years: It is *all* part of the same body of work.

I have been formally and informally gathering material in areas of the supernatural for almost two decades. My interest in these experiences has hardly declined with the passage of time. Some close to me are worried that it is mutating into an obsession. I confess to mixed feelings about this possibility. This book, however, is no more than the latest expression of my current preoccupations (which are still within the domains of Popper's falsifiability thesis). The goal in the present work is to introduce and evaluate a set of disparate arguments on the supernatural, and to enliven these arguments with events that may or may not have happened in the way that they are described by those on either side of the divide over experiences beyond the conventional boundaries of nature. I hope that the book provides a bit of light on some of the most complex, ambiguous, and important experiences we can have.

((One))

DOMAINS OF CONSCIOUSNESS

I

Think of sensations that can occur in an ordinary day: The feel of a wooden table under your hand. Seeing a single shaft of sunlight across the floor. The sound of traffic on a busy street. Smells of cooking food. Each exercise of the senses is a complex amalgam of thought and feeling. We perceive and comprehend events in terms of a language—table, sunlight, traffic, food—that may not be fully tangible or visible, yet provides meaning for experiences. In some fashion, not easily understood, we all use sensory and abstract instruments that function in tandem to negotiate human experiences while remaining at least partially in the background, away from our immediate attention.

The divisive question is, What do we make of our conceptual and sense experiences? Everyone has known a believer and a skeptic on the supernatural. Both of these individuals will feel the table, see the sunlight, hear the traffic, smell the food. They may also share much common ground in making these experiences intelligible, even relying on the same assumptions and employing similar methods of inquiry. That we must test descriptive statements with evidence drawn from only partial knowledge of our surroundings, for example, is a working premise that both the believer and the skeptic endorse. But the scope of reality, and the inventory of objects within the real, differ radically for these two individuals. Those who believe in supernatural phenomena testify to powers of clairvoyance, precognition, and telekinesis, to at least partial knowledge of higher planes beyond full human understanding, and often report the presence of various types of spiritual figures, sometimes including God. The skeptic describes and explains, and sometimes speculates on, a world that has been emptied of extraordinary individual powers and spiritual presences. Touch, sight, sound, and smell represent different universes for the two individuals. For the skeptic, all can be explained by natural laws within our powers of knowing. For the believer, there exists a world behind the sensations, the reality that counts most of all but can never be fully reached.

Modern versions of skepticism take the form of scientific temperaments. Science aims to describe and explain a set of knowable realities that yield their features to theories built on falsifiable statements. It is understandable that scientists doubt the existence of realities assigned a standing beyond human comprehension and offered as the source of meanings for human experience. Doubt is the working attitude of science, and the visible is the natural foundation of scientific reality. But doubt is contrary to the faith that typically characterizes spiritual communities. Those who see the supernatural in experience believe in a reality that can only be partially seen and explained, and in important ways is not falsifiable.

Scientific and psychic communities are operating not just within different understandings of the boundaries of reality, but also of the methods for gaining access to the real. The most readily visible worlds of science are in the realm of light. The unaided eye sees items as light illuminates them. We can expand this realm with instruments. The invention of the telescope in the early seventeenth century extended the visible world by enlarging distant objects, allowing access even to objects entirely beyond the range of unaided sight. Instruments can also reapportion dimensions. The solar system is technically within the visible world of the unaided eye but, like so many macro systems, cannot be seen all at once. The telescope and later, more sophisticated instruments that gather and collate data scaled planetary configurations to manageable proportions.

Instruments also can remove natural and artificial impediments to sight. The vision of damaged eyes can be improved with corrective lenses. Cameras can record that which cannot be seen directly, as when photographs of the developing fetus provide dramatic presentations of a gestational sequence—a scene which would be accessible, if only the human body were transparent. Instruments also provide visual records of the micro world—site of the fertilized ova, among other entries—presenting events that the unaided eye cannot see even when no impediments exist.

Yet all vision relies on knowing. It is a truism that we often see what we expect to see, and what we see depends in some measure on what we know. The art expert has a different visual experience of Velázquez's *Las Meninas* than does the novice looking at the painting with no understanding of art theory and history. In part because of the intimate connections between knowing and seeing, authorities often mediate visual experiences.

The medical expert must tell the viewer, at least at first, what is seen in X rays of the kidneys or photographs of the fertilized ovum. Astronomers had to interpret direct representations of the solar system until the heliocentric view was generally understood and accepted.

Believers in the supernatural dimensions of experiences accept an unseen and unseeable reality and are comfortable respecting this reality as a limiting condition for human understanding. The foundation of all beliefs in the supernatural is an acceptance of alternative realities unknown *and* unknowable in their entirety to humans and governed by natural laws so different from human experience that we cannot fully understand the events covered by these laws. According to many spiritual communities, alternative life forms exist in other realms and can be summoned for Earthly appearances. But these forms of life need not be temporal or even substantial. Both objects and life forms in alternative realities may be so different from temporal expectations that humility quickly becomes a proper attitude for believers: Supernatural realities exceed the grasp of human beings. The controlling thought within these communities is that we can have only partial access to the invisible worlds that occasion our beliefs, and this will have to do. For those who believe in the supernatural, the limits of the visible world disclose nothing more than the conventional boundaries of human understanding, not the limits of reality.

2

The belief that reality extends beyond the conventional limits of the natural world appear in one form or another in all human communities. We know this belief as a common and acknowledged feature of religious cultures, but it is no less familiar in modern secular life. Surveys in Western social practices consistently indicate widespread beliefs in the reality of supernatural phenomena. A Gallup Poll published in October 1988 revealed that 50 percent of the American public believe in angels, 46 percent in extrasensory perception (ESP), and 37 percent in devils. The poll reported that college graduates believe in clairvoyance in greater numbers than do those who did not go to college at all (27 vs 15 percent). Another Gallup Poll, in 1991, expanded those findings: 52 percent of Americans believe in astrology, 46 percent in ESP, and 42 percent in communication with the dead. A Time/CNN poll in 1997 found that 64 percent of the American public believe that creatures from elsewhere in the universe have been in touch with humans. The data go beyond just beliefs. Opinion polls report that from one-half to three-quarters of the American population report that they themselves have had some type of psychic experience.

Those who study psychic matters tell us that reports of psychic experiences are inevitably winnowed down to lower percentages when they are investigated. The acceptable range after explaining away the obvious (and sometimes the non-obvious) is more modest: 10 to 15 percent of the population have had a psychic experience for which there is no conventional explanation. Yet anyone familiar with the size of the American population knows that these lower percentages still cover between 25 and 40 million people. The supernatural seems to be a generalizable commodity in American life, suggesting that a recent president's attractions to biblical predictions and astrological readings were yet more proof that he truly did represent the settled convictions of the people he served. The data are also caution lights in exploring beliefs in psychic powers and experiences. Phenomena so deeply embedded in the belief systems of a culture must be examined with critical care in order to avoid routine subscriptions to its authenticity.

The question inviting our attention is, Why? Why do so many people *today* believe in the supernatural at a time in history when science, arguably the dominant way of thinking in the modern age, has presented a world that does not contain supernatural (in the sense of "beyond nature") features?

One answer is that these beliefs are still exceedingly attractive, sometimes irresistible when one considers the substantial advantages of suspending natural laws even in a technological age. In Woody Allen's movie *Alice,* a Chinese acupuncturist administers a drug that renders individuals temporarily invisible. When Alice doubts the effectiveness of such a fantastic therapy, the acupuncturist dismisses her doubts with the observation that Alice is Catholic and "Catholics believe in ghosts." Though Allen has missed the historical divide between magic and religion, the invisibility scenes illustrate the benefits of overriding the body's cumbersome form. Alice drinks an herbal concoction that, like Gyges' magic ring in Plato's *Republic,* makes the body invisible. The ring and magic potion each provide the unnatural advantage of seeing without being seen. Both Gyges and Alice understand their opportunities, though each has a different schedule of ambitions. Gyges uses his invisibility to seduce the queen and become king, suggesting to the reader of Plato's story the political uses of sex in ancient Greece. Alice merely spies on friends and her husband, who thinks his own extramarital seductions are occurring away from his wife's unfriendly gaze.

Privacy is obviously a fragile principle in fantastic experiences, ancient or modern. Natural laws at least ensure against nosy invasions across the barriers of space, time, and a locked hotel room. But the trade-offs are obvious for those who have the right powers. Invisible persons escape many of the onerous restrictions of nature's laws. More of the world is available to fulfill their wishes, meaning that individual power has increased dramatically. How welcome are such possibilities when compared to the more limited prospects of ordinary life.

Some psychic experiences are terrifying. For every Allen movie, there are many more (like *Flatliners*) that trade on the frightening possibilities of life beyond temporal existence. But the prospect of escaping the limits of conventional experience is always tantalizing, even when things go wrong. The sad truth is that natural laws are often burdens, especially when they track the decay and eventual death of the human body. It can be comforting and even exciting to have access to worlds where limits are routinely escaped and where humans can have powers to secure what normally counts as only wishes or dreams. We may believe in the supernatural because such beliefs make the natural world tolerable by promising a way out of it. Just having these fantasies is a strong sign of mental health. Psychotherapists routinely look at the imagination as a source of stability and an indication of the individual's abilities to cope with the environment.

As part of the research for this book, I interviewed a psychotherapist on the subject of psychic beliefs and on fantasies in general. His words echo widely held views:

> As early as a year and one-half, children are already inventing things. Not only that, but they're being encouraged by their parents. There is a great value placed on being able to pretend and make things up in our culture for various reasons, one of which is that we start very early to bombard children with fantastic ideas. Most of culture is unreal, just things that people have made up to support their way of life or rationalize what they have been doing. So I think that what happens is that kids learn that they're going to have to become experts with illusion, and they begin to sharpen their abilities almost immediately to get acquainted with this whole process of making things up. They become very, very expert at doing it. It's also a very important way that the culture uses for blocking immediate motoric expressions—that is, by giving

an individual a layer of functioning which is fantasy, they become warehouses for storing things that are unacceptable. We encourage our kids to become experts at having this kind of fantasy storehouse for making things up as a substitute for doing what they want to do. . . . Scholars have suggested that there can be no mental health without illusion, seeing it as basic for being able to function in this world of ours. Many no longer see illusion as a deviation, but as a necessity for adapting to the world. . . . It has been shown that de-pressed people are more realistic than nondepressed people. So if you want to be happy and not depressed, you have to have illusions. People get depressed in the world because they do not have enough of an illusory buffer.

In traditional research vocabularies, we would say that beliefs in the supernatural may persist because they provide a kind of adaptive or coping power to their holders that has remarkable endurance. A second answer is also persuasive, however. Individuals may believe in the supernatural because evidence for its existence is both palpable and convincing. Inter-views with survivors of near-death experiences, for example, reveal a certi-tude not easily shaken by psychological or neurological explanations for what they have seen and felt. Such individuals *know* that the person leaves the body for a blissful existence after death. This second explanation is as compelling as the first: Beliefs in the supernatural may be influential and widespread because they are true, not just because they promise unusual advantages or are psychologically comforting.

Complicating the task of explaining beliefs in psychic events is the prob-ability that experiences of the supernatural may be variable with proximity, real to the participant but forever elusive to the impartial spectator seeking an objective truth. It is precisely this distance between experience and ob-servation that creates difficulties in replicating and cataloging supernatural events in a laboratory setting. Another obstacle to scientific treatment of these beliefs is the risk that individuals incur when they report supernatural experiences. Testifying to the validity of psychic events, or just plain admit-ting that one has had a supernatural experience, can be unsettling—for one's job, family, and standing as a sane and competent member of the community. If you believe that magic can be real, that psychic powers are occasionally genuine, that spirits from alternative realities can be contacted from time to time, then, simply put, there are those in both religious and secular societies who will see you as a crazy person. Or worse, considering that the Salem witch trials are hardly an anomaly in human history, you may be subject to unbearable sanctions. Any reasonably prudent person may find it rational to shield experiences with the supernatural from public scrutiny, at least on occasion, in order to maintain professional standing and personal integrity, and even to ensure survival. The acknowledgment of these risks means that the outcome of every empirical study of the supernatural may contain errors originating in a rational under-reporting of the experiences.

These are frustrating problems, for beliefs found in the domain of the supernatural affect almost all parts of human communities. At stake in the way we regard these experiences (whether valid or invalid, for example) are some of the basic terms of social practices, including the nature of the self, the scope of human experience, the rival explanatory powers of science and mysticism, the meanings of life, health, death, the relationships between church and state, and the boundaries between our imagination and substantiated beliefs about the natural world. How a community explains the supernatural helps underwrite its understandings of itself, and its capacities for addressing the known and unknown in human experience. But the issues are broader even than signature statements. The foundations of secular and technical civilizations are challenged by the possibility of supernatural realities beyond human understanding. If a spiritual domain exists outside the boundaries of secular experience, a purely material culture is an absurdity. It is hard to imagine higher stakes with any other set of issues in contemporary life.

3

Karen Armstrong argues in *A History of God* that the idea of God has no objective meaning, but like all terms means something only in context. It follows that an atheist may be asked what conception of God he does not believe in, and the theist may be similarly questioned about which version of God she does believe in. One may say something like that about the believer and the skeptic of the supernatural. Which of many versions of the supernatural does one believe/not believe? These questions can be parsed on both poles: a true believer may be skeptical in order (like the apostle Thomas) to confirm the truth of the supernatural with hard evidence; or one may believe in the supernatural but question particular cases and claims; or one may be chronically suspicious of all putative instances of the supernatural to the point that no case ever passes a conveniently high threshold of proof; or one might believe without criticism or reflection, thus allowing both the genuine and the bogus into one's belief system. It will quickly become apparent that the work here has an affinity for the critical *and* open minds of the first two perspectives, and little sympathy for the dogmatic skeptic and the credulous believer. It should be an easy matter to see that it is the intellect that must guide us through the terrain of the supernatural, not the sympathetic heart.

But the immediate question that follows a recognition of *both* secular and psychic beliefs is also the one that may have no conclusive answer: How is it possible for the human intellect to yield such disparate understandings of experience? The differences that separate the thoughtful believer and the skeptic, after all, are among the more profound one can find or imagine. To hear a capable believer in the supernatural delineate a reality with metaphysical boundaries and inventories can inspire reverence. To listen to a strict materialist account of experience from a skeptical and intellectually rigorous scientist is always an impressive session. But then the questions: What is it about human perception and cognition that permits such profound differences in interpreting and explaining our existence? How can members of human communities disagree so sharply about the foundations of experience?

Questions about the logic and scope of beliefs about reality are to some degree inquiries into consciousness itself. What are the processes and limits of conscious experience, the neurological powers that render experience intelligible, that admit skepticism and belief on the matter of supernatural phenomena?

These questions are deceptively complex because while consciousness is a commonplace in human experiences, it is also a mystery. It is not an isolated mystery, surrounded by lucid and certain knowledge. Zeno's paradoxes, for example, occur as mysteries in the midst of a logic that, to the point of the paradoxes, can do no wrong. The puzzlement is no less genuine, for the paradoxes incline us to question the formal system that yields the mysteries so suddenly, but the mysteries are local. Consciousness, by contrast, is a large and unbounded mystery. To even begin discussing consciousness is to enter a wilderness, an uncharted land where speculation dominates and puzzlement is a state of mind. This much we know: Consciousness is a power or resource of the brain, probably best understood as a process, yet not explained completely in the terms currently used to account for the biology of the brain. As in one of the numerous thought experiments conjured by philosophers, imagine a color-blind neurologist who has provided a complete and truthful explanation for the brain's powers to discern colors. The neurologist would have full knowledge of the biology of color perception but would not know what it is to experience color. Thought experiments like this one elaborate our strong intuitions that there is a kind of internal side to being conscious that may be (and almost certainly is) entirely dependent on biology without being reducible entirely to biology.

The difficulty is that no explanation of the neurological correlates of conscious states doubles as an explanation of consciousness. The best view is that consciousness is a biological condition of the brain. But a complete biology of the brain does not account for consciousness. Why should consciousness occur on the basis of neurological processes? If we suppose (as Steven Weinberg maintains) that the goal of physics is a "theory of everything," and we imagine that goal achieved in the future, we still would not have an explanation of conscious experience given the methodologies that currently dominate scientific theory. Not to put the point too finely, but a complete theory of the physical world in contemporary terms would not even tell us what consciousness *is*. Consciousness seems to be a state not entirely reducible to the laws that currently explain the physical universe.

We must be very cautious with these observations, however, given how little is known about the brain and consciousness. It may be, as John Searle has long argued, that explaining consciousness is analogous to explaining life. At one time life was a mystery distant from the best explanations of science and philosophy. Then research slowly disclosed the powers of natural selection, the chemical nature of genes, the detailed roles of protean molecules, the mechanisms that control and activate genes, and the full panoply of genetic endowments (soon to be entirely cataloged through the Human Genome Project). No one talks about the mystery of life in quite the same way today. It may be that we are at very early stages of research into the brain and that as this complex organism is mapped to the same level of detail that we have available on life, consciousness will be similarly demystified.

But the puzzling irreducibility of consciousness suggests that it may well be a subjective experience that must be explained on its own terms, not in terms of the laws and principles that account for the objective phenomena of the physical world. Some concepts *may* be generalizable across subjective and objective domains. David Chalmers, a strong advocate of property dualism and the reality of irreducible nonphysical elements, has suggested that organizational invariance may be one such principle. Information theory tells us that the same structure will produce the same (or very similar) patterns of information throughout an organization. We might say (tentatively) that similarity of neurological structures produces similar conscious experiences among persons. The problem with this seemingly innocuous suggestion is that it is contestable. The structure of the brain is conditioned by experience, and the nature of conscious experience is influenced by prior experiences, even if what we can see about brain structure remains constant across different experiences.

Of course if we could use without dissent the familiar concept of organizational invariance in consciousness, the implications would be profound. It counts against the possibility that there are zombies among us, those with normal brains but without conscious experiences. It also renders solipsism an unlikely story of conscious states, reduces some of the difficulties that seem to obtain in bridging the distance from self to others, and, of most importance to some conversations, favors the view that silicon chips (not just carbon-based neurons) can generate consciousness if the right neurological *structure* is in place. But we cannot use the concept of organizational invariance in any easy way. It is as contestable as any term in science. It may be that all basic proposals on consciousness, at least at this point in time, are speculative and easy to demolish. The tentative state of observations and theories on consciousness suggests again that no sound explanation of consciousness is likely to be reductionist, at least in the sense that conscious states are explained by some current, more fundamental theory from another field of inquiry. We have to look elsewhere.

4

The best explanation for the wide variation in beliefs on the foundations of human experience is probably derived from the limitations of conscious experience. Nothing like a linear and complete relationship between stimuli and thought is found anywhere in understandings of conscious states. In visual consciousness, for example, we know that the sensory powers of the brain located in the visual cortex are activated in perception. But the connections between the neuronal processes in the brain involved in perception and the subjective experiences of perception are not adequately understood. The physical side of perception is being documented with research into brain functions. Experiments described by Francis Crick and Christof Koch suggest that visual awareness requires the coordinated firing of a selected subset of neurons in certain higher areas of the visual cortical system that may be thought of as "awareness" neurons. These particular neurons seem to provide the complex representations of stimuli that we know as conscious perception. It is interesting for theories of physiology that these neurons are in parts of the brain physically distant from the sensory periphery. But it is unclear how awareness neurons differ from others in the visual cortex. Nor is there any credible theory on how conscious perception emerges from these neurological correlates, nor any account of the conscious state that is perception.

What is known is that a variety of neurological coping devices act on stimuli to influence visual images. Perhaps the most striking of these devices is the brain's ability to construct information by filling in what we might call the missing patterns in a representation. Look, for example, at the well-known figure of the phantom triangle, below. This triangle appears vividly as a complete geometric figure, indicating that the perceiving subject has a power or tendency to construct a whole form from incomplete presentations. Sometimes the brain represses information, as in a phenomenon called binocular rivalry. When only one eye receives the visual input necessary to perceive an image, any motion introduced to the visual field of the other eye can reduce or erase the perception of the image. In the Cheshire Cat experiment, for example, a viewer separates her field of vision with a mirror that reflects a blank area for one eye while the other eye sees a cat (presumably Cheshire). As the viewer moves her hand across the blank area, the cat is diminished and often vanishes. The brain's attention to the movement causes all or part of the cat's image to disappear. Perhaps the simplest pattern of the brain's influence on vision is its compensation for the blind spot. The blind spot is located about fifteen degrees from the center of the eye and is thought to be caused by an absence of photoreceptors in that part of the retina where the optic nerve connects to the brain. It is evident when both eyes are open and objects enter the blind area. But closing one eye eliminates the hole in the visual field. The brain either ignores or fills in the spot. These kinds of optical illusions are repeated in any number of controlled experiments. They put on display the powers of the brain in influencing a wide variety of sensory experiences, and also some of the brain's limitations in organizing even simple perceptions.

The phantom triangle is so vivid a representation of the brain's "filling in" powers that one wants to say, "See the triangle," as if it is really there in the drawing.

Numerous parallel experiments in psychology have demonstrated that subjects sometimes "see" what they subjectively anticipate they will see. Sometimes the powers of the brain distort visual items that are recognizable without distortion when more exposure time is allowed. The early Bruner-Postman experiments asked subjects to identify anomalous playing cards (red spades, black diamonds, etc.). The subjects repeatedly "saw" the cards in terms of their expectations (correct, or nonanomalous, cards). Only when the subjects looked at the cards for longer periods of time were the anomalies perceived. The work of Tversky and Kahneman documents the widespread use of heuristics to complete events by ordering and simplifying data, often with the use of narratives. Studies of science itself have demonstrated that established theories strongly influence what scientists see. There is no mystery here. Studies in biology and neuroscience suggest that the we must use a priori types and categories to order inductive experience (and that these devices are probably the direct and indirect result of natural selection).

All of this research suggests that the human brain, on all accounts the decisive setting for the parameters of consciousness, is a creative and flawed instrument for managing experience. It gathers, collates, reduces, amplifies, and in general organizes information (even at an unconscious level). Environment counts. Interactions between the brain and sensory material are reciprocal, in the sense that the "data" entering the complex resources of the brain actively affect neurological patterns and arrangements. But the ordering powers of the brain are awesome by any standards. Attempts to describe and explain experiences outside the structuring effects of the brain would be unintelligible since we have no literal access to such experiences.

The neurological resources framing experience seem to be both stochastic and poorly defined, however. They may even contain a program that allows wide latitude in making experience intelligible. Roger Penrose has speculated that the foundations of our cognitive powers may lie in the random (or at least non-algorithmic) functions of quantum fields deep in human neurology. An open capacity to make things intelligible may be yet another survival trait, since both the senses and the intellect are represented by systems elastic enough to permit great variation in seeing and knowing. Or the brain simply may be an ineffective organizing instrument in coping with the complexities of experience, and this inadequacy may leave a remainder of "data" partially unorganized and open to rival interpretations. But we can certainly say that the processes of conscious experiences can comfortably house both belief and skepticism on the supernatural. People may in fact have genuine sensory experiences that indicate to them the existence of spiritual realities. Others, with more orderly, or more limited, neurologies, may experience only secular realities. Nothing tight enough to be an effective and plausible adjudicator of these different views seems readily available in our current understandings of neurology. The human brain seems to be an instrument for both spiritual and secular beliefs.

One conclusion is generalizable across all views of reality. Once we accept the structuring effects of the brain in processing information, we must accept that the nature of experience is dependent in some important way on the active mental categories of the knowing subject. A world without human consciousness would not, could not resemble the experiences that define our existence. We must also accept the possibility, however, of different structuring powers in other types of neurologies, and so of experiences, and *perhaps* alternative realities, that vary with forms of conscious life. In addition, since we cannot know the complete inventory of possible ranges of conscious life, there is no reason to think that our conscious experiences are privileged. If more complex forms of conscious life exist, they may have deeper and more insightful accounts of experience. It is precisely the uncertainty of the full range of conscious life that offers a modest discretion in defining the limits of experiences and allows in part for the play across materialist and spiritual versions of experience that may or may not cash out in statements about reality. All that we can say with reasonable certainty is that the neurological conditions of human consciousness prevent a direct and unmediated access to any sense of the real world expounded in material, spiritual, or indeed any theories of being.

5

Cognitive limits amplify the imperfect connections between consciousness and whatever it is we are conscious about. Even the best science today must be humbled by speculations about the scope of the universe when compared to our understanding of it. The universe detected by astronomers and the puzzling uncertainties of the micro world present ample evidence of the severe limits of our ability to explain and understand the natural world. The spectacles of black holes, distant galaxies, powerful gamma-ray bursts from uncharted regions of the universe, pulsars and quasars, the mystery of the universe's origin, the paradoxes of quantum theory, the limits imposed by the speed of light on our powers to see the edges of the universe, the puzzle over what might be meant by the edges of all physical existence—science is filled with events and theories that testify to how imperfectly we grasp the physical contexts in which we live.

An unsettling conclusion slowly becoming irresistible in the scientific inquiries that mark the end of the twentieth century is that the human intellect is incapable of understanding the full logic and arrangements of experiences. The micro world of quantum theory, which appears on the maps of continuous or linear thinking as an unintelligible experience, provides perhaps the best illustration of these limits. In one of the first presentations of its anomalous character, Werner Heisenberg demonstrated that the position and velocity of a micro object could not be determined simultaneously since the light thrown on an object to determine its position will affect its velocity. A number of other difficulties were later demonstrated, presenting a variety of data and theory that simply cannot be managed by the organizing categories of a thinking that seems to work well at the level of ordinary experiences (which is what makes the data, thought experiments, and principles counterintuitive).

The paradoxes of quantum mechanics have been supported consistently with experiments. For example, in June 1997 physicists at the University of Geneva sent pairs of photons in opposite directions to destinations seven miles apart. Communication between the sets of photons was impossible if we accept the limits imposed by the speed of light. When the pairs of particles reached the ends of their pathways and had to move in one of two random directions, the "chosen" directions were always matched between the pairs even though there was no physical connection between them. Also, the phenomenon of "tunneling" is still utterly mysterious. No explanations exist for the strange ability of subatomic particles to penetrate barriers and arrive at a destination before they depart. Looking into the face of these experiences suggests that humility is a more appropriate attitude than the scientific hubris of the Enlightenment. Humans may not be up to the task of rendering nature intelligible in all of its important dimensions. Even the most robust structuring powers of the brain may not be able to bring under intellectual control the complex phenomena that we must frame and order if we are to understand our universe.

There are other limits. The very theories that we use to make experience intelligible have in this century undermined the classical dream of perfect knowledge by demonstrating the limits of our instruments of knowing. The classical effort to unify theory has always had a malevolent virus in its system. Plato was aware of the paradox of Epimenides when elaborating his theory of forms. In this paradox the self-referential powers of language can yield a paradox when a statement is scrutinized with its own claim: "All Cretans are liars" uttered by a Cretan, or "I am lying now." If the statement is true, it must be false. If false, then it must be true. This paradox appeared again in the twentieth century as a refutation for the heroic efforts to ground mathematics in logic and in doing so to generate a system of mathematics that would be complete, certain, and consistent. In the early part of the century, the great mathematician David Hilbert was sure that a logic would be discovered that could provide a secure and unified foundation for mathematics. But this logic was undermined with a startling proof that elaborated the paradox of Epimenides. A theorem developed by Kurt Gödel demonstrated that no system can be both complete and consistent.

Gödel's theorem traded on the shimmering, back-and-forth reflections found in the liar's paradox. Look at the following two statements:

The statement below is true.
The statement above is false.

Moving from one of these statements to the other and back again is an exercise of simultaneous frustration and enlightenment. The contradiction is produced by the referral force of the statement pairs: as each one refers to its mirror twin, it is clear that the arrangement of the two statements self-destructs. In his theorem, Gödel translated the self-reflective paradox into a mathematical proof that begins with the thought that statements about a system are not within the system, and statements within the system are not about the system. For example, "In a right-angled triangle, the square of the hypotenuse is equal to the sum of the squares of the other two sides" is a statement within the system of mathematics, while "Pythagoras's theorem refers to abstract rather than empirical relations" is a statement about mathematics. Gödel demonstrated that a system representing numbers can always represent its own proof relation, and so a statement that this type of system is complete is outside the system and cannot be proved by criteria within the system (it is *about* the system), and (worse) that one can never be certain that all statements within a system are consistent or true (they may be undecidable). In more exact terms, there can be no formal system representing number theory that can be both complete and consistent. Hilbert's program was gone. The dream of a unified system of mathematics turned out to be just that, a dream, and one without possibilities of being realized.

These and other limits display basic imperfections in the instruments of thought that we use to make experience intelligible. There is more. Persuasive arguments in the sociology of knowledge indicate that all knowing might in some way be an artifact of culture. Even our best explanations may be no more than a theory that is local to social conditions, not a hard and objective look at the universe. But the most telling limitation of human thinking is that provided by a growing understanding of neurological structures. Mystical traditions have always maintained that the objective world is a function of the human mind, not an expression of the universe, and this view folds comfortably into widely accepted understandings that we process sensory data according to the chemistry and structure of our neurology. If we collapse for one melancholy moment our experiences and human forms of reality, then we might say the world is the way it is because we are the way we are. To the sociologist's thesis that all knowledge is from a point of view can be added the devastating restriction that the more incorrigible parameters of this point of view may be hard wired into the brain as it interacts with experience.

The recognition of limits in our powers to manage and know experience does not require subscriptions to traditional realism. Nothing in these speculations takes us to an objective reality outside sense perception that is in some causal relationship to experience. If we have no dependable access to anything outside the structuring framework of our brains, then we cannot know with the proofs and tests that represent our neurological powers if there is any external reality independent of our experiences, or if there is any such reality, whether it is an orderly, law-governed, *objective* reality, or whether such a reality affects in any way that which we do experience. The blind man cannot use the instruments of sight to discern objects. This does not mean that other means of access are not available to the intellectually constrained and the sightless man. One might "see" with other instruments (revelation, touch). But the proofs of the intellect are limited in settling on the possibility and nature of an external reality. These limits are also caution signs for accepting any version of idealism, or any of the currently fashionable "social construction of reality" views. If we live in a limited theater of knowing and perceiving, then we cannot say that all of reality is an artifact of the human intellect and senses. There may well be an "outside" to human experience that directly influences our internal worlds. My point is simply that we do not know enough to support or maintain either view, traditional realism or idealism (old or new). Accepting limits does, however, lead us to a kind of oblique or indirect realism. Internal realism tells us that we must at least occasionally talk as if objects exist in order to use our objective languages correctly. On a similar logic, we must sometimes talk as if a supernatural (in the sense of beyond nature) reality exists because the limits of our intellectual powers in making experiences intelligible indicate the possibility of something external.

Limits in our instruments of perception and thought also invite us to be attentive to experiences that *suggest* some larger reality outside the knowing and sensing powers of the human intellect. The "reality" of human experience is that we routinely encounter events that cannot be fully explained with our best efforts. Anomalies that do not fit our intellectual frameworks (not a surprising occurrence given our limitations) may be as common as orderly phenomena. The open questions are, What points of view are appropriate for the experience of puzzling phenomena? and What kinds of metaphysical commitments (material, spiritual) are reasonable in interpreting the phenomena? Also, Is belief or skepticism a more plausible attitude toward the supernatural interpretations sometimes suggested by such phenomena?

Two paths are open to us in answering these questions. One is marked by a strong version of the anthropic principle: the reality we see is limited to the structure of the brain, is not generalizable to other forms of life, and is the only reality to which we can refer. This first route leads to a dead end that yet may be the actual state of things. It supports a closed human community without even speculative proposals on alternative realities. Here is the limitation stated at the extreme: The inferior parietal lobe, the region of the brain that processes mathematical thought, three-dimensional visualization, spatial relationships, and other mental processes, was significantly larger in Einstein's brain than is the same area in people of average intelligence. What is the significance of this? Did Einstein see more deeply into reality as a consequence of the increased size of this region of the brain? If so, we can imagine constructing computers, or artificially enhancing brain size through, say, genetic engineering, as a way to understand more completely the nature of the universe. But if the increased size of this neurological region simply means that Einstein had superior constructive powers for elaborating a universe that is an artifact of the human brain, then we are back where we started, with no important access to realities that are outside our sensing and knowing powers.

The other path is revealed with the thought that our sensing and cognitive limits permit only partial and imperfect access to any sense (if there is any sense) of the whole of reality, but partial access is parasitic on a more complete access to something. This second path takes us on a short line through science to the fundamental assumptions and beliefs of many religions: reason is a limited instrument of understanding; reality may far exceed our grasp, with the result that the unknown must be both an inescapable and profound condition of human experience; the full scope of possible worlds may include forms and forces that exceed human consciousness; and different and perhaps more effective access to the unknown may be acquired through some combination of science, intuition, faith, and pleas for help (such as prayer). The limiting conditions arising from contemporary scientific inquiry, in short, may take us full circle to a new beginning where scientific and spiritual beliefs are compatible after all. On this route the issue of which are the best methods for gaining access to experiences inevitably bears on the interplay between scientific and religious approaches to experience.

6

Sensory and cognitive limits suggest a hard answer to the question of how experience can yield both material and spiritual interpretations. The current mysteries of conscious experience may allow a catalog of diverse and reasonable beliefs on the supernatural because our seeing and thinking are so deficient that we cannot prune enough beliefs to produce a mutually consistent set. Or, put another way, the believer and the skeptic on the supernatural can hold to their respective beliefs because neither type of belief can be decisively falsified. Also, and particularly important in a secular age, the complex range of conscious experience restricts some of the traditional gatekeeper functions of a materialist science. At the start we cannot dismiss terms like mind, spirit, and soul unless we have a definite fix on a material world that grants us permission to classify these items as ethereal. But the simultaneous elusiveness *and* dominance of consciousness undermine distinctions between the physical/material and the mental/spiritual. For example, we do not have at this time in human history an adequate theory of the self or person. Various dualities that distinguish mind and body are no longer plausible in the face of arguments and evidence in continuing inquiries into the nature of consciousness. We *think* currently that consciousness is a biological condition of the brain, perhaps unique to humans, though likely found at lower and perhaps higher levels in other life forms. But we do know that recent work in clinical therapy has questioned traditional distinctions between mental and physical and suggested that the borders between the spiritual and the natural are not as assured as they once may have appeared to be at the height of modern science.

Controlled studies in medicine now routinely deny any distinction between mind and body that asserts the independence of one from the other. Here are some familiar causal chains that link mental and physical states: embarrassment causes some people to blush (a physiological reaction); nervousness can produce sweaty hands and a churning stomach; fear can galvanize or paralyze physical responses. Studies have shown that chronic stress can cause hypertension and perhaps brain atrophy, that psychological trauma can actually affect the biology of the brain, sometimes causing brain damage. The causal paths also go in the opposite direction, from body to mind. Chemicals can affect mental states, in good and bad ways. Trauma to the brain can cause psychological disorders (the tragedy of Alzheimer's, for example).

The best part of these causal arrangements is that mental states can have definite positive effects. What used to be called "will power" can summon truly amazing body power. Anecdotal accounts of physically frail people doing physically heroic deeds to rescue loved ones compete with double-blind studies that disclose odd and rewarding causal paths: those who go to church have fewer heart attacks, those with strong religious beliefs recover more rapidly from severe burns. The placebo effect has produced some remarkable recoveries. A century of psychotherapy (unfairly maligned in current discourses) is based on getting mental states right as a way to avoid and heal at least some afflictions of the body and generally enrich one's physical states. We know, for example, that group therapy can prolong the lives of breast cancer patients, that therapy for mild depression can help postoperative heart patients. The unconscious, notoriously receptive to suggestions in therapy, seems to contain a guidance system. A recent study has identified a part of the brain that draws on emotional memories and is activated to guide decisions before awareness occurs—the source of intuition, in short. And then there is the "zone," that wonderful state one occasionally enters in sports, where the mind seems to dominate the physical scene; the ball is as large as the moon; time has slowed to a crawl, and one's opponents are moving at an even slower snail's pace; and one can do no wrong. One wants to say, Michael Jordan's ordinary day on the court when he was a player.

Therapists tell us that the therapeutic powers of beliefs are best triggered by an authority figure, the shaman in traditional cultures, healthcare professionals today. A kind of kinesis is demonstrated: thoughts affecting the matter that we call the body, which contains the thought. Such connections among different regions of the person along mental and physical lines invite us to abandon the binary self. Abundant evidence indicates that we are unitary selves in which the mind and body are one. This steady and unsteady mix of the mental and material presents formidable problems in disentangling the natural in human experience from what are regarded as mental events. But if we cannot segregate thought and event, then even the most fundamental assumptions of our best inquiries—on human identity, the scope of reality, and the commonsense distinctions between mind and body—may be wrong or inadequate when stretched across all manner of events.

The materialist may still maintain that mental events are complex states of the brain, and therefore the documentation of mind-body interactions is a non-issue. But what may be represented in these studies is the possibility that our thoughts are not reducible to a physical state of the body. The problem in defining consciousness, remember, is that there may be a remainder even after the physical brain is adequately described and explained. The problem for a skeptic on the supernatural is that a hard-line naturalistic science, especially one that depends on some precise concept of a material universe, is not much use in a world where conscious states cannot clearly segregate the mental and the physical. Also, the picture of cause and effect drawn up by unconventional medicine is situated in a human experience that cannot be easily replicated in the laboratory. It is too open, too stochastic, and crucially, the "mental" variables controlled by a naturalistic version of science are often the decisive variables in bringing about an effect. This phenomenon is one of the possible explanations for the healing effects of nutrition and therapeutic touch. The problem is that we continue to think that the mental is not somehow as real as the physical. This thinking inclines all of us (including the founders of spiritual and alternative ontologies) to elevate the physical causal chain, and the controlled experiment, over the larger, less cohesive, and noncontrolled experience of the settings in which humans use their natural mental powers and live their lives.

I once asked a physician how he could live with the placebo effect in his practice since its occurrence depends on the physician conveying to the patient a belief in the efficacy of a substance he knows is a sugar pill without sharing reservations about the truth of the "medicine." How does this faked sincerity affect truth in doctor-patient communications? The answer my friend provided: placebos have good effects, and so we are obligated in our fiduciary roles as physicians to help our patients find what works. Fair enough. To this good answer we can add the possibility that mind may be inextricably embedded in the primary variables of human experience. A physics that tries to cancel the mental may be missing the main point. To understand a complete range of human experiences may require a sound inquiry, with a more robust science in place, into the logic and structure of the mind as undifferentiated from a physical dimension that is itself bound with the mental.

No complete definition of human consciousness seems possible at current states of knowledge. But we do know with reasonable certainty that human experience combines what are currently known as the physical and mental, and that this combination goes far in efforts to define ourselves. The lesson that follows this acknowledgment is both simple and important. Materialism has a thin and fragile base. It does not have the intellectual power to deny authenticity to the spiritual on the grounds that spiritual events are mental, subjective, and so only epiphenomena with no foundation in "reality," or are simply just another part of the physical world mistakenly labeled as distinct by misguided dualists. The distinctions between a "real" material world and a "fictional" mental world are no longer plausible and cannot be used to privilege a materialist science over all other species of interpretation. Put another way, it could be no more than a casual adventure, and perhaps an intellectual disaster, to attempt an understanding of what we now call the paranormal by using untenable dichotomies from an earlier age. We need a more secure map that will guide us in making sense of both psychic and material phenomena, and the methods for determining their authenticity. This map must be drawn up on a particular terrain of recognition: persons are complicated arrangements of the very domains that are used today to demarcate psychic phenomena and a materialist account of the natural world—mental and physical. This recognition suggests that when we come to terms with the boundaries of experience, we will also have redefined who and what we are.

The map that helps us negotiate the differences between belief and skepticism in the regions of the paranormal may well point to truth somewhere in the ground that separates the two sets of beliefs. Any such map may hold the key to a deep understanding of human experiences because so much is at stake in the beliefs. The believer maintains that the world cannot be comprehended successfully without the illumination provided by different planes of reality. The materialist draws up the boundaries of knowledge in terms of the falsifying powers of science, claiming they will lead us to skepticism on the supernatural.

One measure of the profundity of these two positions is that they encapsulate most of the means typically used to adjudicate the disputes they produce. So we must begin from a different location. One source for an early sketch of the boundaries of experience that captures both common ground and strident opposition is in the stories told by believers and skeptics. These narratives can guide us toward theories of conscious human life and its true range of possibilities, including science itself. At the very least they remind us of the importance of induction in science, even when inductive research takes the form of anthropological excursions into beliefs and practices that are antithetical to those scientific inquiries based on a strictly defined material universe.

PSYCHICS

I

Francine Bizzari is a psychic. Like many in her profession, she is a freelance practitioner. She approaches the supernatural as material for a business transaction, offering information for a fee to clients who want to see into the future, understand the hidden dimensions of life, and in general acquire privileged insights into matters of health, love, friendship, family, money, and power. Psychics who provide such services are usually easy to find. In the yellow pages of any large metropolitan phone book, there is an entry for "Psychic Life Readings." Some listings include a disclaimer, "For entertainment only." Bizzari's entry does not. She includes only her name, address, and phone number. Appointments are recommended.

On the summer day that I visited her home for a discussion of psychic practices, the weather was agreeably temperate. The temperature was in the low 80s, sky clear, breeze moderate—wholly suitable even if not entirely typical for mid-state New York. Bizzari lives in a middle-class frame house in the village of Auburn and, like most dwellings in the area, her home represents a fusion of country and city styles that seems to characterize life in and near the Finger Lakes areas: verdant surroundings and clapboard houses mixed with cable television lines and two automobiles in most driveways. I resisted all temptations to ask if she knew what the weather would be like today, or the burlesque answer to her questions about my research project: "But don't you already know?" My purpose for the interview session was practical and direct. I wanted to learn how psychics work and what suppositions about knowing they maintain in their work.

Bizzari began by telling me about her childhood. She had experiences early in her life that are common to psychics. She began to see things that others could not see. She cannot describe this power accurately even now as an adult, or even define it, except to say that each individual has an aura that she can see and read. When she was young, the other children would taunt her by saying, "Don't bother to tell Francine anything, she already knows." The problem—a curse then, but a blessing now, she believes—was that she often could see events before they happened. They seemed embedded in some way in the shifting glow of colors surrounding every living creature she saw.

Bizzari's mother was a psychic. Her predictions were drawn from dreams and always seemed accurate to those who heard them. She was born and raised in Italy and emigrated to the United States as a young woman, where all of her eight children were born. Francine is the youngest. The gift, or whatever it was that her mother possessed, was passed on only to Francine. She remembers that she could tell her mother who was calling as soon as the phone rang. She also used to tell her mother who in the family was going to die next—and she claims to have always been right. Her mother did not find these predictions odd, did not question how Francine did it. She seemed to know and accept that her daughter was different. Bizzari's father, an American whom Francine's mother met in a processing plant in the United States where she served lunch to the workers, did not have a chance to appreciate his youngest daughter's insights. He died when Francine was only eighteen months old.

Later Bizzari did not pay much attention to psychic possibilities. She remembers her teenage years as a pleasant blur of social life and work. Then came marriage and children. It was the death of her mother that seemed to release something in her. The event was especially painful because her mother had been both parents for her. Everything seemed to fall apart afterward. She started having unwanted visions, seeing and hearing things that she could not understand. She also began telling everyone around her what would happen to them, and she remembers that her predictions came true. She felt like she was psychotic, not psychic, and that she needed help.

Two things helped her through this chaotic period of her life. One was the appearance of her mother in a vision assuring her that she would be helping people all over the world with her psychic power. The other was the Edgar Cayce Institute in Virginia Beach. Francine Bizzari believes that psychic abilities are best developed in some master-apprentice relationship. Such an arrangement simultaneously reduces the risk that the psychic will collapse mentally and refines the psychic's natural abilities. Bizzari went to the Institute primarily for counseling. She was told that she was psychic and should find a teacher to help her develop her skills. She returned home and found her teacher, a local man who gives classes to those who sense that they have unusual mental powers.

An instructor in psychic skills does two things that are especially important to students. One is screening. Individuals are tested to see if they are genuinely psychic. The test is both informal and easy to administer. The student must simply do a reading of the instructor's current life and future. An accurate diagnosis and prognostication qualifies as the real thing. Second, the instructor teaches the ethics and etiquette of psychic readings. These instructions include rudimentary advice on handling clients, addressing public relations needs, setting fee schedules, and the like. The courses usually last ten to fifteen weeks.

After taking such a course and having her psychic powers once more confirmed, Francine Bizzari began giving professional readings. She schedules her consultations in her home. Clients call and then appear at the assigned hour to receive news that is distinctive in both source and premise. Her fee (at the time of my interview) for a one-hour general session is $40 to $50; for a past-life reading, $45; a full life reading, $150; and $50 plus $3 postage and handling for a reading by mail. She confesses to being very nervous when she began her practice, but her confidence grew as she saw more and more clients. Today she has a successful practice that includes her own classes on psychic awareness, a local radio talk show, and consulting work for various local and state police and private investigators. She has worked on several missing children cases locally and in other states.

The gifts Francine Bizzari claims in a brochure she distributes reflect the range of psychic powers generally. The list consists of "gifts, available to all who seek, [which] drop the veils of illusion, time and space, and help us to see the Unity of Creation"; clairvoyance ("seeing beyond the outer reflection of reality . . . with the mind's eye"); clairaudiance ("clear hearing with the inner ear."); psychometry (sensing and interpreting "the vibrations associated with an object held"); aura reading ("the reading of the energy filed by the variations of [the aura's] colors and patterns, associated with the person for whom the reading is being channeled"); crystal ball reading ("a point of concentration by which symbols or impressions may be received"); past life reading ("reviewing of one's 'past' lives"); and card reading ("a focal point through which to discuss the past, present and future of the person for whom the reading is requested"). Bizzari has also practiced faith healing and engaged in ghost hunting.

She regards the life of a psychic as some combination of trouble and benefit. Friends do not always stay friends. They fear Bizzari will tune into their private lives. Verbal abuse from skeptics is not uncommon. Bizzari also worries about how her church regards her work. She is a Roman Catholic and is unsure whether the parish priests approve of what she is doing. But she is clear in her priorities. If the church does not accept her, she will still continue her psychic practices because she believes that God put her on Earth to be a psychic. Bizzari regards St. Bartholomew, one of the apostles, as her main spirit guide. She believes that this saint provides information and protection for her.

Her success in reading a person depends on how open the client is. If the individual is skeptical or builds a psychological barrier, Bizzari has trouble gaining access to the information she needs. She is quick to claim credit for overcoming resistance on occasion, however. In one memorable encounter, an individual accosted her in a psychic fair in Toronto with the news that he "didn't believe in this crap but show me how good you are by telling me something." Bizzari picked up immediately the fact that the man was from a minimum security prison, out on a weekend pass. He was appropriately shocked at this insight and immediately became a believer.

Bizzari will sometimes hold back bad news if she believes the client cannot take it successfully. The key to her judgment is in the aura she sees around and behind her clients and in what the clients tell her. If someone comes in and says, "Tell me everything—who is going to die, the works— that is why I am paying you forty dollars," then she will probably go the full disclosure route. But a surprising number of people will say, "Please do not tell me if somebody is going to die—I don't want to hear it." Then Bizzari works around whatever tragic messages she might receive. The main sign is unspoken, however. Strength and weakness are signaled by the aura. She lets these silent indicators guide her on how much to tell a client.

She claims to have predicted a wide range of tragic events, including plane crashes, train derailments, bridge collapses. Like most psychics, however, she sees the future without context. She is never sure exactly where and when a perceived event is to occur. Often she dreams about an event. Sometimes she sees things in the aura that must be interpreted. On occasion a vision appears that looks to her like a movie, vague in places but unfolding in strong narrative sequences. The scenes are sometimes so dramatic that she likens them to a soap opera.

Bizzari also heals, an action she sees as cleansing the aura around the client. She tries to remove the negative energy emanating from a person. Her technique is to use holy ashes that she has secured from a mystic practicing in India. (The mystic sells the ashes by mail order.) She blesses the afflicted person and rubs the ashes on the affected areas. At one of Francine's performances, a woman with a sizeable lump on one of her legs came up to the stage. Bizzari put the ashes on the swollen area and claims that the woman awakened the next morning to discover that the lump had vanished.

The first and last impression that one has of Francine Bizzari is that she is an eminently practical woman with a no nonsense attitude toward her gifts and her clients. Giving psychic readings is something she does routinely because she can do it effectively. Like a hair stylist or a lawyer, she provides services that clients pay for because they can use the information Bizzari gives them. But Bizzari believes that the client remains authoritative over the insights and predictions that she offers.

In Francine Bizzari's words: "If a person comes here for a reading, I tell them what I see. That's it. If you don't like it, tough. I don't contradict myself when I say something. I say it once and that is it. . . . You have free will. You can alter any situation. If you go to a psychic, and they are telling you some negative things, well, Sweetheart, you can alter that. . . . That is where your free will comes in."

At the end of our session, Bizzari narrowed her eyes and looked directly at me: "You talk too much in your work. People use it against you." Then, after a pause, she offered the first name of one of my colleagues: "Does [name withheld] mean anything to you?" It did. "He is not your friend." Later, for the record, the mentioned colleague did emerge as one of my most disagreeable adversaries at the University. No thoughts on how Francine Bizzari saw this. I did promise her to try to say less and think more. Seemed like good advice for all of us in professional life.

2

Anne Marie Folger claims psychic gifts but has never tried to make money from them. She believes that individuals can receive information in ways not involving the five senses, and that she has an unusually strong ability to do this. Her technique requires only a written name. She asks individuals to write a name on a slip of paper. The paper is folded and handed to her. Without looking at the name, simply by fingering the folded slip of paper, she claims to be able to receive information on the person whose name has been written down. She has been doing this exercise in clairvoyance for twenty years and says that her accuracy is remarkably high.

Folger's initial inspiration for psychic reading was Peter Herkoff, a professional psychic. Herkoff was appearing at a local nightclub, and Folger went with a group of friends to one of his performances. She visited him later for a private reading. The accuracy of his information on her life amazed her. The following week she did some research on psychic powers at the public library. The material she read convinced her that the vivid images that had always been part of her mental life indicated psychic powers.

Folger began by trying to duplicate Herkoff's act. The performance involves holding some object given to the psychic by a person and sensing vibrations from the object. Information about the person is to come from the vibrations. Folger had no luck at all with this approach. So she asked friends to write down names on pieces of paper. Bingo, she recalls. The images started coming to her as she held the paper.

Her friends tried to trick her in these early efforts. Once her brother-in-law wrote not a name but a word, "cemetery," on the paper. She says she began getting strong images of a tombstone. But the one experience that convinced her that her powers were genuine came in her second reading. Someone gave her a slip of paper. She started the reading by saying that this person loves cookies and doesn't like to be hemmed in, though she is hemmed in at the moment and trying to get out. It turned out that the man who handed her the paper had written, "Cookie," the name of his dog, who was kept in a pen. Folger is convinced that she somehow had entered the dog's mind for the information.

Entering minds is for Folger the key to understanding clairvoyance. She does not believe that psychics, or anyone else, can read the thoughts of another. But she does believe that one can pick up information, and perhaps ideas though not the words in which the ideas are expressed, by going into the mental states of others. To Folger this exercise is like pushing a button on a computer. You simply relax and allow the images from the other person to enter your own consciousness. Folger explains prophecy as access to another's mind in the future. She does not believe that individuals see future events. But they can enter the mental states of those living in the future and gain access to the future indirectly through the consciousness of future persons.

The images she sees are often direct. For example, she might be talking to a person and see in her thoughts a picture of a marriage contract being ripped up, or a ring coming off a finger. No problems in concluding that the person is in the process of separating from a spouse. But on other occasions the image is less direct. Sometimes she might see a rubber band being stretched to the breaking point. This image also suggests an imminent separation or divorce, or at least marital strains, but it also can mean many other things.

The most difficult images for her to decipher are those that are almost entirely symbolic. For example, Folger once saw a train speeding by at night. After talking with her client she understood the image in two ways: as an obsession the client had with his current work and as a prediction that the work would inevitably succeed. But she concedes that interpretation, not just seeing, is the crucial part of such readings. She also admits the unavoidable conclusion of such a concession—that a baseline of knowledge is often decisive in interpreting symbolic images, for otherwise one would not know the technical implications (economic outcomes, say) of the images.

Folger does not believe in the full range of psychic powers. She regards telekinesis as impossible and claims for it as generally fraudulent. For two years she worked in a university laboratory testing telekinesis, extrasensory perception, and other psychic powers. No experiment demonstrated the slightest trace of telekinetic powers, though many efforts were made. Folger also admits that all of the ESP experiments in the lab came up with insignificant results, or results that were only slightly above statistical averages. She still believes in ESP, though not as an objective exercise in a laboratory setting.

Folger believes that four conditions must be in place for ESP to occur. One is the absence of stress. Folger says that her own psychic powers will not work unless she is relaxed and in the mood. The second condition follows closely on the first. ESP cannot always be produced on demand at a certain time. Instead an atmosphere of casual inattention must be created. Clients who are relaxed and patient will have a higher probability of receiving an accurate reading than those who are intense and demanding. Third, there must be a need for the information produced in ESP. The impartial accumulation of knowledge—often the driving force of scientific inquiry—is not enough. A personal need, whether from love, fear, or whim, must transfer the interrogation from an objective to a subjective frame (but the need cannot be excessively egoistic, like winning the lottery). These three conditions explain for Folger the difficulty in identifying ESP in a laboratory setting.

Folger uses a fourth condition to explain how ESP is possible. She believes that all of reality is fixed by design. An omnipotent God supervises a reality that includes past, present, and future simultaneously. Folger accepts predestination. Each person's life is patterned from the first moment in all of its details. God has given us each a destiny, and nothing can change it.

The acceptance of such beliefs leads easily to ESP, for readings of other minds and even the future is simply a matter of gaining access to the fixed patterns governing human experience. The rejection of telekinesis is also understandable. Altering a physical distribution through mental efforts is arrogant, humans trying to be godlike. ESP, by contrast, requires only a heightened sensitivity to God's designs.

Some of Folger's perceptions have exposed false understandings. Once the faculty head of the ESP lab got a call from a man in a nearby village asking for help in ridding his home of ghosts. Normally the parapsychology group avoided such activity, but the man sounded sincere and rational, and also very much in need of assistance. So a group went out to explore matters. The man was an artist who had just purchased a farm. He painted in the barn, which was where he had seen the ghost on several occasions. Folger sensed immediately that there had been a suicide in the barn. It turned out that she was right. She concluded that the artist, entering an altered state of creativity when he worked, had picked up information on the tragedy and then subconsciously transformed that information into a vision of a ghost. When he accepted this explanation, the artist discovered that the ghost stopped appearing.

Anne Marie Folger, odd though this may seem, does not believe in ghosts. She believes in divine plans, including predestination, and the possibility of access to some part of these plans. In this sense, ESP is no more than a natural phenomenon consistent with her view of reality. Ghosts are only human constructions, epiphenomena with no grounding in reality.

3

Nelson Guyette is a professional psychic who became aware of his powers when he was a pubescent child, which he marks roughly at eleven to twelve years of age. The paternal side of Guyette's family was French-Canadian, though his father was born in Watertown, New York. His mother was a Native American born on a Chipewyan reservation in Canada. The cultural and national diversity of Guyette's family provided him with dual Canadian-American citizenship and the chance to inhabit two ways of life.

Guyette spent his childhood summers with his mother's parents. His maternal grandmother was a spiritualist reader. She read tea leaves and also practiced spiritual healing. Guyette's exposure to spiritualism was not part of his New York experiences, which were dominated by strict Catholic traditions. But, as might be expected with any child, he was fascinated by the spiritual rituals he witnessed during his summers in Canada. At an early age he began to appreciate two approaches to spiritual realities, one represented by the psychic and the other by religious liturgy.

Guyette also began hearing and seeing things as he moved into adolescence that his peers in Catholic school were not sensing. He saw white and black images move across his field of vision that were not there for his friends and classmates. His father told him he needed glasses. He did, and got them, but the images persisted and grew stronger.

The Guyette property in Watertown bordered the north cemetery, which was and is the largest cemetery in Northern New York state. Guyette felt drawn to the area and would often stroll among the gravestones reading their brief histories of the deceased. On one occasion when he was twelve years old, he rode to the cemetery on his new twelve-speed bike and stopped near one of the tombstones. A man came over whom Guyette thought was strangely dressed. He began talking literally, and in considerable detail, about the Civil War. He said that his name was Mark. Guyette looked at the gravestone nearest to where they were standing and saw that the middle initial of the deceased was an "M." He looked back at the man and realized, *knew*, that he was talking to an apparition or ghost.

The conversation with the Civil War veteran was the first experience Guyette had of a reality beyond the norm. It began his lifelong puzzlement over the scope of human experience. Soon after the ghost encounter, Guyette's puzzlement was amplified when he began predicting events. Numbers have always fascinated Guyette. In the parochial school he attended, bingo games were held every Friday evening. Guyette would write on the blackboard the total amount of dollars taken in before the games began. Then, on Monday morning, he would raise his hand and ask Father Peter if the church had a good night with bingo. Yes, the Father would answer, we took in $850. Guyette would point to the blackboard where $850 was written. Guyette remembers himself as the class mouth. In eighth grade he would routinely finish the questions that Sister Patricia began, endearing himself to no one but the other smart alecks in the classroom.

At first Guyette regarded his gifts as party tricks. He went into the media at an early age. At the age of sixteen he was a full time broadcaster, working in Watertown, Syracuse, Utica, and San Francisco. He slowly became more involved in management, sales, and programming, but still he kept demonstrating psychic skills before audiences. Basically he was the performer with a gimmick warming up the audience for the main act. One day Peter Herkoff was the main act at the Three Rivers Inn, a famous landmark theater just outside of Syracuse. Guyette was at the hotel bar drinking a cup of black coffee at 4:00 o'clock in the afternoon when Herkoff walked in. At first Guyette thought that he was a stage hand. Herkoff was dressed in an old turtleneck sweater and had absolutely no airs about him. He simply sat down at the bar and, in a very clipped accent, asked if he could have a cup of coffee. Guyette reached over to the urn on his left and poured another cup of coffee. Herkoff introduced himself and said, "I think I'll be working with you tonight." Then he reached over and took the watch off Guyette's wrist. The watch, a twenty-one jewel Seiko, had been given to Guyette by a close friend who later had been killed in Viet Nam. Herkoff closed one of his hands around the watch and immediately said, "Too bad about your friend." Guyette nodded and said, "Yes, very true." Then Herkoff looked directly at Guyette and said that no good would come of his family, that "they will bring you no good." He also predicted that Guyette would marry a dark-haired girl from the mid-Mediterranean and that he saw two children around him and then "an added child." His last observations, still holding the watch, were that Guyette had a gift, that he would start using it and eventually—in his fifties—would do very well with it in Canada, the United States, and Great Britain, and even talk to members of the Royal Family as part of the romance with success.

Herkoff turned out to be right on the money as far as Guyette was concerned. His family disintegrated in the next few years. His mother became a hopeless alcoholic totally dependent on him. His brother entered a veterans hospital completely incapacitated. His sister began having emotional problems and was institutionalized in Florida. Guyette also found out that his father was not his biological father, which meant that his siblings were only his half brother and half sister. The good predictions also came true. He met his wife, whose mother was from Malta and father from Sicily. She had two children, whom Guyette adopted after they married. Later, much later, in his fifties, Guyette began to have the kind of success with his psychic gifts that Herkoff had predicted. He also remarried in the fifth decade of his life and had a daughter, the "added child" that Herkoff had predicted.

Guyette says that his psychic abilities present themselves in different ways. He does not use watches or other artifacts in his work. He simply touches the left hand of the person in front of him. For some reason this touch sets off a kind of movie or video tape inside his head that reveals private information about the individual and the individual's future. His first wife came to him on a lark with a friend. They stayed four hours as the movie in Guyette's head allowed him to describe in detail his future wife's two small children and other events in her life. It was a fortuitous meeting, one foreseen by Herkoff.

Often the client will help with the information, confirming his observations as he makes them, adding to them when appropriate. But once a woman who was almost pathologically secretive came in to see him. She appeared to be in her mid fifties and had a thick accent, which Guyette placed in northern Europe. Something also told him that she was much older than her appearance. He immediately began sensing travel, a great deal of travel, some of it under the sea. Then he began to get images that made no sense to him. He kept saying "Eva Braun," even though he could not understand what that had to do with the woman. "You are with Eva Braun," he continued, "and how you love to type, type, type." Guyette went on to describe silence in the woman's marriage, a wall between her and her husband. He also saw destruction around the woman and heard explosions while she continued to type. Guyette saw her husband on the phone and then did not see him. Suddenly the movie ended.

The woman, who had said absolutely nothing during the session, looked at Guyette and said, "You are amazing." She then told her story. She said, "I was a writer for Joseph Goebbels. Martin Bormann was my uncle. I used to spend a lot of time at the Bavarian retreat. Eva Braun was my idol when I was a little girl. My husband and I went to Argentina in 1945 and then to Canada. We stopped speaking in 1945 when I found out about the atrocities in the Jewish labor camps. He knew about it. I didn't. When I confronted him about it, he just pushed me away. He kept his national socialism pride after the war. He was on the phone all the time—to Buenos Aires, Berlin, Bonn, New York, and Alexandria, Virginia. But every call was in code. Do you know why I'm here?"

"No," Guyette answered. "Tell me."

"I thought you could crack the code for me. Because when I call the numbers my husband used, they want to know what the code is."

It seems that her husband had left their home three months before she visited Guyette. The man was in his eighties. On the New York State

Throughway, on the way to Cleveland, Ohio, to attend a meeting of those few who had escaped from Germany and were still alive, he had suffered a heart attack and died. Unfortunately for the wife, he took the secrets of the money, of the codes to the hidden accounts, to the other side with him. She wanted Guyette to divine and reveal the codes so she could get the money. He was unable to help her and not unhappy that his talents were unusable in this case.

Guyette concedes limits on what he can see. Obviously if he had access to secret codes or critical numbers like the lottery, he would be immensely wealthy. Sometimes he sees numbers and is not entirely sure what they mean. He kept seeing the numbers 7 and 3 jumping around Peter Herkoff. He knew that these numbers placed together do not mean much in numerology, but he suspected that they were morbid indicators. Herkoff died on May 22, his seventy-third birthday. Guyette had reported the numbers to Herkoff in one of the many joint readings they would conduct on each other, but not his suspicions on what they could mean. Guyette compares dying to winning the lottery. When your number comes up, you pass to the other side. But he regards such numbers as privileged information, not generally available to humans even if they happen to be psychics. Still, he says that occasionally he does see these events. Recently he saw his father-in-law laid out in a funeral home. The vision came about in human reality less than two months later.

Guyette bifurcates his visions into karmic and nonkarmic. He firmly believes that life is laid out for individuals from birth forward. Occasionally he sees things like cars going over bridges and has told clients to have everyone in the family avoid that route to work for awhile. They generally do so and in Guyette's judgment avoid possible catastrophes. But he firmly believes that some things have to happen, and that no amount of warning or prudential avoidance can change the course of these predetermined events. He admits that he cannot always see the difference between karmic and nonkarmic events, but from time to time he senses the inevitability of what he foresees. Then the film in his head is like real cinema. No one in the audience, and no one on the screen, can change a thing about what is to occur.

Guyette believes that everyone is born with ESP to a certain degree. But he thinks that the gift is distributed unevenly in the population, which he regards as consistent with the distribution of all talents. He also believes that human civilization was originally seeded by extraterrestrials, which to him means that we are only partially native to the planet Earth. The extraterrestrial system of life shows up in our possession of ESP. Guyette also is convinced that we will be in contact with our extraterrestrial origins at some point in the lifetime of his generation. He anticipates that this contact will be interesting but not beneficial to humans.

Guyette happily claims that he has never had a client whom he could not "see through," no one so psychically opaque that nothing was revealed. Always something comes through. Once he gave a reading to one of his wife's friends, a woman so distraught with her life that she simply sat mute in front of him. Guyette saw it all—the divorce proceedings, the bankruptcy court, the inner turmoil. But he says that he cut through that chaos and saw a better future, one in which he and his wife were with this woman near the Rio Grande River. Fiddles were playing, they were in a lounge with wagon wheels and electric candles. The food was superb, the stories great, and the woman was with someone out of her past with whom she was in love and who was in love with her. What's more, Guyette saw that the vision was karmic.

The reading was in September. In February, he says, they were all sitting at a table in a very exclusive nightclub outside of El Paso, Texas. The woman was with a former boyfriend, who had joined the border patrol. They were in love again. Guyette reports that they were having so much fun. He was telling his nightclub stories, and his wife was laughing so hard the tears were coming out of her eyes. The entire bar turned around on an electric stage, and fiddlers came in playing Mexican music. There were wagon wheels and electric candles. Guyette says that they were all enjoying the experience and each other so much that no one remembered the reading until much later. Guyette reports that this may have been his best prediction and one of the best times of his life.

4

James Randi is a formidable and relentless critic of all who assert that they have psychic powers. On this sun-filled day we have met at the airport in Fort Lauderdale, Florida, as he returned from a trip. I was scheduled to leave Florida for New York the following day, and since I was staying the night at a hotel nearby, it seemed convenient for both of us simply to find a private room somewhere in the terminal to conduct the interview he had agreed to give me as part of my research into psychic matters. I waited for him at his arrival gate, and we were able to find rather quickly a room that had a sign labeling it as a quiet room. We went inside, discovered that it was indeed quiet, and had the area to ourselves for the taped session. What follows is drawn up mainly from the discussion that we had on that day. I found him to be a gracious and candid subject with all of the intellectual powers he has demonstrated in his campaign against psychic pretenders.

The first thing that is clear about Randi is that he has no doubts about where he stands on psychic matters. He has been a professional magician all of his adult life, meaning (for him) that he has been a systematic liar, cheat, charlatan. Before each performance, he admits to the audience that he is an actor who is about to play a specific part, that of a wizard. But, he cheerfully admits, it is a part in a performance aimed is to get the audience to believe for a short time in the reality of what is patently false. That, for Randi, is the appeal of magic. It purposely and skillfully creates illusions, entertaining an audience with contrived falsehoods. It is not and cannot be a truth demonstration. Randi is convinced that psychics, in claiming truth for their performances, are frauds.

Randi's intelligence was evident at an early age. He was a difficult child, chronically unable to fit in, a gifted youth bored with school and teachers. He was always several grades ahead of other children his age, which denied him a peer group in school. He mixed with students who were in their first or second year of college with the predictable results. Some taunted him and most did not have time for him, though a few did discuss items of mutual interest. He remembers spending most of his youth in the library and in a nearby science museum.

One Wednesday afternoon he went to a magic show put on by Harry Blackstone, Sr., who made a lady float in the air, cut another woman in half, and in general so bedazzled the young Randi that he left the theater in a daze. He wondered if the effects had been achieved through hypnotism, the minds of the audience clouded as by the Shadow in the popular radio show of the time. He went straight to the library (as he always did when he was puzzled) and read everything he could find on magic. The research was helpful in showing him how some of the tricks were done. At a later performance he went backstage to tell Blackstone some of the secrets of magic. The old man was duly impressed. He urged Randi to join a local magic club and visit the magic shop. A local impresario running the club took Randi under his wing and taught him how to do magic. Soon he was good enough to perform for a modest fee at parties, bar mitzvahs, weddings, even wakes and funerals.

Randi was fascinated both by the illusions in magic and by why people experienced the illusions. He had seen the woman floating in air at Blackstone's show, had watched as the magician passed the hoop around and underneath her, and yet knew that what he had observed could not be so. The effects were, accordingly, amazing. When Randi began performing, he was impressed with the audience's amazement at his relatively simple tricks. They liked him and what he did. He began to think of magic as a way to make a living and an opportunity to study the reactions of individuals to illusions.

Randi was also constantly on the lookout for real suspensions of natural laws. He went to Spiritualist churches, supernatural performances of one sort or another, and many faith healing sessions. On every occasion he saw through the performance to an underlying reality that was not pleasant or amazing. People would retrieve the crutches they had thrown away on stage and walk out in worse condition than when they had walked in. But they would have large smiles on their faces and be thanking God that they had been healed.

Once Randi went to a Spiritualist church and observed ministers reading the contents of sealed envelopes sent to the front by parishioners. He recognized the exercise as the "one-ahead" method, a trick where the performer reads the contents of the envelope belonging to the parishioner just ahead of the one being addressed. Randi snatched the papers out of the waste basket and showed a lady in the audience that the envelope the minister was holding was not hers since her envelope was at that moment in Randi's hands. The woman covered her ears and started shaking her head from side to side. She didn't want to know the truth that Randi was telling her. For his efforts Randi was arrested and taken to the police station across the street, where his father was called off a golf course to come take him home. Randi was fifteen years old at the time. Two years later he dropped out of high school and left home with a carnival.

Randi has remained fascinated and repulsed by the capacity of individuals to resist what he considers decisive evidence that explodes a belief or phenomenon. Once he was on a panel in Casper, Wyoming, with Charles Tart, a psychologist and parapsychologist (which to Randi's mind is like being a Baptist who plays cards). Tart explained at the opening of the discussion that he first became convinced of parapsychology when a female colleague in Berkeley, California, had a pre-seeing experience in the last days of World War II. She had been sleeping soundly after a long day of work. At 1:30 A.M. she suddenly sat bolt upright in bed and knew that something terrible had happened, though what exactly had occurred she did not know. She got out of bed, turned on the light, and went to the window. The street outside was still. Nothing seemed amiss. Suddenly the glass in the window shook violently. She thought it was an earthquake, except that the reverberations subsided quickly. Her feeling of dread continued as she returned to bed and sleep.

The next morning she learned that the city of Port Chicago, twenty-five miles from Berkeley, had literally been blown off the map in an explosion of a ship at 1:30 in the morning, killing 130 people. Tart had accepted this as a paranormal event because his friend had actually gotten out of bed and gone over to the window with the feeling of dread before the explosion shook her window.

Randi looked around the room, expecting that people would be breaking out in smiles as they solved the mystery. But there was no reaction whatsoever. So he wrote a question on the back of one of his business cards and handed it a couple of seats over to a geologist he had met before the conference began. The man nodded his head and left the room. He came back a few minutes later and handed Randi a card with a single phrase on it, "eight seconds." The question Randi had asked him was, "What is the difference in time in the arrival of a shock wave through rock and air over a thirty-five-mile distance?"

At breakfast the next day Randi went over to Tart's table. Tart, Randi recalls, was sitting there with a plate of scrambled eggs and a cup of coffee. He reached up and shook Randi's hand and invited him to sit down. Randi then delivered the story of the eight-second delay and the observation that his friend had felt the vibration of the shock wave in rock first, which then had alerted her to the fact that something had occurred. Randi remembers Tart smiling broadly, his mouth full of scrambled eggs, and saying, "Mr. Randi, I expect that is the kind of solution you would rather accept." Randi looked at Tart and admitted, "Yes, I certainly would rather accept that," which to Randi meant and means accepting evidence and the physical laws that the evidence supports.

Randi believes that most paranormal events are products of selective descriptions. A few years ago he was the sponsor of a talented youth, Steven, who wanted to learn magic. Steven lived in Randi's home for a year and a half and went to school locally. Steven's mother Elsie lived thirty-five miles away in New Jersey. One night Elsie called at 3:00 A.M. and woke Randi out of a sound sleep to report a terrible dream that Steven was sick. Randi admitted that Steven had a bad fever and was going to stay home tomorrow from school. Elsie said, "There, I was right. I have these psychic dreams." Randi, fully awake now, pursued the claim. "Elsie," he asked, "when was the last time you called me at this hour in the morning?" Elsie considered. "Monday last week." Randi pressed. "What did you say?" Elsie allowed that then, too, she had had a dream that Steven was sick. Then Randi pointed out that the flu was going around and had been widely reported in the media. Also, he continued, "You have called eight to ten times, Elsie, come on now, with this same dream." Elsie finally agreed.

Randi's point is that if someone had been there with Steven's mother and had not known enough about the situation, the selective description of the event would have produced a standard reaction. "How could she possibly have known? She must be psychic." But the reality was that Elsie had called numerous times with the same dream when Steven was well.

Once Randi had what he thought was an out-of-body experience. He had returned home from a trip and passed through his kitchen where some visiting magicians were playing cards at the table. "Hi, everyone," he had called, "I'm exhausted so I'm going straight to bed." He went in his bedroom, collapsed on the bed, and fell asleep. Then, when he went back to the kitchen late the next morning (where the magicians were now eating his groceries in a sumptuous breakfast), he suddenly remembered his out-of-body experience. He insisted on relating it to the magicians before he forgot it.

During the night he had awakened, still too pumped up from the trip to continue sleeping. He remembered switching on the television set with the sound turned down and feeling tired. He fell asleep while watching an old movie. Then he awakened again during the night and was floating with his back against the ceiling. He looked down and saw himself on the side of his king-size bed tucked under the old green and chartreuse cover that everyone in the house hated. Alice, his big fluffy evil-tempered Persian cat, was sleeping in the middle of the bed. The room was lit in the gray flickering light from the television set. The station was off the air, and the set was making a soft static noise. He was definitely up against the ceiling watching himself and Alice when the cat opened her eyes. They were green eyes, and it was like looking at two holes cut right through her. He could see the green of the antique bed cover through the cat's eyes, green against green. Then he closed his eyes and went back to sleep.

One of the magicians leaned back in his chair and grinned at Randi. "I think I can prove that you did not have an out-of-body experience." Randi waited. The proof began.

"First, this is Harry here." Another magician nodded at Randi. "Harry arrived yesterday afternoon. He is allergic to cats. When he came in the house we put Alice out. She's been out ever since. She's out on the patio now." Randi looked out the window. There was Alice on the patio.

"Second, go look at your bed." Randi went back in his bedroom. The green and chartreuse cover was not on the bed. In its place was a cover with a hunting scene (horses and foxes). It was held in even lower esteem than the other cover and was used only when the first cover was in the laundry. Randi looked down the stairs to the basement and there at the bottom in the big transparent laundry bag was the green and chartreuse bed cover. "The cat had gotten a lot of hair on the old cover, so we took it off yesterday for cleaning," the magician told Randi.

Randi had no choice but to conclude that the out-of-body experience had been a dream, probably recalled as real by the one acknowledged fact of the experience. He had left the television on all night, and it was still on when he woke up in the morning. Randi's point is that if the green and chartreuse cover had been on the bed, and if Alice had been in the house, then he would have been convinced that he had once had a genuine out-of-body experience.

Randi doesn't say that the supernatural is always reducible to the natural, just that it has been in every case he has looked at. As a result he places a very low probability on the possibility that a supernatural world of any sort exists. The reality delineated by scientific methods is the only reliable world for him.

5

A man sits in a chair opposite a psychic. They are outside on a lawn under some trees. It is a hot summer day in South Florida, and he can feel both his jeans and his shirt sticking to his skin. The psychic is a tall and very thin man in his late twenties. His hair is pale blond and long enough to rest generously on his shirt collar. Face modestly chiseled with soft areas of skin under the eyes. He is dressed in a long-sleeved white shirt and loose-fitting black slacks and seems oblivious to the heat. Not a single drop of perspiration is evident on his face or hands. A single wasp moves in sharply angled flight down and across the area separating the two men.

"You are in our space," the psychic announces. "Please leave." The wasp swiftly moves away in a straight line toward the trees on the far side of the yard.

The man notices the small plastic container near the psychic's chair. "I'm allergic," the psychic tells him, "though I probably won't have the nerve to inject myself with the adrenaline if I'm bitten."

The man lets his gaze swing casually around the yard. To the left, a wire pen encloses a large gray dog.

"He's a Pyrenees husky," the psychic tells him. "Ten years old." The dog moves restlessly back and forth within the enclosed area. "This breed is quite large, as you can see."

The man looks directly at the psychic. "How does it work? Are we close enough?"

"You're fine."

"Should I take my dark glasses off?"

"Not necessary."

The man leans back. He feels very relaxed, convinced that alpha waves dominate his brain. It is easy for him to imagine his force field opening up for inspection.

"I will say a short prayer to begin the session. Then, when the spirits begin talking to me, I will give you whatever messages they give me. You may ask questions whenever you wish."

The psychic closes his eyes. "Dear God, guide us toward the light to-day." He remains motionless for a few moments. The man has a brief vision during this silence. A juggler appears in his thoughts. She is dressed in blue and yellow tights and is tossing three bowling pins simultaneously.

"I see a feast, a long table filled with various dishes heaped with food. It has been prepared by a man, a relative who died in his middle years. He is fond of you. This vision means that you may pick and choose in your life, that opportunities are dangled in front of you."

The man waits in the brief silence that follows.

"Another figure has appeared. A young woman. She says that you look like her. She is another relative, someone who died young and rather suddenly. She is offering you two metal urns. They contain water. Water is very important to you."

A cat comes over to the man's chair and rubs up against his leg.

"You are in good health, though someone is now having tooth problems." Pause. "I see some recent stomach problems. Lower stomach. Have you ever had an ulcer?"

"No."

"I think you may have had one. Upper right side. But these problems are gone. You are now stronger than you have ever been, more fit, healthier, though you do not know this. You are more aware of your weaknesses than your strengths. This is very common. But you have accomplished many good things. Try to concentrate more on these." Silence for several minutes. "Both of the spirits are concerned that you have a real weakness for alcohol. Someone in your family, probably your mother's side, was a real drinker. You have inherited the tendency. Do you drink?"

"No. Hardly at all."

"Good." Silence again. "I see something ending in your life, something closing off later this summer, then a new beginning in the fall. Your life is definitely going to take a turn. But for the better. The next year will be very good for you. I see you making money, money beyond your salary, that will make you more comfortable." Pause. "I see you moving out West." The psychic smiles. "Sorry about that if you like it here. But you are definitely going out West, to California, maybe Arizona. You have no ties to the East."

The man feels like he is entering his own personal trance. Catatonic almost, his emotions are on a smooth plane, and everything seems to be connected to everything else. At the corner of this holistic space some movement catches his attention. He turns his gaze toward the dog pen at the precise moment the psychic shrieks and stands up.

"The dog. He'll kill her." The psychic lopes toward the pen. The man sees flashing colors, gold and tan, moving across the fence openings in the form of two animals, one large and the other small. He follows the psychic and sees the dog chasing a cat around the pen in concentric circles that seem to be narrowing toward some disturbing point of closure. The psychic is in the pen shouting at the dog to stop, but the dog is ignoring the commands, and the cat is too deeply in shock to see a way out even with the gate open.

"Let me help." The man enters the pen and grabs the dog by his collar. The animal's strength is immense. The man digs his running shoes into the dirt and is drawn into the fence, where he grabs the wire mesh with his free hand. This halts the animal long enough for the psychic to pick up the cat and get outside. The man releases the dog with a curse on his soul and exits also.

"Lucky he didn't tear us apart." The psychic's arms are shaking as he releases the cat. "Stay out of there, Jennifer." He shakes his head and settles once more in his chair. The man also sits down.

"The spirits." Several moments pass. "Something will happen in August, late August. I see a contract of some sort. You are very demanding, precise. You must not ask for too much. The contract will be good for you." Pause. "An elderly man, someone close to you, will not be able to communicate with you. In late fall he will pass over to the other side." The psychic looks directly at the man. "Does this mean anything to you?"

"You are describing my father."

"We are not allowed to predict the death of a particular person. Only remember that death is simply a passing over. Nothing more." The psychic pauses. His voice then drones on with other predictions and observations on the man's life. The statements continue in a kind of stream-of-consciousness that lasts almost a full hour. At some point he pauses again. "Do you have any questions?"

"I have no questions."

"The consulting fee is forty dollars."

On the way out to his car, the man notices a couple waiting to the side. The psychic greets them brightly. They must be the 1:00 P.M. appointment, the man thinks. He multiplies six (the number of hours in what he assumes is a modest work day) by forty to calculate the psychic's income and concludes that, even in a bad year, psychics do better than instructors in the social sciences, even at prominent universities.

Later the man sits at his desk and carefully lists the various predictions of the psychics, organizing them under three categories: (1) most impressive observations, (2) uncertain observations, and (3) least accurate (or furthest from the mark). Under (1) he places the following: the declaration that someone is having a tooth problem at the time of the seance (exactly the moment when the man's father is having a broken, embedded tooth extracted by an oral surgeon); the observation that the man's mother is having mental problems but that the condition is an electrolyte imbalance and not Alzheimer's; the judgment that the man values freedom and cannot work regular hours in an office, is creative in his work, and that his life is changing (something ending, something beginning); that someone on the maternal side of the man's family is vulnerable to alcohol; that the man has had recent stomach problems but is now healthy and stronger than he has ever been; that the man's older daughter will marry late, possibly live with a man first, and go into entertainment or the theater; and that the man's younger daughter is a humanitarian and will go into some form of public health work (and possibly disappoint by marrying early).

The man realizes that many of these statements go against the inertial movement of current events—his older daughter is going to law school in the fall, the younger is a philosophy major who plans to be a journalist— and several statements, for example the observation on his mother's health, could only be confirmed or falsified over the long term. Still, the reading of his own needs and his daughters' characters impress, and the observations on life change, family history, and the like seem accurate.

Under category (2) the man lists the following: the man's wife loves him and is afraid of losing him; a contract of some sort will be offered to him in late August; the man will make independent money the following year and also begin publishing in magazines; he will buy a car in that year because he wants to, not because he has to; his father will die in late fall; and the man will resettle in the West in the near future.

All of these statements are possible, though most seem unlikely and some just remote. Since the man cares little about cars and has never bought one in the absence of overriding need, lavishing money and attention on a new car would seem to require a metamorphosis of his entire being. Also, the man's track record for making money outside of his salary would not induce even reckless speculators to bet much on the prospects. And since the man's love of the eastern coast and indifference to western styles and values are legendary, the predicted geographical move is highly unlikely. But each statement is coherent and possible, including his wife's fears and the death of a beloved eighty-year-old man within six months.

The least accurate statements are not predictions (which, however outlandish, could turn out to be true in some possible future world), but observations. Among these are: the psychic's statement that the man could be in, or have enjoyed, law enforcement; that the man is a bit dour and needs to use his good sense of humor at a deeper level; that the man is a perfectionist who needs things just right while tolerating laxness in others; and that the man needs to work harder and find a way not to procrastinate too much.

Since the man has been anti-authoritarian since birth, the thought of law enforcement is ludicrous. The man also perceives himself as (a) a maniac in play and things humorous, and (b) an individual obsessed with his work (though definitely engaged in sweet procrastinations at the time of the reading). Still, at least some of the reasons for relegating these observations to the least-likely category are self-perceptions which could themselves be erroneous.

That same week the man visits three other psychics and compares their statements. Within four minutes in each of two of the other readings, the psychic tells him without the slightest uncertainty that he will be relocating in the West, "probably California, but possibly Arizona or Colorado. But definitely a western state." Both of these psychics also tell the man that he will succeed wonderfully in his work in the coming year, and they offer observations about his marriage and his two daughters that sometimes seem right on the mark and other times are not even close. Two of the three psychics caution him about his eating habits and some lower stomach problems and mention a seminar in Toronto, Canada, that will benefit his work. One of the psychics introduces the first names of individuals, warning the man about some and encouraging closer relationships with others. This psychic also warns the man that something will be stolen from his car in the near future. Another psychic tells the man that he is too impatient, and that he gets down when his work is not going well. Still another tells him that she can see a cloud over his head, but this is not something he should worry about because artists and writers sometimes do their most creative work under such a cloud.

At the end of the week the man records the following observations on psychic readings drawn up from his own experiences. First, psychic sessions establish a rapport between psychic and client that helps the psychic to read the client's responses to observations and predictions. Sometimes a psychic will key off responses in direct ways. One psychic, for example, would interrupt a stream-of-consciousness run of statements with the phrase, "Does any of this mean anything to you?" A negative response would lead the psychic to say, "I don't know where that stuff is coming from" and begin a different line of thought. Second, almost every psychic statement is general enough to fit somewhere in anyone's life. We all have health problems, and most of us suffer gastric disturbances from time to time. Also, every marriage has strains and uncertainties, and children can be fitted into almost any prognostication given the undefined nature of their lives and the robust scope of possibilities in the long future ahead of them.

These two observations suggest the obvious. Psychic readings are so general that anyone wishing to do so can find truth in them. But, also, the sessions are pleasant diversions that can fill leisure time in harmless ways so long as (a) important actions are not undertaken on information derived solely from psychic readings, and (b) the monetary fee can be paid without hardship or discomfort.

Clients should also realize that psychics differ in abilities claimed and services offered. But even the weakest psychic believes two extraordinary things. One is that the sensory world does not exhaust reality but is only a limited entry in a larger universe that exceeds human experience. The second is that psychic abilities provide special access to dimensions of human experience that are normally inaccessible (the future, the deeper intentions of others, states of health, and so on) *and* to a spiritual realm that furnishes privileged knowledge about human experience. One must be thoughtful about the possibilities. If psychic powers are genuine, then readings are very important events.

The one event that continues to puzzle the man as he reflects on psychic powers is the absence of commentary on the dog attacking the cat during the South Florida reading. If all occurrences are taken as meaningful for particular lives, even as partial expressions of a grand design, then attempted homicide on a summer afternoon even among animals must signify something. But the psychic made no mention of the frantic action between the two pets. The man is left with memory fragments only: small pockets of dust arising from the pursuit and flight; the heavy strength of the dog; the smells of animal excrement and sweat. The event remains random and untranslated.

((Three))

EXPERIMENTAL CONTROLS

I

The scene used to occur almost daily in Greenwich Village. Two men in their early twenties are running a shell game. Six pedestrians, all reasonably well attired and apparently visitors to New York City, have stopped to watch as the shorter of the two men, tersely referred to (only once) as King by his partner, places a silver ball under one of three shells and begins slowly moving the shells over the top of a table designed to be folded up quickly if need arises. His associate is the pitch man, urging the witnesses to place bets, to win the easy money that will be theirs if they guess which shell covers the ball. One member of the crowd places fifty dollars on the table. He guesses correctly and wins. He bets the same amount again. Another, a young man urged on by his two friends, quickly counts his money and also lays down fifty dollars for the next round. King slows the movement of the shells and then stops. Both bettors point to one of the shells. He turns it over. The silver ball is underneath. High fives all around as the two men take their fifty and the fifty they have won.

But wait. The ante goes up and the odds get better. Now the invitation is to bet one hundred dollars at two-to-one odds. Win and collect two hundred dollars. Both men accept and place their money on the table. The pitch keeps up his patter, trying to draw more spectators into the game while King moves the shells. This time the movement has increased in speed, at first imperceptibly and then obviously. The human eye cannot accurately track the movements of the shells. King stops and leans back. There is a pause as the two men look at the three shells, now immobile and arranged in a rough triangle. Each guesses a different shell. Both are wrong. King lifts the third shell. Underneath is the silver ball. Quickly the pitch gives even better odds. Three-to-one on another hundred. The young men quickly place the money on the table. King is a no-nonsense player on this iteration of the game. He deftly moves the shells with a speed that makes locating the ball pure guesswork. Both men are wrong again. They leave the game. One walks up Fifth Avenue talking animatedly with his two friends. The other returns a few minutes later to discuss whether they could have milked another bet from the player. He is the shill for King and the pitch, there to encourage the spectators, to increase the betting by his own "success."

Suckers, the skeptic would say. But the scam works on commonsense beliefs and gut feelings. The spectators believe in the shill. They also believe in the intuitive powers of the human mind to divine and perhaps even control the physical location of the silver ball, and they accept the conceit that the eye is the dominant instrument in sense experience. King knows better. He bets his resources on the speed of his hands.

Now let me describe another scene. A magician is on a stage, a single spotlight encasing him in a white light. He is dressed in a dark blue suit, white shirt with yellow tie, black socks and shoes. He is pulling one small rabbit after another out of a top hat that could not hold even one of the rabbits. An assistant, a young woman dressed in a white dinner jacket and black shorts, and wearing boots that extend to a point above her knees, takes each rabbit from the magician as he removes it from the hat. After a dozen rabbits have been extracted, the magician places the hat on his head. It begins moving immediately. He removes it and looks inside. Then he reaches in and takes out a white dove. He throws it into the air, and it flies up into the darkness above the stage. When the audience looks back at the magician they see a cloud of smoke filling the stage. When the smoke clears the stage is empty.

Now see this scene: A magician is sitting at a table. She is performing a card trick made famous by Ricky Jay. The trick involves producing playing cards, say deuces, one after another from one's empty hands, then placing the cards between one's teeth until, say, four have been produced. Then the cards are removed to show that they have become the four aces. The magician does the trick successfully. A silence follows. Then she proceeds with a variation on another Jay trick. She asks one of the spectators to select a card from a deck that she has fanned across the table. He picks up a card, looks at it, then replaces it in the deck. The magician shuffles the deck, then spreads the cards out on the table. The target card is missing. She suggests that the man look in his coat pocket. He does and retrieves the card he had selected. The group of spectators smile almost as one and begin applauding. They are not sure what they have seen, except that the experience has been a source of deep and unexplained pleasure.

This joy in encountering powers that seem to be outside the limits of the natural world yields both a gift and a test for any exploration of the supernatural. The gift is a range of experiences enriched by possibilities beyond the "normal," which allows us to spin out fantasies about doing better and greater things in life. But the fantasies can be seriously considered as practical guides for experience only if the powers are genuine. Like the gambler armed with the foolproof system, the rewards of the evening's wagers are in direct proportion to the validity of the system. For me, the key to understanding King's game (I was one of the spectators) was the collapsible table. A quick disappearance may be one of the safety nets needed for all practices that work too well to be anything but scams. Maybe the caveat required as we assign truth tests to various claims for supernatural powers is this: pay attention to the collapsible table. If arguments and events need an escape mechanism, we have reason to doubt the validity of the game we are inspecting.

2

Magic, according to *The American Heritage Dictionary,* is "the art that purports to control or forecast natural events, effects, or forces by invoking the supernatural." It is an art present in the earliest human experiences. Paleolithic cave drawings portray magic ceremonies in the hunt. Spiritual shrines for magic are found throughout the Neolithic period. The Ionians of ancient Greece regarded nature as animated by spirits that could be influenced by spells, divinations, incantations of various sorts. Magic and religion were closely aligned in all early human communities (though some scholars, notably Frazer in *The Golden Bough,* regard magic as the more primordial practice). The pre-Christian worlds of Egypt, Greece, and Rome were dense with magicians who claimed access to the divine, not to be confused with the moral, and were prepared to provide supernatural powers for a fee. All fundamental theory seeks the codes that can explain experience and provide instruments to control events. The earliest forms of these codes were framed by the magician summoning the secrets that unlock privileged powers.

Gonzáles-Whippler draws several distinctions between magic and religion. The shaman using magic is drawing upon the supernatural on his own, while the supplicant praying for a miracle is subordinating his will to a higher power. Magic in general is more oriented to the individual and the human community. Most religions, certainly Christianity, defer to the higher purposes of God and define human goods in terms of a divine plan contrived by more powerful and knowing beings. The magician absorbs and uses power as a kind of demigod trying to dominate natural forces. Humans are celebrated in magic, the gods are the primary variables in religions.

Magic, more than religion, represents what appears to be a basic component of the human species: a need to establish dominion over the natural environment. What is curious and complex about this need is that it must fail at the earliest stages of individual experience. Attachment theory and studies of cognitive development indicate that infants acquire identity in two ways: bonding with caretakers and encountering the resistance of the world to simple wants and intentions. Put simply, the human self is a product of love and an awareness that thoughts do not have natural kinetic powers. This almost paradoxical combination of early union with another and a separation of self from surroundings formed on the differences between thought and act seems to be required in all cultures that nurture humans from children to competent adults. But the impulse to close the distance between thinking it so and making it so is also a feature of all mature human communities. Most of the dazzling machines of Western technology are instruments to extend and translate nonkinetic thought into practical control over the natural world. Pretechnological civilizations do not have such toys. They do have magic, however, to pursue the primordial dreams of mastery over the natural world. The code presented in magic fulfills the desire to control nature by realizing thoughts through intentions and speech acts.

The supernatural powers that promise a mental dominance over nature have always been dualistic: white and black, good and evil, high and low. The simple powers of the magician may be morally neutral, but the goals are not. The shaman who tries to restore health and defeat death aims to help the patient. The sorcerer who casts a spell to paralyze or kill an adversary proposes an evil result from his craft. It was white magic that entered religion in early human communities. In the origins of Christianity, for example, miracle cures were combined with a moral theology to draw followers. The miracle of the loaves and fishes is a familiar (and immediately practical) intervention to allocate more of the scarce resources of the natural world to believers. Black magic followed a different and underground path. It has represented an assemblage of powers that promise returns indifferent to the parameters of religion or morality, and often hostile to our better impulses. Its parallel today is science for bad ends.

Science became magic's adversary in the modern era. Science is the practice of observation, of explaining relationships among variables drawn initially from the visible worlds of human experience. Modern science originates in the spiritual quest for a deeper code that can explain nature. The great scientists who discovered and created the substantial texts of mathematics and astronomy in the seventeenth and eighteenth centuries were continuing the inquiries of magicians and priests into the laws and principles of fundamental matters. But the methods changed. Instead of using intuitive insights and divine texts, the scientists relied on observation and inference to generate empirical laws.

Some forms of scientific inquiry can be tracked back at least to early Greek thought. The Ionian philosophers of the sixth century B.C. attempted to explain the universe with methods that were objective for the historical period and reasonably independent of religious vocabularies. The leading thinkers in the Ionian School searched for a permanent feature of reality, some code that was reliably fixed in the chaotic flux of human experience. The controlling question was, "What is the world made of?" With this question, Ionian scientists sought to explain nature as an external reality. Pythagoras, a disciple of Ionian natural science, suggested arithmetical correlates for qualitative differences in nature, shifting inquiry away from a defining substance in nature to the structures by which nature is organized. Pythagorean science united mathematical principles with natural substances, explaining differentiation in nature in terms of distinctions among mathematical forms. It is also reported that Pythagoras introduced the view that the Earth is spherical. The deeper explanations of nature were artifacts of deduction and observation.

The long romance that scientists have had with mathematics and nature continues in contemporary times. Early in the twentieth century, D'Arcy Thompson tried in a twelve-hundred-page book to link numbers and biology, basically life itself represented in mathematical systems (Pythagoras in modern guise). More recently Ian Stewart has proposed that life actually accords with mathematics, and that the universe itself is organized according to mathematical principles. In Stewart's view of reality a snowflake is a hexagon, a cauliflower is a fractal, the number of petals in flowers is (more often than not) a Fibonacci sequence, and so on, including the possibility that all of creation follows mathematical rules. This framing of nature in mathematical terms is seductive because it suggests an orderly arrangement of experience according to axiomatic systems of thought that humans can master. The secret of life then resides not in the sometimes unruly products of inductive reasoning but in the deductive elegance of math and logic. In some ways the extremely complex structures slowly being disclosed in DNA (see the Human Genome Project for lessons in dense details) represent the formal order long sought by those who want nature to meet the beauty and rigor of mathematics. It is not surprising that so much effort traditionally has been expended in claiming an isomorphism between nature and numbers. When a system is both beautiful and rigorous, it is irresistible.

A nonmathematical version of the heliocentric theory of the solar system, a theory credited to Copernicus (and others) much later in history, also can be found in early Greek thought. In the third century B.C. Aristarchus, a Greek philosopher, suggested that "the earth revolves about the sun in the circumference of a circle." The social response to this strikingly modern idea prefigured the Inquisition's public trial of Galileo in 1633. Plutarch reports that Cleanthes, another Greek philosopher, "thought it was the duty of the Greeks to indict Aristarchus of Samos on the charge of impiety for putting in motion the Hearth of the Universe [that is, the Earth]."

But early Greek thought is not a precursor of modern science. Greek culture did not recognize the sharp distinctions between body and mind (or spirit) that are basic to scientific inquiry today. Matter is not dead or inert in early Greek thought, but alive with a spiritual vitality. Soul is real, and infused nature. The theatrical expression of an animated nature is the spectacle of Homer's gods, who live in nature and make events happen. But the deeper understandings of thought in nature move through all of the Ionian philosophers. The Pythagorean idea that numbers *are* things is faced with strong objections on its own terms, but it can be viewed as unintelligible only from within modern distinctions between mind and matter. Plato defined being in terms of forms, transcendent ideas that are the locus of reality. Aristotle regarded the forms as immanent, thought in nature rather than transcendent to it. All of early Greek science occurs in a culture without the more recent understandings of nature as a mechanism, *matter,* devoid of what we would call today the mental.

The sharp dualisms between mind and matter that inform modern science would not dominate Western sensibilities until the thought experiments that Descartes introduced in the seventeenth century. Contemporary science, with the use of instruments unavailable and perhaps unimaginable at earlier times in history, has described and explained an objective world at macro levels that is distinct from the subject and free of the spiritual qualities animating nature in early Greek culture. The explanatory codes of modern science reveal a *physical* reality. The spiritual in modern secular societies was natural in the Greek culture of the ancient world, but today the dominant inclination is to depict all of nature in terms of matter, not mind.

It is this more materialist version of science, with its revised understandings of the physical world, that has subverted the prospects of a realistic magic. Nature was redefined in (roughly) the seventeenth century with empirical laws that could be discovered and organized by human reason. The secret to sovereignty over the natural world seemed to be in using and eventually controlling this empirical code, not in the magician's prowess. As a lasting consequence, all versions of the occult in the West fell under the scientist's skeptical gaze. Every ritual and belief of magic realism—seances, spells, extrasensory perception, and more—are scrutinized today by the powers of modern science. As these powers of observation and testing have entered the professions, the assertions of magic have been increasingly marginalized. The influences of the natural sciences on the medical profession in the nineteenth century, for example, led to the expulsion of the shaman and apothecary from the ranks of licensed physicians.

Today magic has entered mainstream culture as entertainment. The professional magician is an admitted fraud, a performer who creates illusions with sleight-of-hand or mechanical devices. The differences and rivalries are considerable. The dexterity of Ricky Jay and the technological versatility of David Copperfield share the stage of contemporary magic, but are as different from one another in their conceptions of magic as the craftsman is from the corporate expert. The source of success in all performance magic is the same, however. The audience has to believe, at least momentarily, in the ancient possibilities that human powers can alter the natural world with the right words, the right thoughts, the properly crafted intentions. The magician on stage nourishes this belief with the same speed of movement and art of concealment that deceives the spectators in the shell game. Like King and his shell game, the magician is a skilled surrogate for the dormant belief that occult powers can reveal the world's secrets, and that nature will yield to wishes and rituals, phrases and spells, if only the thoughts that matter can be found and sent in suitable form toward human experiences.

The narratives that describe the powers and exploits of the great psychics of the late nineteenth and early twentieth centuries are filled with supernatural events. These stories, still read and accepted today among the faithful, represent the beliefs in realistic magic that modern science opposes. The individuals celebrated in the tales exercise extraordinary powers that defy the natural laws that we know and accept. The evidence for the events that these stories report, however, is deep in the realm of controversy. The "data" are usually anecdotal, eyewitness testimony at best, turned into reinforcing commercials at worst. But the narratives are beautiful and suggestive, and remind us of what we would believe in if only the stories would somehow turn out to be true.

The story of Daniel Home is one of the more impressive entries in this narrative history. He was born in Edinburgh, Scotland, in 1833. The city has one of the oldest and distinguished universities in the West, and in the twentieth century, the campus would house one of the world's leading centers for psychic research. This touch of academic irony and historical coincidence might have amused Home. His own progenitors were a mix of the practical and the metaphysical: his father was a carpenter and his mother a clairvoyant. As a child Daniel exhibited the unusual perceptual gifts that seem to mark off psychics, among them the macabre ability to foresee the imminent death of another person (in Home's case, at the age of four, the death of a cousin). Home moved to Connecticut with his family in 1842. His psychic precociousness barely kept pace with his mother's gifts. In 1850 she correctly predicted her own death, though Daniel also reported seeing her in a vision at the time she died. According to Daniel she continued to appear to him as a guiding figure throughout his life.

Home was said to have had a kind of special kinetic power that allowed him to bypass certain natural laws, including the constraints of gravity. At the age of nineteen (according to the stories) he would levitate sizeable objects such as tables and chairs, usually in the homes of wealthy individuals. He soon began conducting seances, again almost always in private homes, and more than a few of these sessions oscillated between the frantic and the bizarre. On occasion Home would enter a frenzied state, playing the piano or accordion as if possessed by spirits, or at least infused with an inexplicable energy. He also produced writing he claimed came from the dead, and more than a few people reported that he could alter at will the size of his body, from what seemed to be his normal height of 5 feet,

7 inches to a stretched 6 feet, 6 inches, and then to the shrunken dimensions of 5 feet or less. Most of these performances were conducted in well-lit rooms, and sometimes with the spectators holding Home's hands and feet.

A typical session with Home began with immense and unexplained physical volatility. Most of the objects in the room, and often the room itself, would begin violently shaking and moving. Soon the table where those attending the seance were sitting would begin moving, tilting one way and then another, slowly making its way upward toward the ceiling with the objects on its surface solidly in place. A panoply of effects might then occur. These included table rappings (from spirits), spontaneous and unaided music from instruments, and truly spectacular effects with fire. Home seemed to be immune from burns even when he was in intimate contact with burning materials. He would handle hot coals with his bare hands for sustained periods of time, sometimes placing his face into the coals. His skin would remain unmarked. Home also frequently levitated during his seances. Some witnesses claimed to see him fly on occasion.

Home was tested by several professional investigators. On all occasions they came away convinced that his powers were genuine. Skeptics did question Home's abilities, but supporters were usually able to counter the arguments. The validity of Home's powers has always seemed more plausible than the conjectures that deny them. To the present day no critic has ever refuted the claims for Home's powers or proved that the demonstrations were false or fraudulent. He continues to be the one early grand psychic who remains genuine for believers and an irritating puzzle for critics.

4

Another grand psychic, Eileen Garrett, was said to have had a troubled personal life. She was born in the natural and almost lyrically green surroundings of County Meath, Ireland, in 1893 as Eileen Jeanette Vancho and became an orphan six weeks after her birth when her parents committed suicide. She was adopted by an unsympathetic aunt and uncle, who, she always remembered, spoke of her dead parents with a mixture of pity and disapproval. At a very early age Garrett began seeing things that others did not. Patterns of light and energy seemed to her to envelop the normal contents of visual experiences. Imaginary playmates, staple items in many lonely childhoods, were real and perfectly ordinary companions to Garrett.

At some point in her early years she began having prophetic visions. Like those experienced by most psychics, these visions inevitably gravitated toward death and dying. In one well-known story, Garrett saw her favorite aunt walking toward her carrying a baby. "I am going away now, and I must take the baby with me," the aunt told the young Garrett. The next day word reached Garrett that the aunt had died in childbirth. The baby had perished also. This visionary preoccupation with tragedy found a parallel in the afflictions of Garrett's early experiences. She suffered chronically from tuberculosis and attendant respiratory disorders. At the age of fifteen she settled with relatives in England. There she married an older man after a brief courtship. Their first three babies, all boys, died very young, two of meningitis. A daughter, born later, survived. But Garrett's health deteriorated. Her marriage ended in divorce.

Garrett's second husband was a young officer who was called to the front during the First World War. Another tragic vision told her that shortly he would die in combat. He did, along with many others in the war, in his case in Ypres during a fierce battle. A third husband survived, perhaps because he and Garrett married shortly before the Armistice ending the war. But this marriage dissolved just about the time Garrett began her career as a professional medium. Later, as health problems were becoming increasingly discouraging to her, she became engaged for a fourth time. Garrett and her fiancé fell ill together. He died of pneumonia. She survived.

Garrett's main psychic skills were in channeling, meaning that she was a medium whom other spirits used as an instrument of communication. These spirits were in three categories: persons who lived at a much earlier time, metaphysical entities, and recently deceased persons. The spirits from more ancient times were two: Uvani, a fourteenth-century Arab soldier who functioned as the medium control, and Abdul Latif, a twelfth-century Persian physician who instructed on matters of healing. The metaphysical entities were also two: Tahotah and Ramah. These entities advised on abstract matters and had no incarnation in human experience. The recently deceased were random spirits who manifested themselves in Garrett to provide specific information.

The trances that Garrett would enter to channel spirits began almost casually. In the revival of spiritualism in England shortly after the First World War, Garrett joined a group of women who had been meeting to contact the dead through the then popular method of table tapping. Garrett immediately and easily entered a trance at the start of her first session and began describing the dead persons she saw sitting at the table with the other women. In the days following this startling experience, Garrett visited a hypnotist, who induced a trance that produced the first appearance of Uvani. This spirit announced that he would henceforth exercise control over Garrett. She began seeking guidance to resist the new, unwelcome presence. Her guides at the beginning were drawn from the leading psychics in England at that time. They included James McKenzie, who helped her over a period of five years (1924 to 1929) to develop skills in telepathy, clairvoyance, clairaudience, and poltergeist communication; and the well-known psychical researchers Sir Oliver Lodge, Hereward Carrington, and Nandor Fodor. But the door allowing Uvani to enter was kept open rather than closed.

A tragedy served as the pivotal event that publicly established Garrett's psychic gifts. During the years 1926 to 1929, Garrett had reported premonitions about the crash of a dirigible. In one particularly vivid experience she saw a dirigible in the sky over London engulfed in flames. In a seance in 1928, she was said to have channeled a message from a dead officer to his friend, scheduled to be the navigator on the maiden voyage of a dirigible named the R-101, warning him not to go on the flight. The British dirigible R-101 crashed in flames over France in 1930. Later, on October 7, 1930, Garrett participated in a seance at the National Laboratory of Psychical Research in which Uvani supposedly guided the dead captain of the airship to enter her person and communicate detailed technical information about the fatal flight to all who were at the session, including a description of the gas leak that the spirit asserted was ignited by an engine backfire caused by the dirigible's excessive weight. Much of this channeled information was reported to have been both detailed and accurate (though the official inquiry into the crash predictably did not consider this account).

Garrett emigrated to the United States in the year following the dirigible disaster. The New World was kind to her. She was able to make a number of helpful connections with influential individuals in both psychic and scientific communities. At the opening stages of this fresh start, Garrett was primarily a willing subject for experiments on the paranormal in both Europe and America. Investigators in a variety of institutions, including Johns Hopkins University and Roosevelt Hospital in New York, conducted physiological and psychological tests on her that seemed to disclose some remarkable psychic abilities. At the Foundation for Research on the Nature of Man, she was highly regarded by J. B. Rhine and by William

McDougall. Rhine deemed the experiments conducted with her "a turning point in parapsychology." In 1941 she became a permanent resident of the United States, acquiring citizenship in 1947.

Garrett had a keen and highly organized sense for business. In 1951 she established the Parapsychology Foundation in New York City. It has flourished over its history while other similar foundations have struggled. The Foundation is known for sponsoring numerous theme conferences on the paranormal and supporting research on psychic phenomena. Garrett also started her own publishing house and began *Tomorrow*, a monthly magazine of literary and public affairs that later became a quarterly journal for psychic research. Garrett herself was by all accounts an intellectual who was uncertain about the sources of her psychic insights. She read voraciously and was relentless in searching for information on psychic abilities. She wrote six books and many articles, all testimony to an inquisitive and restless intellect. She regarded her powers as an inexplicable gift, a mental power originating in her own unconscious instead of in the spirits that seemed to occupy her mind from time to time. But even this restriction of psi to the inner nature of a person required important revisions in understandings of reality.

The full revisionist effects of Garrett's abilities were developed by Lawrence LeShan, an American psychologist. LeShan, formerly a clinical psychologist, turned toward psychic studies when the futility of conventional psychology became clear to him. He has believed throughout his career that Garrett's psychic powers were genuine and not fully appreciated even by those who accepted the reality of paranormal experiences.

5

Edgar Cayce claimed the powers to see and read auras, diagnose medical ailments, read past lives, and communicate with ancient civilizations, Atlantis in particular. He was born in 1877 on a farm in Kentucky and did not receive much formal education even by the expectations of the time and place (ceasing his schooling shortly after grammar school). But he was by all accounts an avid reader from childhood until his death in 1945. He favored occult and medical literatures (especially osteopathy). Cayce's family was sympathetic to the paranormal experiences that would come to dominate his life. His grandfather was the county dowser, his father an acknowledged psychic. The youngest Cayce prayed one Sunday afternoon to be given healing powers. He later reported that a radiant visitation had assured him that he would indeed become a healer.

Cayce's earliest diagnoses and cures were directed at his own maladies. One of his children related that Cayce was hit in the spine with a baseball when he was fifteen. The blow seemed briefly to change his personality, making him irritable and noisy. Cayce slipped into an unconscious state on the evening of the trauma and, while seemingly comatose, instructed his parents to place a poultice at the base of his brain. They did, and Edgar awoke in the morning restored to normal. Later, as an adult, Cayce lost his power to speak. He consulted a hypnotist and, while in the hypnotic trance, diagnosed his own malady as nervous stress. He then instructed the hypnotist to suggest to him while in his trance that circulation was being restored to the larynx. The hypnotist did, and Cayce's vocal cords were returned to full service.

Cayce's powers were most effective while he was said to be unconscious. The Cayce Foundation in Virginia Beach includes records for over 14,000 readings that Cayce conducted in his life. Almost 9,000 of these readings were medical, meaning that the majority of Cayce's efforts were devoted to diagnosis and treatment. But the truly unique feature of these readings was the state of mind of the seer. Cayce's followers and detractors alike called him "the sleeping prophet" because he seemed to go into self-induced trances in every session with a subject. Believers maintain that he was in contact with a higher consciousness during these psychic readings. But whatever the explanation, the readings were provided by Cayce in words spoken while he seemed to be unconscious.

Accounts of Cayce's life afford numerous case studies of his readings. Thomas Sugrue describes the general form of a session as a kind of friendly conversation requiring faith on the part of the subject. The main point that Cayce apparently emphasized at the beginning and throughout the session was the mind-set of the patient. Success in both diagnosis and treatment was in the hands of the one being treated. Most medical seers regard themselves as conduits for higher powers. Cayce saw himself as a guide (and no more) to a higher consciousness, and then seemed to diminish even this instrumental role by elevating the patient to an authoritative position. The participating attitude of the patient was to be the decisive variable in enlightenment and remedy. Cynics and those desperate for a last-chance, anything-goes alternative were not good candidates for a cure. Sincere and sympathetic believers were because they were able to recognize the *spiritual* nature of the healing exercise.

The records at the Cayce Foundation illustrate the techniques used in the sessions. Cayce would first engage in a series of readings of the body of the subject, and after each reading he would recommend a course of treatment. In one case described by Sugrue, a young woman with what was then known as intestinal fever did not respond to the conventional treatments of the time (the year was 1935). Cayce performed his readings and urged therapy organized around grape poultices combined with massages and enemas administered by an osteopathic physician, and then a diet regimen. The young woman responded to the treatment and survived. The case was typical of Cayce's approach: unorthodox diagnosis in the sense of intuitive readings, and treatment that corresponded with many of the homeopathic therapies of the day.

Some cases were read at a distance. Sugrue cites a case of epilepsy resolved with letters sent back and forth between the subject and Cayce. This correspondence led to a reading in absentia that (the documents say) resulted in treatments leading to a permanent cure of the ailment. At other times a direct reading was followed by a letter or telegram outlining treatment. In another case described by Sugrue, a woman paralyzed from the waist down, with hardened abdomen, swollen face, and in severe pain, was given a direct reading. Afterward, Cayce sent instructions for a course of treatment consisting of applications of Atomidine, Chloride of Gold, and Spirits of Camphor by telegraph to the family. These applications (which were modified as the woman's condition changed) were administered by a nurse and later a doctor following Cayce's recommendations. Reports by the woman, her mother, the doctor, and the nurse testify to great improvements in her condition as the treatment proceeded.

The striking feature of Cayce's treatments was the joining of intuitive diagnosis with medical therapy. Cayce was never a pure spiritual healer, either in the older sense of a shaman who casts out the spirits of disease, or in the more modern sense of one who heals by shifting the attitudes of the patient or by invoking the powers of an alternative reality. Cayce's diagnoses and treatments accepted conventional medical definitions of illness and resorted to therapies that were often endorsed and carried out by healthcare professionals. His emphasis on a proper diet was a mainstay remedy in homeopathy, and one which contemporary medicine is stressing once again (at least as a preventive). The use of laxatives, either the old drugstore over-the-counter mineral-based types or those found in natural foods, was also quite fashionable at the time. Other Cayce remedies were less conventional, such as fasting and hydrotherapy. But even Cayce's more extreme variants were well within the parameters of medical practices that were themselves much more pluralistic than the stricter regimens of the post–World War II period. Some of the more heroic stories about Cayce's experiences depict him as being vindicated by the medical authorities of the time. He was a psychic in diagnosing illness, but his remedies, and the tests of his powers and therapies, were drawn from criteria accepted in medical science.

6

Stories like those of Home, Garrett, and Cayce are mainly (though not entirely) anecdotal. They fill the texts of those who believe in psychic practices with narratives that are told ritualistically for comfort. But they are tales that please the eye and ear, not the intellect that requires strict controls along causal pathways. In a scientific age such accounts, with the exception of LeShan's work with Garrett, are displaced by more systematic and falsifiable reports. Controlled studies of the paranormal today begin with a binary organization of psychic ability (psi): extrasensory perception (ESP) and psychokinesis (PK). ESP is the general term for clairvoyance (discerning objective states), telepathy (discerning the thoughts of others), and precognition (seeing the future). PK is mental influence on objects, or thought affecting the external world. These distinctions absorb realistic magic into the wider fields of psychic experiences. Both ESP (seeing and forecasting) and PK (controlling natural events) fall under the dictionary definition of magic, and both abilities are tested currently in parapsychology laboratories. The powers of modern science have been employed today by parapsychologists to determine, and ideally confirm, the reality of abilities that material approaches to experience deny.

The introduction of science to psychic experiences was the mission statement of J. B. Rhine, who, with his wife and colleague, Louisa E. Rhine, and the psychologist William McDougall, is generally acknowledged as the founder of parapsychology. Rhine's earliest goal was to be a minister, a vocation that gave way under Louisa's critical discussions in their early acquaintance. Banks (what J. B. used as a first name) considered ecology and genetics, but finally joined his future wife in deciding to study botany. Both of the Rhines entered graduate school at the University of Chicago in 1920. Banks was never content with a mechanistic view of the universe, however. Even as a graduate student in the natural sciences, he was drawn to stories of clairvoyance and precognition. In their third year of graduate work, the Rhines attended a lecture given by Sir Arthur Conan Doyle in which Doyle expressed his belief that the dead could communicate with the living. Louisa and Banks were impressed. When other students were openly skeptical, even scornful, of Doyle's claims, Banks argued that an open, scientific mind would allow the topic to remain open until studied with the proper methods. Other claims and stories intrigued Rhine. Once, the professor in a plant morphology course Banks was taking at the University of Chicago described an episode in which a neighbor woman "saw" her brother commit suicide in a dream, and the event turned out exactly as she dreamed it. Banks was amazed that anyone could find fulfillment in botany after hearing of an experience like that. Both of the Rhines completed their doctorates in botany at Chicago, Louisa in 1923, Banks in 1925. In 1924 Banks had begun teaching at West Virginia University. He returned in 1925 as chair of the botany department. It was to be a very short teaching career.

What Louisa described later as a change in direction started almost as soon as Banks was ensconced in his new position. He entered the critical discussion over a famous case that occurred in response to a prize of $5000 offered by *Scientific American* for a "psychic manifestation." A Mrs. Mina (Margery) Crandon, the attractive wife of a Boston surgeon, seemed to be able to communicate with her dead brother and conjure a variety of mysterious physical effects. She fooled the prominent skeptics of the time, including Houdini. But Rhine expressed doubts. He even resigned his position at West Virginia in 1926 to investigate the woman. His critical account of one of her seances was rewarded when the woman was exposed as a fraud. One of the more prominent claims of psychic powers and (it turned out) the scandal of the day had demonstrated the importance of reliable tests. Rhine's evaluation of Crandon's powers impressed McDougall, a professor in Harvard's psychology department. The case fortified Rhine's inclinations to retreat from the nineteenth-century reliance on nonexperimental events. He resolved with his wife and, later, McDougall to test psychic abilities with the most rigorous scientific methods.

The Rhines settled into the Cambridge, Massachusetts, area and began looking for jobs. It was at this time that Banks began what would be his life's work in devising scientific methods to test and identify psychic experiences. He never changed his views on the importance of scientific inquiry and consistently regarded parapsychology as one of the psychological *sciences.* He intended it to be identical in methods with clinical psychology, and distinct only in the subject to be studied: psychic ability and its phenomena. Rhine (and others) acknowledged the *reports* of psychic experiences that are common all over the world. He also recognized the modern conflict between the spiritual in human experience, represented most poignantly in religions, and the materialist sciences that had become so influential in contemporary experiences. But Rhine's approach to the paranormal was uncompromising and to the point: expel the spiritual from the methods of inquiry and use science to test the psychic experiences that have been so prominent as folklore throughout history.

Rhine's dreams of a psychic laboratory with proper test conditions were realized when McDougall came to Duke University in 1927 as chair of the psychology department. McDougall had been a traditional psychologist vehemently opposed to the new behaviorism that would come to dominate the discipline through much of the twentieth century. His interests in vitalism were part of his resistance to the mechanistic psychology of the new order. It was at Harvard, shortly after the Crandall experience, that he met the Rhines, a young botanist going through a transition to parapsychologist, and his wife. The acquaintance, though distant at first, eventually led to explorations of more robust human powers of cognition and perception than the behavioral school of psychology allowed. But the commitment of all of the principals to science demanded a rigorous testing of these powers.

The Rhines followed McDougall to Duke, ostensibly to deliver some research material. Banks was offered a position in teaching and research. He and his wife decided to stay. It was at Duke over the next four decades that they and McDougall developed and set up the famous series of experiments to test psychic abilities statistically against chance success. These experiments evolved into a center for psychical research, designated in 1935 as the Parapsychology Laboratory. Banks became the director. For the next twenty-eight years, the Laboratory functioned on the Duke University campus, affiliated for the first fourteen years with the Department of Psychology and then continuing as an independent academic unit until Rhine retired in 1965. At that time the Laboratory separated from the University and became the Institute for Parapsychology. Its faculty and staff continue to test psychic abilities with scientific methods of inquiry.

One of the more important distinctions in psychic experiences is between the grand and the precise, which corresponds roughly to a distinction between the natural happening and the controlled experiment. Though Rhine recognized this distinction, he consistently favored the precise over the grand. He regarded case studies of spontaneous psychic experiences as scientifically flawed because the evidence for natural occurrences, which are by definition outside controlled settings, is anecdotal. Even the reports of planned occurrences in non-laboratory settings failed Rhine's standards because he was doubtful that observers could reach any reasonable certainty on what it was they were observing. The main "controlled" studies in the nineteenth century, for example, focused on the activities of mediums and the powers of levitation, automatic writing, telepathy, and ectoplasmic and poltergeist activities that they asserted or reported. The methods of science were used in many of these studies, for example by members of the Society for Psychical Research (which was established in London in 1882), but the studies were inconclusive. Some evidence favored telepathy, but the counter-explanations were as plausible given the open parameters of the experiences. One problem was that nineteenth-century inquiries into the activities of mediums were controlled primarily by the medium, not the scholar, and so were objects of derision by critics. The tone of these critiques was repeated in the twentieth century by professional magicians like Randi, who scoffed at the gullibility of scientists in allowing Uri Geller to set the conditions for his spoon-bending tricks. The skeptics have been persuasive because the controls in such inquiries were loose, nonexistent, or even worse, in the hands of the subject being tested.

The Rhine programs of testing psi have celebrated minimalism with an emphasis on standardized procedures. A typical early experiment, for example, used a special pack of cards that allowed subjects to respond to five single geometric designs. Each of these cards, called Zener cards after their designer, Karl Zener, was imprinted with either a circle, a square, a star, a plus sign, or wavy lines. The ability of subjects to identify these symbols without seeing them was measured against chance guesses. This type of research was conducted for over thirty years. Most of the experiments used volunteers from the Duke University student body. The volunteer subjects would in some way be isolated from the staff members handling the cards, or (later) dice or sealed envelopes that were the targets of the ESP efforts. Sometimes screens would separate the two groups, though separate buildings were also used in later studies, to avoid contacts that would contaminate the experiment. Early research emphasized clairvoyance, but research interests in precognition and psychokinesis are found in experiments conducted as early as the mid 1930s.

The Rhine laboratory's minimalism has strongly influenced all studies of psi, but especially research into psychokinesis. The traditional claims of realistic magic connected human consciousness and macro events. Scripture contains stories of the psychic powers of will and thought to part seas and wreak havoc on one's enemies. The miracles of the New Testament involved spiritual cures of the worst afflictions of the day, including resurrection from the dead. Even the secular spiritualists of the late nineteenth century claimed the mental abilities to move large tables and chairs. In the Rhine laboratory, experimenters turned to the effects of thoughts on micro events and designed experiments to test the abilities of subjects to influence in some statistically significant ways the random movements of artificial or biological occurrences.

Helmut Schmidt's work in the 1970s was highly regarded for devising machines (now called random event or number generators, or RNGs) that independently generate a sequence of random events, like a red or green light, which then allows the researcher to test the subject's powers to influence the random sequence using nothing but thought. One such experiment, for example, gives subjects the opportunity to bias a computer program that "throws" dice patterns across a screen. In effect the subject is engaged in a contest with the program and "wins" if a bias is introduced in the probabilities through his or her intentions. A typical session places a subject in front of a computer screen that displays a random distribution of numbers when a console button is pushed. The subject tries to influence the distribution of numbers by punching in her own numbers and willing her distribution to appear as the random selection of displayed numbers. No connection between the random and selected distributions is possible except through the "will" of the subject. A recent overview of RNG research suggests that there is evidence for mental influences on the target systems.

Another recent, and promising, extension of minimalism by controlled experiments tests ESP with the use of sensory deprivation in what is called a Ganzfeld procedure. The subject is placed in a sound-attenuated room next to a separate control room. Perceptual isolation of the subject is increased through a variety of devices, usually including pink plastic objects (like halved ping-pong balls) gently taped over the subject's closed eyes and a sound system that plays white noise. The subject then tries to describe randomly selected target pictures viewed by a sender in a control room. The subject provides these descriptions in a running commentary on the mental images or associations he has during the session. Then, afterward, the subject is shown a set of pictures and tries to identify again the targets the sender viewed during the period of isolation. The Ganzfeld experiments have produced favorable outcomes not reasonably explained by chance.

The validity of the data collected and the conclusions drawn by the Rhine experiments continue to be debated, however, and it is fair to say that the overall efforts have at one time or another disappointed even the most partisan advocates for ESP. Professional psychologists were only rarely supportive of Rhine's efforts, and most were highly critical. B. F. Skinner, for example, wrote in his 1937 review of *New Frontiers of the Mind* for the *Saturday Review of Literature* this statement: "The result is that Professor Rhine is always very close to presupposing what he undertakes to prove, and his account is thereby seriously weakened for the critical reader." It was Skinner who first discovered that the Zener cards could be easily read from the back in a certain light. After regaling the Minnesota Students' Forum with his new psychic gifts by "calling" one hundred cards correctly in succession, Skinner informed Rhine with some amusement of this possible source of error in the experiments. Skinner's tone was deferential when compared to some of the more strident critics. The reviews of the work that appeared in the late 1930s were vicious. Part of the resistance to the Rhine experiments emerged as the turf war that seems to occur when any practice becomes a profession. Skinner was particularly concerned that the press attention given to parapsychology would damage the profession of psychology.

Some supporters continue to believe that many of the Rhine experiments provide evidence of psi, but even sympathetic critics (and there are many) have concluded that the controls in the experiments were inadequate, that alternative hypotheses that might explain the phenomena were not adequately excluded or explored, that the tendency to use ad hoc hypotheses to explain failures compromised the experimental outcomes (the subject's powers were not present on a bad day, for example), and that the statistical significance that was occasionally demonstrated can be explained in terms of normal ranges of distributions in a set of individual responses that easily converge toward an average in the long run. The last criticism is especially telling in explaining the acknowledged tendency of psi abilities to level out over time. Consider: Any test for psi will produce a common bell distribution, with some individuals exhibiting psi at higher levels than others. This statistical pattern is to be expected in all displays of traits. If "gifted" individuals identified on a first test of psi are selected out and retested, a second bell curve typically appears that is roughly approximate to the chance distributions of correct-incorrect guesses in the experiment. Then, if the new gifted individuals are selected again, the pattern can repeat at tighter levels until, over time, even the most gifted will slide back to the statistical norm of the chance distribution assumed as a benchmark in the experiments. On a longitudinal model of distributions the spectacular early successes and later failures of some of the subjects in the Rhine experiments could be seen as patterns of responses leading to a normal distribution expected in any studies attaining statistical validity with repetitions.

The issue of controls has over time produced the most acrimonious disputes, which is understandable since it goes to the delicate matters of integrity and competence. Critics like James Randi and Martin Gardner have always maintained that the experiments permitted the subjects to cheat. The early experiments, for example, seemed to lack the foolproof controls that would have ruled out subjects peeking at cards or gaining information from biased experimenters. At times the possibilities raised for cheating were remote. In one set of extravagant claims, C. E. M. Hansel maintained that the Pearce-Pratt experiments, in which the experimenter and the subject were in different buildings, were compromised on the possibility that the subject (Pearce) might have walked from one building to another and looked over two transoms at the small card symbols. Even diehard skeptics regarded these speculations as outlandish. But some (very few) critics still reminded the public that the possibility of such Herculean efforts makes cheating a possible explanation for the outcomes of the experiments. The better, more reasonable point is that the design of the experiments ought to anticipate earnest efforts to cheat. The designs on the whole did not contain such anticipations since Rhine and his associates were honorable persons who expected a similar integrity from others. Put simply, they believed that they were conducting scientific (read: honest) experiments among individuals who genuinely wanted to assist in testing for psychic abilities. The critics have maintained that honor is not a reasonable assumption in a controversial science, especially when the stakes include getting a precise fix on the full range of human perceptions and the effects of thoughts on material bodies.

An even more sensitive, and important, point was the critical reminder by the skeptics that independent testing is required to ensure impartiality in any field of inquiry. One of the more successful demonstrations of ESP, for example, was a test conducted by Rhine on Hubert Pearce, the divinity student at Duke University who appears as a subject in many of the experiments. Pearce, according to observers, correctly identified twenty-five

Zener cards in a row after Rhine promised to pay him one hundred dollars for each successful identification. A second experiment under similar conditions, conducted by Rhine and J. G. Pratt, had a similarly successful outcome. The problem for skeptics was not only that the controls on these experiments were inadequate to protect against a skilled magician, but that Pearce demonstrated such extraordinary powers in no other setting under different conditions (though he seemed to score significantly above chance results on a number of other experiments). Nor, according to the critics, was there ever any independent testing of Pearce (along the spectacular lines) by individuals who were *not* true believers. The critical point is fairly basic: objective results are attained by replication of experiments by more than one set of experimenters, and by those who have no vested interests in the outcomes.

The ad hoc explanations that Rhine offered for the phenomenal scores of some of the early subjects are both intriguing and exasperating. He (correctly) pointed out that the atmosphere of the laboratory in the formative years was very supportive of psi, and that subjects could carry out the tests in conditions of comfort, encouragement, and trust. Rhine saw these conditions as conducive to the realization of psychic abilities. The later imposition of stricter controls, with the presupposition of fraud, presumably undermined the very ambience that made the demonstration of psi possible. Sympathizers could rationally acknowledge this point because it is simply true that relaxed and confident subjects in conditions of trust perform better on a wide array of tests. But critics also rightly pointed out that Rhine's entire professional approach to the psychic emphasized the importance of rigorous controls that would eliminate the possibility of specious outcomes.

One of the outcomes of the mixed test results from the Rhine laboratory, in particular the puzzling abilities of some subjects to score consistently in the negative on tests, was a fresh look at the role of personality in psi. Gertrude Schmeidler suggested in her own later review of the data that subjects could be divided into sheep and goats. Sheep, accepting the possibility of psi, could be expected to score positively on the tests. Goats, who reject psi, would score in the negative. One implication of this distinction is that personality traits must be factored into success on psi testing. A long range research goal of the current laboratory, renamed the Rhine Research Center in 1993, is a search for personality correlates of psi abilities. The results so far have been (in the tantalizing language so common to these controlled experiments) promising but inconclusive.

There also were, and are, problems with the fundamental variables being tested in controlled experiments. Laboratory research on psychic phenomena tests psychic powers in controlled settings, meaning that the relevant variables are isolated and effects are attributable to causal influences, not extraneous events. The results of successfully controlled experiments tell us whether psychic powers are genuine, and what antecedent conditions allow them to be expressed. Unfortunately, the distinctions among types of psi occasionally fold into each other in both theory and practice. Precognition, for example, may simply be telepathy extended to the future (reading the thoughts of future persons—a common explanation among psychics for pre-seeing), and clairvoyance may be a reading of the thoughts of those with access to the objective state that is the target of ESP. Any remote viewing may be an out-of-body experience, with the astral body of the subject traveling to the viewing area. A subject identifying Zener cards successfully could either be demonstrating ESP or exercising PK over the random process governing the choice of cards. The individual in charge of the experiment could inadvertently be influencing the distribution through the unconscious effects of psychokinesis.

These curious overlaps undermine controlled experiments by chronically obscuring causal variables, for example the indeterminacy of cause-and-effect resulting from simply not knowing whether the subject of an experiment is engaged in remote viewing or telepathy. Even the basic concepts are contaminated. Rhine regarded ESP as entirely mental, but any definition of ESP and PK can easily and completely absorb ESP into PK, leaving mental *control* over the physical world as the dominant psychic power. Even those sympathetic to controlled testing of psi must admit that experimentation cannot successfully define basic terms and influence paths, which then means that there are problems in describing and interpreting laboratory results. Put more strongly, the problems of identifying causal chains seem to compromise all formal testing of psi since it is impossible to say with reasonable certainty either *what* or *who* is causing the effects recorded in the experiment.

Yet, in spite of these seemingly insurmountable difficulties and breakdowns, something seems to have been discovered in the long line of controlled experiments on psi that Rhine began. Dean Radin, in *The Conscious Universe,* reports on a number of meta-analyses of the research into psi. In one, conducted by Edwin May, the set of all psi experiments (in this case, remote viewing) at the Stanford Research Institute (later the SRI International) from 1973 to 1988 was analyzed. Even allowing for design flaws May concluded that chance explanations of the positive results of the experiments were unlikely at odds of 10^{20}. A more general analysis has been provided by Julie Milton. Milton (in Radin's words) examined "all free response psi experiments [as opposed to, for example, the forced choice experiments with the Zener cards used in the Rhine experiments] conducted in the 'ordinary' state of consciousness [not depending on altered states of consciousness such as dreams, hypnosis, trances, sensory deprivation, etc.]." This particular meta-analysis extended to seventy-eight studies published from 1964 to 1993. Here an explanation by chance occurrence of the overall positive results, according to Ms. Milton, were on the order of ten million to one. One particularly intriguing meta-study compared experiments with the use of hypnosis to those using subjects in "ordinary-state" conditions. In Radin's summary of the meta-study, "[t]he hypnosis condition resulted in psi effects significantly greater than chance, with odds of twenty-seven hundred to one." The ordinary state conditions yielded odds against chance of eight to one, suggesting that if we can invoke deeper states of (unaware) consciousness then psi can be enhanced. Radin cites additional meta-studies with impressive results. These different and impressive odds against chance interpretations of the experiments indicated with various meta-analyses are probably high enough to offset design and control problems, though the problems of disentangling causal paths make it unlikely that we will ever identify psychic powers along the categories set up by the Rhine laboratory (whether, for example, ESP, precognition, or psychokinesis).

An unbiased and fair conclusion is this: The studies of controlled experiments indicate that human powers of perception and thought are more considerable than we normally realize, even though we do not understand exactly what these powers are at the levels disclosed by the tests.

7

Critical thinking is the lifeblood for skeptical views of the paranormal. A critical inspection of psychic experiences often seems to reduce them to commonsense events or extinguish them as false experiences. But the effective use of the intellect can also benefit from an appreciation of revisions in any field of research. As well as the addition of truly controlled experiments, current psychic research is guided by a different set of concepts. Researchers today consider ESP and PK as unconscious faculties that may have evolved as survival traits through natural selection. In this framework psychic abilities may be (a) distributed unevenly through the general population, and (b) found at more pronounced levels in individuals who are successful in one way or another in life, or seem to be just plain lucky. (This research agenda is an offshoot of the search for personality correlates of psi.) Two consequences follow. One is that the traditional Rhine assumption that everyone has ESP or PK at some impressive level may be false. As with the possession of musical ability, most may be psychic at modest ranges while some may be extremely gifted. Second, the key to discovering ESP and PK may be as simple as identifying successful people and providing them with real-world equivalent incentives in laboratory tests. Only in such settings might the unconscious evolutionary powers of ESP and PK be demonstrated in controlled conditions. Survey efforts to link personal and social characteristics with evidence for psychic abilities may help to identify distributions of psychic powers in the general population.

Problems of interpretation and meaning continue, however. Statistical techniques are now reasonably good, and fewer claims of cheating are made today. But the inadequate understanding of psychic abilities, and the possibility that they are omnibus traits at an unconscious level, create intractable problems. Remember that once ESP and PK are linked to human needs or purposes, it must also be kept in mind that the individuals with the greatest needs and strongest incentives to have experiments succeed are the researchers themselves. How can anyone say that successful results are produced by the subject and not from the unconscious use of powers wielded by the experimenter? Also, the difficulties in separating ESP and PK have not been resolved. The tendency of recent research is to regard PK as the basic power, with all other powers seen as derivative, but this tendency is the result of a failure to disentangle the causal chains.

Finally, while the view of ESP and PK as unconscious abilities evolving in response to human survival and competitive needs is more congenial with modern biology, it may also be a view hostile to a range of controlled experiments. Intentions may be inappropriate devices to express the unconscious, especially if concealment helps in the effective exercise of psychic powers. Perhaps those with psychic abilities even consciously resist exposure, fearing the restrictions and exploitation that publicity might bring. Without the subject's cooperation, however, most ESP and PK tests cannot be performed.

For these and other reasons, some Rhine supporters believe that the natural evolution of the Rhine laboratory is toward the larger nonexperimental worlds of social practices. Richard Broughton, at this writing the director of the Rhine Research Center and a strong advocate of nonexperimental research, says that Rhine's singular accomplishment was to cut psychic research away from the loose and primarily observational techniques that had dominated up to that time and to bring rigorous controls (and Broughton believes that they were rigorous) to studies of the paranormal. Broughton maintains that Rhine did definitely prove that people receive information without using sensory channels, that the phenomena are there, and that they can be studied with scientific methods. One result of the controlled experiments that Broughton stresses is that after Rhine we can see psychic powers not as something weird, different from anything else that humans do. Broughton believes (and has driven home this point in his writings) that psychic abilities are just abilities, and very much like all other things that people can do. They are exhibited in the full range of human performances even when, like all abilities, they are not fully present in any given moment or action.

The continuing problem is that we do not know with certainty what exactly these abilities are. Broughton regards them as similar to creative powers in the sense that they are to some degree uncontrollable and not always on call. A great poet, he says, cannot always summon her creative powers in writing poems. For these and other reasons he sees the legacy of Rhine as moving naturally and effortlessly away from the lab to test ESP in real-world situations. He favors talent searches similar to the remote viewing project organized by the U.S. government. In this project a number of psychics were assembled to describe (primarily) military installations in the Soviet Union by mental efforts alone. Broughton reports that these psychics produced useful information roughly 10 to 15 percent of the time, a figure that Broughton regards as astonishing given the difficulties of such exercises. At the moment Broughton is trying to construct psychological profiles on people who are successful as day traders in the stock market. These individuals seem to know little about the technical side of the market, yet some are strikingly successful. Broughton speculates that such individuals are intuitively advantaged. They may have a kind of precognitive ability that allows them to know when to sell, buy, stay put. Again, psi is regarded as a natural human ability that some persons have in generous amounts.

The general program that Broughton endorses maintains scientific testing, but the testing is directed at selected individuals who are successful in social practices that are random, not rote organized. In these practices the natural psi abilities of the psychically gifted can flourish because the rules do not mandate conclusions: the gifted medical diagnostician of hard-to-define cases, the psychic detective successful with ambiguous and scarce evidence, perhaps the creative Hollywood accountant, certainly the intuitive player in an unstable stock market, who may even be well trained in the technical side of economics, but in a volatile market is making good decisions on gut feelings. Broughton wants to move outside the laboratory without giving up the rigor of scientific inquiry in psychic matters that Rhine began.

8

Psychic claims and beliefs seem always to be more comfortable outside the laboratory, in part because larger and more dramatic events are often spontaneous and not containable by experimental controls. Many claims for psychic experiences cannot be tested easily in controlled conditions: premonitions of disaster, sightings of ghost, poltergeist, and other spirit occurrences, and the equally dramatic (and unsettling) phenomena of out-of-body and near-death experiences. These kinds of human experience, that galvanize witnesses and convert skeptics, may be impossible to duplicate in controlled conditions. The spectacular effects achieved by D. D. Home, for example—which included levitations of enormous tables, rooms shaking, spirit contacts—may have needed special settings (whatever the effects in fact were). Sightings of saints on sacred grounds are another species of event that must occur outside a laboratory. These are the grand events that the Rhine tradition of controlled testing set aside as anecdotal, not scientific.

The thought informing many beliefs in psychic or supernatural realities has a metaphorical expression that may finally be directly and unalterably opposed to the controlled experiments of any narrow version of scientific inquiry. The expression is this: Human reality occupies a small stage in a theater filled with dramas that can be only partially glimpsed by our powers of sensing and knowing. If we accept this framework, then scientific inquiry must be limited. The primary aim of science, after all, is to describe and explain a set of visible realities that yield their features to testable statements. The knowable is the natural foundation of scientific inquiry, not realities that are beyond human comprehension. Orientations that accept a larger, and to some degree, invisible world, rely on the limiting condition that reality cannot be fully explained *even in principle*. It is a simple and thoughtful proposition: Psychic powers may originate in alternative realities. This would mean that the full range of psychic experiences is outside the dimensions of human experience, even when they are exhibited as abilities in ordinary life, and, by definition, they are certainly beyond the parameters of experimental science.

We may want to say that the expansive nature of psychic events, their tendency to exceed formal limits, is not only part of the logic of grand experiences, but of psi itself. Even the more modest abilities indicated by ESP and PK may not be capable of full expression in formal settings, or even adequately tested with field work. Like any of a number of human traits, talents, and virtues, psychic powers may well be organic capacities, products of evolutionary development that contributed to human survival. But like many of these traits their natural homes may be in spontaneous experiences. The capacity to love, for example, is a genuine human power, widely acknowledged by lay and professional people. Imagine, however, an experiment which introduces two individuals in a laboratory or controlled setting and gives them a certain number of hours (or days) to "fall in love" to test the validity of the experience. It may work. But the failure of such an experiment does not falsify the capacity. Controlled experiments may be unable to examine those variables that occur only or primarily in the non-laboratory settings of ordinary (read: real) life. It may even be difficult to break down such experiences with an examination of real-world practices. Psychic powers may be as genuine as the capacity to love and as unsuitable as love to formal *and* informal testing.

Nothing, however, is simple in the world of psychic claims. The general qualifications we might place on all evidence for testing spontaneous psychic experiences are complicated by other validity concerns. At a basic level is the problem of precision of expression. Informal psychic statements are often stated in such a way that even in principle they cannot be falsified. The researcher who visited a set of psychics in a brief period of time was rarely provided with the kind of precise statement that is routine in conventional empirical science. Instead the observations and predictions were vague and general, congenial with a range of data that might even contradict itself, and usually protected with a wide range of qualifying clauses. Statements in science must always, at least in principle, be falsifiable. Psychic claims often are not.

It is true that scientists are sometimes, perhaps often, warranted in protecting fragile but vital statements from falsification. But falsification must still be the ultimate test of retention or dismissal, and the most welcome statements in experimental science remain those that can be subjected to multiple falsifying tests. Resistance to such tests authorizes the scientist to maintain the statement in conjunction with other statements. But the statements offered by psychics and found throughout psychic practice often suggest no critical tests to dismiss or maintain them. Even when a falsifying test can be identified—as with the statement that a contract will be offered to an individual within six weeks—the elasticity of the controlling terms (what is a "contract," for example) can always provide an exception to the prediction.

Perhaps the most extreme examples of belief overriding falsification occur in "end of the world" predictions. Christian religious groups throughout history have selected any number of dates for the apocalypse: 110, 1000, 1260, 1533 (among others). The Millerites designated 1844 as the ending date. That we can list the dates at the end of the twentieth century proves that the predictions were false (unless we are living in an alternative reality). But the capacities of the faithful to produce auxiliary hypotheses to escape falsification are remarkable. Edgar Whisenant, a retired NASA engineer, predicted that the end of the world would occur September 12, 1988. The day passed uneventfully, at least from a doomsday perspective. Undeterred, Whisenant allowed that his calculations were wrong because he had miscounted the years in the first century. The correct date was September 1, 1989. Nothing happened on the corrected date either, prompting Whisenant to issue a new date in 1990. At last check the world has survived this projected doomsday also. (The title of this pamphlet notes the passing years: "The Final Short Rapture Report 1990, 1991, 1992, 1993"—and counting?) The thought that the predictions are wrong apparently has not been factored into Whisenant's theories. It is no wonder that outsiders become frustrated with such tests. They seem worthless as devices to determine whether statements issued from psychic insights should be maintained or dismissed.

Nonexperimental evidence is also subject to exactly those errors in perception and recall that controlled experiments are designed in part to avoid. Eyewitness testing is notoriously unreliable, and witnesses to paranormal events are often biased in favor of the reality of psychic phenomena. A cautionary note must be entered here, however. Skeptics may be prone to dismiss eyewitness testimony too quickly. Sometimes powerful evidence is ignored on the basis of discrediting accounts—for example, citing mass hypnotism, for which there is often even less theoretical support than that buttressing psychic events. The climate of skepticism dominating secular societies may even keep sound eyewitness experiences from the public record. Many individuals admit to psychic experiences very reluctantly for fear of being labeled eccentric or even insane.

More damaging to psychic claims is the widespread evidence of fraud that has been uncovered by critical investigators of spontaneous paranormal experiences. The list is long and at times sensational. Nineteenth-century spiritualism included beliefs outlandish by any reasonable standard. It is surely revealing that the aggressive spiritualism flourishing in past centuries is largely dormant now that technologies can confirm or falsify the phenomena. Mediums are interesting case studies on this point. Seances are standard examples of practices that professional magicians today can duplicate and expose. Crystal balls seem to be useful only as props in television commercials.

The insouciance of the practitioners is sometimes startling. A leader of a cult named Mankind United, Arthur L. Bell, testified to a California State Legislative Committee that he not only had powers of precognition and rapid personal transport all over the Earth, but that he could walk through walls and levitate through roofs. At its peak in 1949, Mankind United had 75,000 members. Contemporary psychics include fortune-tellers who read crystal balls in storefront offices. A number of faith healers, past and present, use patently false techniques. Psychic surgery, for example, seems to be pure nonsense that any competent magician can duplicate.

The case of Peter Popoff is one of many egregious instances of fake healing. Popoff was an itinerant preacher who crusaded across the United States "healing" the afflicted and milking a mailing list for a considerable monetary return. James Randi, who regards faith healers as an affliction that must be eradicated from the human landscape, sent in his own operatives to examine Popoff's evangelical techniques. They sat in the congregation armed with electronic receptors. These devices picked up an interesting voice during the part of the service in which Popoff approached members of the congregation, diagnosing their ailments and telling them private things about themselves. This disembodied voice was not an angel, but Popoff's wife providing information to him through a small wireless microphone the reverend had in his ear. (His wife had obtained the information by reading the cards that members had filled out upon entering the tent.) Later, in one of the more delicious moments in the history of the *Tonight Show,* Randi showed two taped segments of Popoff's performance, one the official ministry account of the "healing," the other his own tape that included the voice of Popoff's wife guiding the minister through his information and ministering sessions. The revelation effectively terminated Popoff's career, sending him into bankruptcy.

The question that occurs to anyone surveying the wide and various frauds in paranormal experiences is, If the powers and events are real, why are the charlatans so prominent in the field?

If this extensive fraud is joined to the widespread exploitation of the vulnerable in the field of the paranormal, it is difficult to regard spontaneous psychic experiences as in any way legitimate. Numerous studies, especially of faith healing, reveal any number of psychic practices as scams that victimize the gullible. The combination of fraud and exploitation is a strong indication of pseudoscience, so strong that the burden of proof can be reasonably transferred to the practitioners to demonstrate the validity and value of what they are doing.

Another problem is that some psychic beliefs deny established theories with insufficient evidence or theory to support the denials. Precognition is one set of such beliefs. It seems to require reverse causality and an understanding of reality as timeless. Both requirements may be possible. But they go to the heart of our most basic ways of understanding the world. Time's arrow, which locates the past at one end of a spectrum and the future at the other end (with the present as a moving point in the middle), makes experience intelligible. Persons who deny time's arrow are often afflicted with severe psychological disorders. To accept reverse causality, which implies that a future that has not occurred can affect the present, is a stunning redefinition of human experience. Enormous quantities of persuasive evidence, joined to elaborate reconstructions of our basic theoretical understandings of reality, are required to make such a case even at the rudimentary level. One cannot just say that reverse causality occurs, period. Another set of ambitious claims are those for various out-of-body experiences, which require subtle theories of dualism, proof of a separate spiritual dimension, the dismissal of materialism, sometimes evidence for an existence after death—all possible, but needing precise elaboration and connections to the relevant experiences.

This particular critique of psychic or paranormal practices rests on a common strategic view of science. A statement is accepted into a body of empirical knowledge if (1) it coheres with established statements, or (2) displaces rival statements with superior evidence and theory. The extravagant beliefs in psychic practices often contradict some of the core statements of science with almost nothing to replace them. Since many scientific statements offer reliable understandings of human experience, we might say that psychic research owes us something comparable in return.

Also, as Zusne and Jones argue, empirical explanations that are consistent with science—in areas of sociology, cognitive psychology, neurology—can account for a wide range of psychic events. Examples are numerous. The somatic nervous system (brain, sense organs, skeletal musculature) is now understood as capable of subtle and complex patterns of disassociation that may explain many psychic experiences. Mainly, we know now that there can be functional distinctions within the self, as in hypnosis and glossolalia, where one self does not know what the other selves are doing. Such disassociation may account for a wide range of psychic phenomena, including out-of-body experiences, spiritualism, witches, access to "past" lives, lycanthropy (the alleged ability to change into, or assume the characteristics of, a wolf), and much of what passes for faith healing.

The sensitivity of the autonomic nervous system (heart, endocrine, etc.) to emotional states is now more widely appreciated. The emotional bases of many diseases and disorders are documented. These include insomnia, some pain, eczema and some levels of psoriasis, various allergies, warts, ulcers, and some colitis. What is called conversion hysteria is identified in many sensory symptoms (some forms of deafness, anesthesia, partial blindness), forms of motor paralysis, and a variety of disordered movements (tics, constipation, vomiting) and eating disorders (bulimia, anorexia). Biofeedback, a conscious control of parts of the autonomic nervous system through mental states, is now taught and practiced in conventional medical settings as a form of therapy.

No physician would maintain that all, or even most, of what counts as illness or physical disorders is emotionally caused, or that attitudes can cure all physical problems. But the role of emotions in influencing and fixing "bodily" states, and even the distinctions between emotional and physical systems in the human body, are now understood in more complex ways. Part of this recent sophistication is an appreciation of therapy directed at attitudes—exactly what faith healers try to do. In simplest terms, the placebo effect is supported by experimental data.

Much faith healing, in fact, can be explained empirically without resorting to psychic or paranormal explanations. Certain disorders respond to emotional stimuli, and certain individuals are especially suggestible. In the right atmosphere, and where (a) the healer and petitioner share the same basic view of the world, including beliefs in the effectiveness of faith healing and a supernatural being, and (b) there is mutual affection and regard between the healer and petitioner, then healing can occur through suggestion. But there is nothing mysterious about such a process. It occurs within the range of ordinary human experiences and simply reflects the functioning of the human body generously defined to include mind and physical state.

What more can be said? This: the fiction-and-fact accounts of the lives and abilities of Home, Garrett, and Cayce and the documented successes and failures of the Rhine experiments carry us *in different ways* away from the controlled experiments of scientific testing. Even with the demonstrations of psi in controlled experiments, the range of psychic claims and experiences does move reasonably beyond laboratory conditions. The general conclusion must be that we need a better framework than experimental science to examine claims for psychic experiences, and a template that will order and critically inspect the reports of those who claim the supernatural as part of their own lives. At the very least we must be able to identify and isolate the *non-fraudulent* experiences of those who assert powers beyond those recognized by a formal and materialist science. We really need a more robust understanding of science as a set of very broad inquiries, governed by multiple sets of research methods that exceed simple experimental techniques. Inquiries into the supernatural must be able to move comfortably into a wide array of human experiences outside the domains of the laboratory.

The guiding questions in these inquiries are indisputable even if the answers are not: Are we able to see beyond the parameters of the conventional world? Can thoughts control natural events? Do we have access to realities that exceed the boundaries set by the best of our natural sciences? Or is an objective material reality that is impervious to our mental efforts the defining limit on our powers to see, know, and control?

((Four))

INTUITIVE SCIENCE

I

Throughout the Rhine experiments, there was an awareness of a parallel universe of psychic phenomena in spontaneous experiences. Louisa Rhine once surveyed these experiences with the thought that case studies might be addressed with different but perhaps still rigorous methods of analysis. She carefully defined her subject as "personal experiences in which an individual gets information about, or causes effects on, the external world without the use of the sense or muscles," and employed a simple typology in separating cases into recurrent (mainly poltergeists and various hauntings) and nonrecurrent (such as veridical dreams and premonitions). The burden put on "muscle" is quaint now at a time when technology follows the causal paths of brain waves, but the study is a sound examination of many reports of psi experiences. In the survey, Mrs. Rhine concludes that spontaneous cases can never *prove* anything by themselves because they are outside the controls that science requires to confirm and interpret events authentically. Cases can only suggest the ways in which psi may manifest itself in human experiences.

The grand psychics of the past represented different approaches to psi. Their ambitions for the reality of the paranormal were nurtured outside laboratory conditions, and they were exclusively interested in the ways that psi could be manifested in human experiences. The biographers recording their lives describe events that are among the more vivid and dramatic of all accounts of the supernatural, magic at least as narrative and, to the faithful, testaments to magical realism. Two invitations are prominently displayed in the traditions of grand psychic experiences: look for the domains of the supernatural outside the boundaries of controlled experiments, and be open to events that are beyond the comfortable parameters of ordinary life. In their better days the grand psychics represent the belief that human experience is filled with supernatural occurrences that can only be seen by abandoning the precise measurements of scientific naturalism and the restrictions of established beliefs. If it is science that one requires in studying psi, the traditional psychics would demand a more expansive version than the Rhines applied.

Charles Darwin, in the flat and appealing language of *Origin of Species,* tells us that nature simply *is.* Reality is a design without a designer, a world without moral purpose, to be chronicled by humans. The modern and postmodern inflections on knowledge extend this view by reminding us that nature *is* what we describe and explain in our chronicles. Nature becomes a human construct, with all that this deceptively simple statement entails. Still an open question is the scope and content of nature, and whether a materialist or spiritual chronicle of experience is more intelligible. Are natural laws complete when they depict a cold and objective world limited to conventional understandings of the human intellect and senses? Or are there natural laws that represent multiple and extensive realities that exceed human limitations and occasionally intersect with our seeing and knowing?

2

To Will Provine, a biology professor in the science program at Cornell University, the luminous powers of science explain a world emptied of spiritual presences. Provine is regarded as a gifted teacher, and one of the few teachers on any campus who will routinely extend classroom discussions to other venues. I have been to social gatherings at his home where students join faculty in the kind of critical argumentation that Provine loves to nurture in his students. Even the most casual encounters at these sessions is charged with a keen sensitivity to rules of evidence, inference, and argument. It is easy and pleasurable to fall into these energizing verbal patterns of attack and defense. John Stuart Mill might have written *On Liberty* as testament to the exploratory discourses that mark these occasions. It is no secret to say that Provine sees this kind of give-and-take as vital to good science. One afternoon in early fall, I sat with Provine in his home in a one-to-one session to explore his views on the limits and possibilities of scientific inquiry.

Observation and reason are Provine's chosen instruments for exploring life itself. For him, what we know starts with what we observe. The senses manage experience by arranging phenomena in causal chains. These chains are connected to general statements assigned to sets of events. Empirical theories provide the abstract vocabularies that relate observations and causal chains. Explanation in science is for Provine a complex and powerful sequence of statements, a linear arrangement of concepts and observations that structure human experience in intelligible ways. He believes that the full and consistent use of this apparatus is the most effective way to make sense of the world we live in.

Provine grew up in a religious family. A tradition of four consecutive generations of Presbyterian ministers on the paternal side of his family was broken only when his father decided in divinity school that the life of a clergyman was not what he wanted. He earned a doctorate in philosophy instead and went on to an academic career. But he continued to believe in God and in religion, and these beliefs influenced the entire family. Will's mother was also deeply religious and attended church services all of her life.

Like most children, Provine absorbed his family's understandings of human experience. His critical intellect soon began to dominate his faith, however. He was a brilliant and precocious child with an interest in the natural world. At the age of sixteen he began his freshman year at the University of Chicago, joining other brilliant young persons who were sometimes even younger than he was. The conversations were wonderful, exciting, and excelled at a kind of critical introspection that characterized the University of Chicago for Provine during his undergraduate years. Every belief, every cherished thought, even one's understanding of oneself, were up for scathing critical inspection. It was impossible to rest one's convictions on faith. Reason defined the boundary of the intellectual playing field, and the play on the field.

The work he did in biology pushed his faith to even more defensive positions, many of them untenable in the face of the empirical evidence he was encountering on life and its origins. His religious beliefs had been formed on the premise that the universe is organized by design and that this design provides everlasting meaning for human experience. The key to his life had been to discover and connect with that meaning. Provine discovered that evolutionary biology is directly hostile to this premise. Modern biology is built on the rejection of Lamarckian design and the acceptance of chance variation and random selection. As Provine immersed himself in this intellectual framework, his religious beliefs began dying from what he regards as natural causes.

His abandonment of religion did not occur suddenly, no reverse cathar-
sis of Paul-to-Saul. First he gave up belief in a personal God. He could
see nothing even in an orderly universe that suggested a deity interested
in human affairs. Then he abandoned design itself, and with it the belief
that any kind of God could exist. For Provine biological organisms obviously develop with no purpose whatsoever. Natural selection is the controlling mechanism for the organization that we see in nature. There is finally
for Provine no point to nature except that things *are*. And with no overall
design there cannot be a designer, a God whose governance of the universe
is expressed through the patterns of the natural world.

Provine has explored the traditional escapes from these conclusions.
One is the relocation of design to natural selection: Darwin simply discovered God's true directing principles. But Provine cannot find anything
helpful in this relocation. He regards natural selection as a principle at
some polar extreme from design since it is used to explain random events.
He cannot understand how random processes support design. He finds it
appropriate that no one since the generation of Julian Huxley has bothered
to look for God's handiwork in evolutionary biology.

He also rejects a second exit route—the thought that design is in the
universe, but we have only partial access to it right now. He sees this
proposition as a version of the "God-in-the-gaps" argument: so much
about the universe is unknown and God is lurking in the gaps in our
knowledge. One proof of this argument would be an increase in knowledge
disclosing the workings of God, at least in some circumstances. But Provine
sees the opposite occurring every time. Embryonic development is the case
study he uses to make this point. During the 1930s, most of the leading
embryologists were vitalists of one kind or another who saw purposes in
organic development. Yet when embryogenesis was finally explained in
reasonably complete fashion, no purpose or design appeared. No God
could be found when the gaps were closed.

In Provine's view, God has retreated mightily in the last 300–400 years.
Earlier, God was everywhere, propping up the planets, holding forth in
the Milky Way, displaying infinite powers on Earth by means of complex
natural laws. Now, Provine observes, God does not do that sort of thing.
The longer and more accurate our vision of the universe, the less evidence
we have of God's presence. When asked on another occasion why so many
biologists are atheists and why astrophysicists so frequently refer to God,
Provine pointed out that our knowledge of the Earth is so much greater
than our knowledge of the stars. He is confident that when and if we

adequately explain stellar phenomena, the cosmos will turn out to be the same type of natural, Godless reality as biological life on Earth. No positive argument has ever appeared to Provine that rests on empirical evidence for God's existence, in particular a designed section of reality that must have been the creation of God.

He is even negative toward a more subtle form of the partial-knowledge approach to God. One strong version of the anthropic principle limits accessible reality to the parameters of the human intellect. The world is the way it is, according to this principle, because we are the way we are. But there is no reason to think that the human world exhausts all possible realities. A form of life with radically different neurological endowments would know different realities. Perhaps God is not so much in the gaps in human knowledge as in the alternative realities that are accessible only to different forms of consciousness.

Provine accepts the possibility of different perspectives on reality but is inclined to see these differences as aesthetic. Cultures may have different perspectives on reality, and alternative realities may be explained by different forms of consciousness. But for Provine the natural world has a bottom line that extends across perspectives. He regards natural science as a generalizable intellectual commodity, the only type of inquiry that can always communicate across cultures. So while intellectual styles may differ, the natural world speaks to humans through experiments, and these experiments lead to theories uniformly true across human differences. Provine believes that if creatures with different neurological endowments could talk to us, they might be appalled at how little we know about the hard sciences. But they would be comfortable with the scientific method, and with its explanatory theories and principles. Provine is certain that they would not use God as an independent variable in explanations, and they certainly would not have abandoned evolutionary biology. If they asserted that evolution is false, then on Provine's understanding of the world they would simply be wrong. He believes that "the evidence is overwhelming that evolution has occurred."

There is an obvious objection to this line of thinking. Strong evidence suggests that human science is noncumulative, with clusters of theories retained for periods of time and then totally or selectively rejected and modified with shifts in scientific paradigms. Since a noncumulative view of science allows *human* dismissal of scientific truth as understandings of the world are displaced with new evidence and theory, it certainly seems possible for creatures endowed with radically different intellects to have scientific theories incompatible with the best theories developed within human communities.

But Provine does not accept the strong relativism on which this objection is developed. He regards at least some of science as cumulative. He admits that problems thought to be solved are often revived. He concedes that speciation was at one time considered fully explained in biology, but that now the splitting of lineages and even definitions of species have been reopened for investigations and fresh definitions. Provine even allows that the best science is chronically skeptical, always challenging established theories with critical attacks that sometimes succeed in bringing down core theories. But he sees parameters to these challenges, most of which are fixed by the *physical* locus of science. A purposeful universe, designed by God, is never entertained seriously even by the most radical of scientific critics.

Provine has explanations for why so many people believe in God. One is the hope of being linked to something grander than oneself. These links to a more comprehensive meaning introduce the palliative beliefs in life after death and foundational ethics that comfort people in a cold and indifferent universe. Provine considers these comforts simply useful fictions. The main explanation he offers for belief in God, however, is the fact that people are told that God exists from the time they are very young children. In a society with official atheism—he uses the Soviet Union as an illustration—Provine thinks that very few people would believe in God.

He admits that he cannot say with certainty that there is no God or angels, or that paranormal experiences are completely false. But he sees no evidence for these realities and much to convince him that the material world defines the limits of reality. The thought that our limited knowledge may be used to indicate higher life forms is acceptable to him. He thinks it probable that there are organic forms of life elsewhere in the universe that are vastly more intelligent and advanced than humans are. But to say that these life forms are angels or Gods is to Provine another version of the "God-in-the-gaps" argument. It also seems unlikely to Provine that such life forms have access to God.

He is understandably skeptical about all beliefs in mystical or extrasensory experiences. He doubts that the near-death experience indicates a life after death. For one thing, he sees in the experiences wide differences that he believes are not appreciated by many who look at the evidence. For another, he takes seriously the biological side of near-death. He points out that the brain produces chemicals that are hallucinogenic in various ways when it begins to shut down. So he is not surprised that individuals have visions at the point of death, seeing things pass in front of their eyes that might include previously dead friends or relatives, a dazzling light that draws the individuals on, and so on. To Provine that kind of experience would not be atypical for those with higher levels of neurotransmitters soothing their brains at the end points of life. But to infer life after death from these hallucinations is pure nonsense for Provine.

The dismissal of God and all spiritual explanations is neither more nor less fulfilling for Provine. He simply finds it more honest, more in tune with everything else that he knows. He would not mind if there were a God "to hang around and give me life everlasting and an absolutist foundation for ethics—all those wonderful things that a benevolent God can give. I would not object to that at all." But he feels no sense of loss whatsoever that this, or any, God does not exist in his understanding of reality. His dominant concerns are with the visible and (eventually, he believes, transparent) worlds of scientific inquiry. He regards the mysterious domains of spiritual approaches as largely a waste of time and intellectual energy.

3

The slope that takes us from the metaphysical orientations of the early psychics to the deep skepticism of Will Provine is a reminder of how easily human experience admits rival interpretations. But sharp distinctions between a materialist science and a more mystical approach to experience, as stressed by Will Provine, cannot always be maintained. Suppose that you encounter a scene that resembles a conventional event but is inexplicable in terms of known natural laws. You are strolling in the woods and come upon a figure, enveloped in what looks like white gauze, seated in a large upholstered chair. The figure is a human form and unmoving. Is the figure alive? Is it a person? The sun is directly overhead and is illuminating the scene with a light that casts almost no shadows. You slowly move toward the setting until you can see exactly what it is. Suppose that on closer inspection the figure turns out to be a plaster cast mannequin from a nearby theater troupe. You put your hands on the material and know it as a familiar instrument in staging a drama. But suppose the drama intensifies. A movement occurs under your touch, and you realize that the appearance is a life form of some sort. You step back and suddenly know that the mannequin of a moment ago is alive, and with slow and symbolic gestures it is giving you a message. Now you are entering a scene that has combined the familiar with the unfamiliar. You have used a comfortable framework to render an experience intelligible, and the framework has found its limits. The imagination must be used to make sense of what you are beginning to experience. Intuition may have to dominate your interpretations at first, balancing the familiar and the strange, as you come to terms with what is happening.

A curious mix of intuition and reason, of mystical insight with observations that are eventually testable, is an abiding part of scientific traditions. The uncomfortable point (hammered home by Imre Lakatos) is that sometimes an unreasonable and intuitive resistance to falsification turns out to be right in the long run in preserving important theories. Wolfgang Pauli's postulation of the neutrino to maintain critical parts of the theory of radioactive nuclear decay (long before any evidence or theoretical justification for the particle) is clearly such an example. Then, at a more recent, practical level, consider the lonely battle waged by Dr. Judah Folkman, director (at this writing) of the surgical research laboratories at Children's Hospital in Boston. Folkman, as a young researcher in the early 1960s, intuited that tumors must induce the body to build blood vessels, a process known as angiogenesis, so that they can be nourished. The doctor maintained this view in the face of years of negative evidence and abundant criticism until he and others could put together the proofs his insight required. Now, over three decades later, the thesis is accepted, and researchers are developing inhibitors of angiogenesis as a cancer treatment. Researchers announced in early May 1998 that two new drugs, angiostatin and endostatin, had eradicated all types of tumors in test experiments on mice with no side effects and no drug resistance. The drugs had accomplished this by blocking the blood supply to the tumors. The National Cancer Institute immediately made the drugs its top research priority. But, like many maverick movements in science, Folkman's work initially encountered replication problems: In November 1998, officials at the National Cancer Institute announced that their scientists had been unable to reproduce the results of the experiments. Folkman counseled patience. Then, in February 1999, scientists at the Institute announced that they had finally confirmed some of Folkman's experiments. Plans were put in place to begin testing the drugs on people.

Charles Gant is another maverick in medical practice, with all the opportunities and controversies of the unorthodox. Gant began his professional life in medicine as a psychiatrist. But his growing understanding of the body as a complex homeostatic system led him to his current practice in a field that he and others describe as orthomolecular medicine. Gant bifurcates the practice of medicine into diagnosis and treatment. He admits that traditional medicine is best for diagnosis, but he is adamant in maintaining that alternative or complementary medicine is superior in therapy. Gant traces his orientations in medicine to the classic dispute between Bernard and Pasteur in the 1840s. Bernard regarded disease as the product of internal changes in the body. Pasteur was the originator of the germ theory of disease and the modern view that illness is the result of external causes. The use of vaccinations to establish immunity to toxic viruses and of antibiotics to destroy certain bacteria is predicated on the thought that invasive agents cause some disease. Gant sides in complex ways with Bernard. He accepts the role of invasive agents, but believes that disease from such agents can be fully explained only by introducing internal causes.

The questions that interest Gant begin with a well-known puzzle. Why are some people resistant to certain diseases? Gant uses the example of food poisoning. In a recent case, 1,000 people consumed meat contaminated with E-coli bacteria at a restaurant chain. Of this set of afflicted individuals, 700 got sick and 10 died. But 300 did not get ill. Gant wants to know more about the immune systems of those who resisted the effects of the E-coli bacteria. Or, he asks, what about the individuals infected with the HIV virus who do not develop AIDS, even after extended periods of time? Gant argues that the Pasteur model, which focuses on the external causes of diseases, cannot account for patterns of resistance to illness. To explain the patterns one must see disease as caused by a breakdown in homeostasis *within* the body.

A shift from external to internal causes, even if just to introduce an additional set of variables in explaining and treating disease, has important implications for the practice of medicine. Western medicine, as a system for the diagnosis and treatment of disease, is unparalleled in history for its scope and effectiveness. In the United States, one-seventh of the total economy is involved in disease management. Gant observes that the largest building in many middle-size towns in America is the hospital. (He half believes that over time the monuments constructed for modern health care will rival the pyramids as cultural artifacts.) Students of British politics are bemused to discover that, with the fall of the Red Army in Russia, the largest employer in Europe at the end of the twentieth century is the National Health Service in Great Britain. But in an important sense this overreaching, and perhaps overbearing, system works. The main microbiological agents of diseases that brought civilizations of the past to states of disarray and even collapse have been largely controlled, or at least contained, by modern healthcare systems. Even with the recognition that disease prevention has been poor, most observers regard contemporary medicine as a superb assault on the traditional diseases that have been the important enemies of good health.

Gant's approach takes on the very foundations of this system by questioning its effectiveness *and* the states of mind that produced it. On effectiveness he likes to use a simple chart of census data. In 1897 the life expectancy in the United States was 55 years. In 1997 it was 75 years. Most readers of this chart would applaud the extension of life (with reservations about prolonging morbity at life's end) and attribute the improvement to the advances made in medical care. But Gant invites us to look more closely. The life expectancy in 1897 for individuals at the age of 45 was—73 years. This latter figure tells us that those who made it to the age of 45 had roughly the same life expectancy of those in the year 1997. What can explain this pattern? Gant offers both medical and ecological variables as explanations. Improvements in prenatal care and childbirth, and inoculations against viral diseases, have dramatically lowered the number of early deaths of women and infants in the United States (and the West in general). But also, the population of 1897 lived more physical lives than is the case presently, with exercise imbedded in work and patterns of play. More people had agrarian lives, with considerably less stress. And the environment of all people in the past was less toxic, including the food and air consumed. (Gant is especially concerned with the increase of carbon dioxide in the air, which to him means a reduction of oxygen.) We might extend this last variable with the recognition of those important public health programs at the turn of the century that disposed of sewage and ensured a safe water supply. Of course these accomplishments in ecological maintenance were based on Pasteur's germ theory of disease.

These variables make the transition from the last to the present century more complex than a first, cursory look at the census data reveals. Yes, Gant concedes the accomplishments of modern medicine. The mortality rates and general horrors of childbirth have been dramatically reduced by antiseptic surgery, effective birthing techniques, and widespread use of antibiotics, which provide an enormous advantage for women and children. But having conceded that important change, Gant believes that the health of those living under the protective and interventionist practices of modern medicine may be no better than the past, and perhaps is worse. The fact of similar longevity at the age of forty-five indicates to Gant that at best medicine today is compensating for lifestyle and ecological decline, at worst is ineffective in modifying a death rate constant across cultures and may be obscuring some very large problems in areas of health and healing. We live in a less healthy world, and Gant believes that contemporary medicine is helping to maintain this world by fighting a battle against the diseases that are its by-products.

Gant sometimes fears that medicine is losing its war against disease and that modern health care may be on the verge of a complete collapse. He keeps seeing the equivalent of the canaries that are kept in mines to warn of danger: the spectacle of auto-immune diseases, the growing frequency of modern illnesses like chronic fatigue syndrome, and the reality of micro-organisms increasingly resistant to the best weapons of modern medicine. Gant wants us to reject the very mindset represented by the idea that we ought to be engaged in a war against disease, that we must *kill* a specific disease with some magic bullet. Gant believes that the physical disorders we call disease are caused by a variety of metabolic abnormalities. In his practice of medicine, he tries to level the homeostatic imbalances in the body that he sees as the true sources of illness. His guiding metaphor is different: not a pharmaceutical war, but a nurturing of the body's natural defenses to allow it to cope with disease in the way it has (successfully) for all of human history prior to Pasteur.

Gant's version of scientific medicine is based on nutrition. The four factors he is concerned with are nutrients, antinutrients, stress, and genetics. Genetic variables are the sources for some forms of vulnerability and resistance that are still not well understood and reside largely outside the pale of therapy (a situation changing almost daily). But the other three factors are variables open to modification. Nutrient molecules include amino acids, minerals, essential fatty acids, water, and oxygen. Fibers are required to aid the digestive system. The nonnutrients are the potentially toxic substances that constitute what Gant calls the toximolecular economy of the contemporary world. These substances range over the products of the food industry (processed foods, caffeine, the current romance with carbohydrates), alcohol and tobacco, pharmaceuticals (especially psychotropic drugs), and the illicit drugs of the underworld. In Gant's view of things, the stress created by the modern world chronically triggers autonomic response of fight or flight. These responses disrupt the natural balance among nutrients and, in breaking down metabolic processes, decrease the body's capacities to handle toxic loads. The combination is all bad.

The natural resources of the body are compromised exactly as they are most needed in an increasingly hostile environment. Gant treats patients by helping them find a diet that will rearrange the molecules of their bodies to encourage natural powers of healing.

Gant's treatments rely on nutrients to trigger the natural molecules of the brain (and body) instead of introducing to the body the molecules found in the external substances consumed by patients treated by modern medicine. But critics warn that *medicines*, not just diet, are needed to control and/or cure a large number of diseases. One of Gant's claims is that diabetes is an autoimmune reaction to milk and can be managed by diet. Medicine routinely distinguishes type 1 and type 2 diabetes. The former is a childhood disorder in which the immune system kills insulin-producing cells. So, yes, this is an autoimmune disorder. Diet was the only treatment available for this disease before insulin was isolated, but children died under this treatment, usually within two months of its onset. Modern medicine has allowed children afflicted with type 1 diabetes to live almost as long as nondiabetics by treating them with *both* diet and insulin. Type 2 diabetes is an adult disease in which the body develops a resistance to insulin. (Insulin levels can be quite high in this disorder.) It is not an autoimmune disorder but, yes, it can be treated with diet, weight reduction, and various medicines. The point made by the critics is that medical advances are considered beneficial because they in fact often *do* provide acute life-saving and life-sustaining treatments. Abandoning treatments such as insulin would simply restore the mortality rates that modern medicine has reduced. Gant responds with the perspectives of the holistic practitioner. Insulin and medications, he maintains, are needed in crisis because of carbohydrate excess. He believes that insulin allows people to continue their bizarre dietary habits and not die. The holistic take on these matters is that although crisis medicine may require ambitious interventions, we must look at the background conditions of lifestyles that create the crisis in the first place.

The critics want two things from the practitioners of orthomolecular medicine. One, they want more nuanced approaches to illness that recognize distinctions like those between type 1 and type 2 diabetes. Two, they want controlled experiments to determine if in fact the nutrients work as intended. The problem here from Gant's point of view is that there are few profits to be made for the pharmaceutical industry from dietary management, and so there is little incentive in a market economy for the drug industry to test nutrient alternatives to costly medicines. On the other hand, he is content with the studies that have been done on diet since he believes that they support his arguments. The more general problem moving through all of these views on diet and therapies, from the impartial critical perspective, is that there is no effort to separate out the placebo effect from genuine causal effects. People may be getting better with nutritional types of treatment because they believe that they will, and this says nothing about the physical effects of the nutrients *so long as mind and body are viewed as distinct.*

Gant makes a special plea. He asks us to trust life and the scientific method applied without profit incentives. He believes that we can nourish biological systems into a correct (read: healthy) state of homeostasis, and that this will be a better way to secure health than the risky efforts in allopathic medicine to control the body. He wants to find a way to bring the body back to its natural state of harmony, an effort that he believes combines preventive and therapeutic medicine at the highest levels. The battles he wages with critics mimic the disputes between believers and skeptics in paranormal research. Gant is moving along a dimension of healing that asserts natural powers for the body, and he is closing the points on that space with a mixture of intuition and science. His research uses both controlled and noncontrolled conditions, and he is prepared to accept the healing powers of the mind documented in the placebo effect. He treats the whole patient, and the whole patient lives and breathes outside laboratory settings.

4

Therapeutic touch, a recent practice with ancient roots, is an example of both mysticism and empirical claims. One of the earliest and most familiar of healing techniques is the "laying on of hands." It is found in ancient and modern versions of religious healing and fills the textbooks on secular forms of holistic medicine. Therapeutic touch evolves from these origins with an interesting mutation: the healer using TT does not actually touch the body of the subject (or patient). Instead the practitioner adjusts the energy field that is assumed to be emanating from all forms of life, removing blockages that cause illness by impeding the flow of energy. The technique was developed in the early 1970s by Dolores Krieger, a PhD and RN at New York University's Division of Nursing. Krieger used the Āyurvedic term *prana* (for "life force") to designate the energy field. She saw disease as an interruption in the movement of prana from and around the individual, which could be alleviated by manipulating the energy field, massaging it back into its natural, unimpeded flow.

Therapeutic touch is part of mainstream nursing practices today. It is practiced in at least eighty hospitals in North America and taught in more than one hundred colleges and universities in seventy-five countries. The American Nurses Association has demonstrated the techniques of TT at national meetings and promoted TT with books and videotapes. It has been estimated that over one hundred thousand people worldwide have received training in therapeutic touch, including forty-three thousand healthcare professionals. The Department of Defense has allocated in excess of $350,000 for a study of therapeutic touch in treating burn patients. But the sure sign that the techniques of TT have been accepted as conventional therapy is that some HMOs now financially cover the practice.

The proponents of therapeutic touch defend it in scientific terms while relying on a vocabulary that can only be called metaphysical. The basic term in use, *energy,* is not defined in any precise way, and the notion of an energy field is both unclear and unproven. It also recalls the ether that was thought to envelope the Earth, at least until the Michelson-Morley experiment performed in 1888 demonstrated that an ether does not exist. Teachers of TT urge that the practitioner become centered, which seems to be a meditative state where the spirit of the practitioner is at rest. Krieger has described therapeutic touch as centered on the will of the practitioner, who can act "as a transference agent for the flow of prana from himself to the ill person." These assumptions and phrases are grounded in a spiritual perspective on experience where the practitioner, patient, and surroundings are defined in etherial terms (energy fields, centering, will). Yet it is Krieger (in the style of Rhine earlier in this century) who has consistently denied the spirituality of therapeutic touch and insisted on rigorous scientific testing as a way to understand and explain the technique. She conducted a series of studies in the 1970s testing the effects of TT on hemoglobin levels (as a measure sensitive to oxygen intake and an indicator for a range of biogenetic changes) and concluded on the basis of experimental data that TT does relax patients in significant ways.

The combination of spiritual and scientific terminology in therapeutic touch presents some unusually productive inquiries into the meanings of supernatural experiences. Scientific challenges to TT have been made, at least one in the form of a critical test. On April 1, 1998, the *Journal of the American Medical Association* published an article based on the fourth-grade science project of eleven-year-old Emily Rosa, which claimed to undermine the central assertions of therapeutic touch through a series of simple experiments. Practitioners of TT claim to be able to sense an energy field around their patients, which is what then makes the shaping of the field possible. The objective of the Rosa project was to investigate whether TT practitioners can actually perceive this energy field. The design of the experiments was eminently simple. In the words the authors use to describe the design, "Twenty-one practitioners with TT experience for from 1 to 27 years were tested under blinded conditions to determine whether they could correctly identify which of their hands was closest to the investigator's hand." In terms of the experiment, the TT practitioners, located behind a screen, were to say whether the investigator's unseen hand hovered above their right or left hand. The placement of the investigator's hand was determined by flipping a coin. A score of 50% in sensing the unseen hand could be expected through chance alone since only two answers were possible in each trial. The assumption was that the validity of TT requires that practitioners should be able to identify the hand of the investigator nearly every time by detecting the energy field around it, which Krieger has said feels like "warm Jell-O or warm foam."

The results of the experiment were decisive against therapeutic touch. The practitioners identified the correct hand in only 123 of 280 trials, or 44 percent of the time. This result was even slightly below a chance outcome. There was also "no significant correlation between the practitioner's score and length of experience." The conclusion of the experiment was that the TT practitioners could not detect an energy field around the investigator, thus falsifying the most fundamental claim in therapeutic touch. The authors reminded readers in their concluding remarks that in 1996 the James Randi Educational Foundation offered $742,000 to anyone who could demonstrate a human energy field in controlled conditions. Though over forty thousand people in the United States claim to be able to sense such a field, only one person came forward to try a demonstration. She failed. The offer is now more than $1.1 million. No one else has tried to win the money with a demonstration. The authors of the study suggested in their conclusions that TT claims are groundless.

Little controversy surrounded the statistical analysis of the data, which is sound. *Who* was doing the investigation raised some questions. Linda Rosa, Emily's mother, is a nurse who has been a strong critic of therapeutic touch. She is listed as one of the authors. Larry Sarner, another author of the study, is (along with Linda Rosa) a member of the National Therapeutic Touch Study Group, which has long been critical of TT. The final member of the team of authors is Dr. Stephen Barrett, board chairman of Quackwatch, a nonprofit group that places information about questionable medical practices on the Internet. The investigators, in a word, were not impartial, but came to the study with an agenda hostile to TT. But too much can easily be made of the partisan views of the author team. The study itself is a simple and elegant investigation that is not biased by the strong starting values of the investigators. This much must be conceded by all parties.

The serious critiques of the study centered on the variables being tested and the conditions set up in the test. Practitioners reacted to the experiment by stressing other powers used to detect the human energy field: intuition and sight. Obviously if sight is needed in TT, the blind study set up by the Rosa team fails to satisfy. Other critiques stressed the differences between the experimental controls and the setting of therapeutic touch. What might be discernable in a therapist-patient relationship might be utterly obscure in a controlled test. Practitioners and teachers around the world say that they can sense the energy fields of their patients as a part of treatment. There *may* be no reason to think that these conditions of treatment are replicable in the laboratory. The reminder for all critics who make this argument is that it requires excluding strict or formal versions of science from a medical therapy, and thus the possibility of securing clinical data on the efficacy of the treatment. The most aggressive criticism of the Rosa team experiment, however, may be the argument that therapeutic touch is finally a deeply intuitive and even spiritual exercise that requires an acceptance of alternative realities incompatible with all manner of controlled tests. This last criticism abandons the program of scientific testing endorsed from the beginning by Dolores Krieger.

5

Stuart Ledwith practices therapeutic touch. He is a precise and careful exponent of the advantages for his patients of his techniques. But his background and beliefs are spiritual in orientation. I visited him in his professional and definitely casual offices for an interview and began by asking him to describe how he came to be a TT practitioner. He answered with the same time frame used by everyone I talked to who claimed psychic powers: something in his early life set him off in a different direction. For

Ledwith the defining experience was what he calls his relationship with his own soul, an inner knowing that he says allowed him access to knowledge undisclosed and unavailable to others. He reports that he could tell when people were sick, when they were going to die, when they were not telling the truth, when secrets were being kept. He began kindergarten in a Catholic school at the age of four. There was a girl in his class that he knew immediately he would marry someday. It seemed like a contract that he would fulfill in the future. (He did.) These privileged insights made his parents very fearful. To Stuart the powers he wielded seemed perfectly natural.

Then, at the age of five, on December 21, 1951, to be exact, his world went from color to black and white for no good reason that he could see. He simply lost his supernatural powers of discrimination. He could still make plants grow just by touching them, make sick animals well. But he could not communicate with the hidden conditions that yielded his special insights. In his words, it was not fun anymore. He grew to adulthood trying at every moment to restore his powers. One vision stayed with him from his childhood. At eight or nine years of age, he began having a recurrent dream that he had been a Finnish soldier in some previous life. He now regards this experience as soul memory. In the dream, which Ledwith says he can relive though it hurts too much to do that, he is a man named Edward in the Finnish army, in a Finnish uniform, on a recreational break from hostilities. Edward (Ledwith) spends a very fun afternoon, evening, and night in a sauna with a young woman named Ariekel, where they do everything one can possibly imagine except prepare for the advancing Russians. At three in the morning, as Edward goes running for his clothes, a Russian bullet enters his right temple and kills him. Ledwith can still feel the bullet entering his head, crushing his brain with hot metal, the bone fragments from his own skull helping to destroy the neural tissue. That memory was too much for Edward, who with this quick exit had now been killed in three consecutive lives. He joined with Ledwith in this life in order for the two of them, host and visitor, to resolve the unhappiness of violent death. Edward has remained as a presence with Ledwith from childhood throughout his life.

Ledwith describes the presence of Edward as another full-fledged being inside himself. This being is very much like his host (Ledwith), with a full set of thoughts, words, actions and is fully capable of living on his own. At first Edward's demands were militaristic. Ledwith says he was fulfilling Edward's war mission by joining the American army in the late 1960s and going to fight in Viet Nam. In that war Ledwith was a guerilla fighter. He claims that he would have been Special Services except that he couldn't pass the swimming test. He says that he could not carry himself and someone else (Edward), plus a full set of gear, in the water for five hundred yards without drowning. He reports that he did two tours in Nam, both of them short, in 1969 and 1970. Some of his experiences were predictably brutal. Once his unit was overrun by a large force of enemy soldiers who were so high on drugs that they did not, he reports, know that they had holes in them and should fall down and die. Ledwith says that the team he headed accounted for more kills than any other unit in the 25th division. But the tours honored what Edward had to do, and Ledwith hoped that other opportunities would open for both of them later.

After military service Ledwith accepted a friend's invitation to join the American Legion, but at the first meeting (oddly enough) someone called him a baby killer and asked him to leave. He was more welcome at the Lion's Club, which at that time was engaged in a number of community projects. Ledwith was asked to take a blind girl out on some activity. The young woman wanted to go cross-country skiing and Ledwith obliged. Out in the countryside, she began asking Ledwith to tell her what he was seeing. He described rabbit tracks. She asked what the rabbit had been doing. Ledwith said that he thought the rabbit was running from something. She asked how he knew that. And so on. It occurred to Ledwith that he might try this gentle interrogation on Edward, getting Edward to think certain things that Ledwith could work through and in doing so hear with more accuracy what it was that Edward was saying to him. So he and Edward practiced that for a week, and then they got it right. Ledwith says he found out later that this process is ancient, a self-interrogation that led people eons ago away from the river banks onto the plains as they received internal guidance and energy. Ledwith used the process to open up lines of communication with the inner being he calls Edward. It was in this special type of meditation that Ledwith discovered he wanted to be a healer.

Ledwith credits Edward with the power to change experience. One day Ledwith decided to play golf with his sister. They went up to Saranac in New York to play on a nine-hole course that would allow them to avoid the long lines at his favorite golf course in the north country. When they arrived it was raining, "heavy-duty rain," and the only person in the clubhouse was the pro, who had earlier sent everyone home because of the rain. Ledwith paid for two green fees and assured the pro that when they arrived at the first tee it would not be raining on them. The pro just grinned and took their money. When Ledwith and his sister reached the first tee, the rain stopped. In the next five minutes the rain stopped all over the course, the clouds literally parting on the west end of the course. The pro come out on the clubhouse porch, hands on hips, with a "how are you doing this" look on his face. Ledwith and his sister played the full nine holes with the rain coming down on both sides of the course, on the road and the fence, on the tree line north of the course, but not on the course itself. Ledwith says that Edward could do these things.

Edward, according to Ledwith, has always worked for the Lord God in every one of his lifetimes. But in every life, when he brought messages to the church, the church killed him. So in this life Edward/Ledwith are teaching people, not the church. The lessons are about souls—who and what souls are, and what the life of the soul is. Ledwith prepared for this healing and teaching mission by going to nursing school, graduating in 1976. Later he earned a doctorate in pastoral counseling. This training and reflection informs his therapeutic touch practice. He treats individuals both mentally and physically. If someone comes in to see him with problems that seem to him to have no basis in this life, Ledwith explores the previous lifetimes of the individual. He claims that in a session or two he is usually able take the soul of his client back to the event that caused its current problem, and then bring that soul back to the present where a quick healing follows. Ledwith believes that souls tend to work toward perfection more than humans do, which makes therapy easier when he does this type of regression with his clients.

The regression itself begins with relaxation therapy. Ledwith wants his clients to "sense what they feel from head to foot, everywhere . . . in their heart, reaching their gut, their pelvic region, feet, knees, arms, shoulders, neck, head—and pay attention to it." Then he guides them to thoughts of simple things like a lady in a pink dress. He tells them to just think the thought and pay attention "to *where* in your head you think it." At this point Ledwith urges clients to have their souls join them "just by taking a couple of deep breaths." Just picture it happening, he tells clients, and it will. Normally, Ledwith reports, the souls of the clients do appear. He believes that souls do not do a full body exposure all the time. They sit and do a head thing, which leaves them dormant since a typical individual normally does not do anything in depth, does not communicate with a deeper self. The soul, according to Ledwith, sits and waits until the body is ready to listen. When summoned, it appears and is ready to do an assessment of the body.

Ledwith seeks an accord between soul and body in diagnosis and treatment. He asks the complete client to tell him out loud what the soul and body think. Often this joining of soul and body will reveal symptoms almost immediately. At that point Ledwith takes the willing client back to the time and place where the problem originated. He does not hypnotize anyone because he believes that this creates too narrow a channel. He wants his clients to go wherever they want to go, and he will go with them. Sometimes he will just touch a body in regression and a kind of video will play for him that presents the occasioning moment. Once he had a client with a major back problem, which felt to Ledwith like a huge gaping hole that resisted treatment because the "wound" was too painful for the client to allow anyone to touch his back. Ledwith just touched him with one finger in the regression and a fantastic video rolled in Ledwith's head about something that happened on one of the ships in the Battle of Trafalgar. The client was shot in the back by one of his friends, a fellow officer, and his soul had brought that early and surprising death forward through several lifetimes, where it now appeared as a severe back problem. When the client forgave his friend, the problem was resolved and the back pain disappeared.

Ledwith says that sometimes he can trace a client's problems to events in this lifetime. On a recent afternoon a young woman appeared in his office who wanted to get pregnant and could not do so. Ledwith says that he turned on all of his energy centers and touched the woman. He saw the problem immediately. At the age of sixteen she had begun having abortions, poorly performed and without proper counseling, and she could not get pregnant until she had taken care of the abortions. By this Ledwith meant that the woman was blocking a resolution in her mind of these actions, and it was this blockage that prevented her from getting pregnant. He says that in one long session he helped the woman remove these psychic impediments by encouraging her to forgive herself. The technique he uses in this kind of session is interesting and (to a skeptic) more than a little odd. He calls the souls of the aborted infants and invites the woman to ask the unborn souls for forgiveness. He reports that the woman usually does go through this ritual, that the infant souls always forgive, and the woman goes away from the session released from the burden. Ledwith expects the recent client to get pregnant in the next few months.

Ledwith accepts that he is helping individuals come to terms with themselves, build an identity if they don't have one, and achieve an internal harmony by shifting the imagery of how things work within their own bodies. All of this head work precedes the actual therapeutic touch session. Put simply, he tries through meditation to get the soul and body of his client connected and going in the same direction before he begins the body work. His offering is elegant by any standard: information and energy so that the client can see a road map, a path, that will allow him to identify what exactly he is doing on Earth. The source of energy for Ledwith is truth accompanied by unconditional love. He says most clients tell him that they reveal things to him that they have never told anyone else, not mothers, lovers, husbands or wives, and that they feel comfortable in this confessional mode of communication. Ledwith believes this comfort derives from an understanding shared by him and his clients that they are arriving at truth in the sessions and that "finally getting truth out is one of the most healing things in the world." He is always asking his clients one thing, asking their bodies and souls, "What do you want?" He wants to know what his clients' dreams are, what energy drives their engines. In practical terms, he asks them what gets them up in the morning, why they go to work. He has found that most people are using fear-based energies because they do not know how to use energies drawn from love. He believes we live in a universe where the main energy is unconditional love, but our societies are fear-based. He wants to shift the energy of his clients toward love and away from fear.

Occasionally he sees clients who want to die. They tell him that, in exactly those words. If appropriate he gives them the permission they are seeking to just go. He once had an eighty-one-year-old woman come into his office and say, "I want to die, but I can't go now because I have a daughter who is a little wacky, and there is no one to take care of her." Would Ledwith take care of her daughter if she has a problem? Ledwith replied that he would be glad to help. Have the daughter call, and he would get something done for her. The woman gave Ledwith a big hug, taking (Ledwith says) all the energy from him that she needed to let herself go. Her daughter found the woman dead an hour after she left his office. In her possession was the note Ledwith had written promising to care for her daughter.

Sometimes he gets individuals who are not finished with life. He finds that they cannot die. One such soul showed up (sans body) at his office last November. She was in agony. Her mission in life was to come here to Earth, live for a very short time, and die young. The point was to teach her brothers and sisters how to handle such a difficulty. Two of her brothers were Southern Baptist ministers, very fundamentalist in their views.

Another brother, who would not speak to the two ministers, was a casual soul with no religious beliefs shared with his brothers. Then there was a sister who did not believe in anything except doing her own thing. The woman charged with teaching the lesson had a severe brain hemorrhage. Right on target. But the body did not die. The doctor in the emergency room in the north country where the woman was stricken arranged for a plane to fly her to a hospital with more advanced equipment. The plane ran off the runway. So they transferred the woman to an ambulance for the four-hour drive over icy roads to the hospital. There were no life support mechanisms on the ambulance. At the hospital the surgeons immediately operated, placing a small coil around the aneurism that had burst. The woman stayed in a deep coma for three weeks. Death still did not come.

The problem was that the soul could not make up her mind whether the lesson plan had been completed. At one point the woman's family decided to shut off the respirator and allow her to die. Ledwith found himself counseling the distressed soul. He pointed out that the family had indeed gathered and agreed to "pull the plug." Was this not what they were supposed to do and learn? Yes, the soul conceded. Then, Ledwith asked, do you have anything else to do? No. Then why not try living? The soul thought that the idea sounded good. On the same day that Ledwith was gently interrogating the soul, the brother-in-law designated by the family to shut down the life-support systems came into the hospital room to carry out his charge. The woman asked him, "Why?" Not a word for the three weeks of deep coma and then a spoken question. The family went crazy, not having a clue about what to do next. Within three days, the woman was sitting up and eating. The physicians sent her off for six months of rehabilitation, which she completed in three days. She returned home and resumed her life. The soul had decided to stay around and do good works on Earth. When the woman later found her way to his office for a therapy session, she seemed to remember that she and Ledwith had talked but was not sure when and how the conversation had occurred. Ledwith was properly bemused.

Ledwith believes in a universe of personal growth. Souls arrive on Earth with a purpose set by a goal and shaped by a sense of mortality. The goal is to live in such a way that the universe is a better place as a consequence of their actions, and they are closer to God at the completion of life. The eventual reward, after a maturity secured through a series of lives, is entrance into God's mansion, "the new Jerusalem." The required price of admission is mastery of unconditional love. Ledwith believes that there is evil in this universe, since light must be balanced by darkness. But the freedom of souls to master unconditional love produces a design that makes both good and evil part of the lesson plan. Individuals can become closer to God in learning how to cope with evil. It is this grand design that guides Ledwith and crafts his counseling sessions with clients in his practice of therapeutic touch.

6

During early childhood in England, Ada saw people that she realized others regarded as no more than her imaginary friends. But to Ada they were real. She would see someone sitting on the edge of her bed at night and start screaming. Her mother would rush in and of course see no one. Her family attributed the sightings to nightmares that would go away over time. But the dreams did not recede into memory, and as they persisted she began to realize that she was different. She also had a good number of what she learned later were déjà vu experiences, seeing and doing what she thought she had already done in some other experience elsewhere. Then there were the auras. She could see different colors around people, as if there were another figure standing behind the person. The background figure was not a shadow because there was always a bright light around the person, with colors moving around the surrounding area. Once, at a very early age, she was at a meeting with her grandmother and pointed to "that person standing behind that man." Her grandmother told her that what she was seeing was normal, natural. Ada later realized that her grandmother said that because she was the only other member of the family who also could see auras.

Once, as an adult, she was in Cornwall with her husband and some friends. They were walking around some of the churches in the area. They went inside one, where they found a coffin. Her husband, who did not like anything having to do with the dead, said "Let's get out of here." Later that evening, after she and everyone in her group were asleep, Ada went back to the church in a dream state. Everything was exactly the same. But this time she went down into an area that resembled a mausoleum and began talking to the people who were gathered there. They were life-like, very real in their appearances. After a short time, however, she realized that the people she was talking to were people she had known who had died. There were lots of people she had worked with in the Labour Party as counselors, older people who had been very helpful to her as she became involved with politics. Except that they were dead.

Ada looked around and could not find a way to get out. She began to panic. Then from out of nowhere her sister Renée's deceased husband, Jimmy, grabbed her hand and told her that she was there before her time. She looked up and saw "sort of a hole in the sky with bright lights." On either side of the hole were Jimmy's daughters, Irene and Patsy. Jimmy lifted Ada up, Irene and Patsy each took one of her hands, and they took her away in one movement from the scene of the dead. The last words from Jimmy during the escape were, "Ask Renée who your father is." Ada woke up screaming in a terrible state. She asked Renée the question, and Ada found out that the woman she had taken as her sister was actually her mother. Jimmy was her father, and Irene and Patsy were her half sisters. The dream had helped illuminate a vital part of her life.

Later, after years spent working for the Labour Party, she tried to reclaim the spirituality that (she is convinced) erodes in political activity. Once, while traveling with a friend in Turkey, she woke up one night and saw her friend up by the dressing table looking at her. The problem was that her friend's physical body was still on the bed. Ada was witnessing another person's out-of-body experience. Later, on a different evening, Ada saw the friend's astral (or travel) body actually return to her physical body. These experiences made Ada think that she might be a good medium. But another friend, more practical than she, suggested healing. Ada began by doing some self-healing, trying to develop her diminished spiritual self.

Her spiritual visitors drop in on occasion. Ada reports that they always appear with beautiful music. If she is asleep she cannot keep her eyes closed because the power of her visitors is overwhelming. On one particular night she opened her eyes and saw the most beautiful face looking at her. It was a child's face, and the child began to smile and move closer to her. The face became brighter and brighter, and the music was (in Ada's words) "wonderful," but when the child's face came nose-to-nose, Ada screamed. The face receded quickly but before fading completely a voice said, "Start healing." She did and even joined the National Federation of Healers.

Her techniques are classic therapeutic touch (though she did not recognize that movement when I used the phrase). The healer first attunes herself with the life force, an energy that Ada calls (with others) unconditional love. The important part of healing in Ada's program is the belief system of the healer, not the person receiving the healing. She channels the energy of healing through the chakras, the seven healing centers of the body. At first she believed that the physical side of the person had to be healed first, and she will still put her hands on a painful area to facilitate healing. But she now realizes that of the four levels of healing—physical, mental, emotional, and spiritual—the spiritual is the most important. Heal that, Ada maintains, and the rest of the person will respond.

Ada runs the healing center where she works and opens the program each day with a prayer. She opens herself as well as the program and always includes a prayer of protection for the center itself. She says that the protection is very important. "You must really, really protect yourself with lots of light around you." She asks God to protect her when she is working. Once a friend and colleague, Katherine, had a patient who was into drugs and other things. The drugs had an effect on his mind, and he had experienced possession. He seemed to want to possess the healer in the sessions. Ada made sure that there were always two healers in the room with this young man. This all occurred when they had first opened the center and did not have many patients or healers in the building. There were just Ada, Katherine, and one man, Stan. The young drug user appeared one evening with a proposal. He had found a spirit guide, a healer, and he wanted the guide to possess the center's healers so that the guide could heal him through them. Ada said, "No way, nobody around here works like that." Then Stan came out and agreed to the possession, but only "if the guide is a five-foot, six-inch lovely blonde woman." The humor defused the situation, but Ada regards this proposal as the nearest the staff ever got to perhaps malevolent spirits.

The first physical moments of a healing session will find the healer placing her hands on her own shoulders and then entering the energy field of the patient. To Ada this field feels elastic. She says that she can feel the energy, and in the place around the patient's body where she finds no energy, that is where the blockage is located. She lets the energy field guide her hands. Sometimes her hands pour out sweat; at other times they are cold, and she asks herself what's wrong with them. When she is attuned, when she is healing effectively, she gets a cold sphere around her face. Her head and face are total ice. She sees cold. A very tight pressure is around her nose as if she's been in the wind, and her eyes feel tight. But always her hands are very hot. To Ada, they have a blue light all around them.

She sees a wide range of patients in her healing practice: AIDS patients, people suffering from cancer, a large number of people with stress-related illnesses, a lot of depressed persons. At the start of all of her healing sessions she asks the patient why he is there. The answers always lead away from the pain in the shoulder to some deeper routes in the spirit. After three or four minutes, Ada will be with a patient who is crying, letting out emotions that have been bottled up. That is when she finds that the physical pain is just the symptom of problems experienced and repressed throughout a lifetime. Sometimes, when she visits terminally ill patients in hospitals, she finds herself just holding the patients, giving them the spiritual healing that they need to prepare for the next step. She does not do miracles. She helps people find the release that they need to experience a healing that is both physical and profoundly spiritual.

Ada believes that some of the problems she tries to heal originate in the past lives of her patients. When someone first comes to her for healing, she just conducts the normal therapeutic touch routine, smoothing out the energy field to remove blockages. But then, over a number of sessions, she gets more involved with the patient. She will not allow her patients to be passive in these sessions. They must take an active role in their own healing. She encourages meditation, and of course talking at length with her. At some stage they start to become responsible for themselves. This is usually the point at which the patient begins discussing past lives. Ada does not consider herself an expert on regression analysis of past lives. She says that there are individuals in London (where she practices) who do that type of work as a specialty. She prefers to let the patient develop this line of analysis.

There are problems that she will not address. First, she will not address any problem until the patient introduces it in a session. But, second, she will not try to heal illnesses that can be handled better with an allopathic physician. Once an associate in her center was healing a young woman who was fatigued after childbirth. The healer told Ada that something was not right. Ada advised the healer to recommend that the woman see a physician. The woman became hysterical when the suggestion was made. She was adamant in not wanting to see a doctor. Ada was called in and was able to convince the woman that a visit to the doctor was best. The woman finally did see a doctor, and it turned out that she had leukemia. Ada says that she and her staff provide healing services, but these services complement conventional medicine. At no time would she go against the advice of a patient's physician.

One of her most gratifying cases was a young man in the terminal stages of AIDS. The man was very attractive, in his late 20s, and very, very angry and bitter. He came to the center for over six months. He gradually became physically worse and spiritually better. The last time she saw him he could barely walk, his lungs were almost gone, but he was serene. She had continually offered to come to him but he said no, that he loved the center and enjoyed his visits there. On the last visit he held Ada's hands and told her how much she had helped him. He had arrived at the knowledge that he was just going to open a door and walk through it, and that this view of death was the spiritual healing that he had received at the center. Ada was fighting back the tears. The man died in the spring. To Ada he was healed spiritually. At the end of the day, she believes, we are each responsible for what happens to us. Whatever we are here to learn this time around, we must learn.

Ada also believes that we are all spiritual creatures, and that the spiritual is all around us even in secular cultures. As children we can look into the teacup for signs, have our palms read, deal cards for insights into the future, all conducted as games but revealing indicators of an early realization that there is something else other than the here and now. She does not specifically recall her own past lives, but whenever she goes to regression sessions with friends she is able to summon the same place from her memories. It is beautiful and green, with lots of space. Her friends regress to painful experiences, and they break down and cry during these sessions. Her memories are all pleasant but with no details. There is just a wonderful place she goes to that is very peaceful and loving in some way she cannot explain.

Ada was very religious as a child. She remembers saying her prayers and thinking, Who made God? God made God, she would answer. But that implied an infinite regress. This made her think that there is a God for different levels. She believes that some persons here on Earth have moved through multiple levels and evolved into profound spiritual healers. One time a healer came to the center, and Ada could see six or seven people behind her as she was talking, sort of multiple auras. Ada believes that such people are more powerful spiritually than others.

7

What are we to make of these stories? And how can we negotiate the hostilities between the uncompromising science elaborated by Will Provine and beliefs in the spiritual world? Perhaps with half-way houses. The slide from hard science to the fantastic stories that Ledwith and Ada tell may be a slope, but it is not what a stylist would call slippery. The resting places along the way are filled with hybrid sciences, inquiries that examine a wide range of events and assertions with broader and less defined understandings of truth than found in experimental science.

Look again at the medical practices of Charles Gant. He is doing science in monitoring the effects of his therapies on his patients. But the settings for his assessments are also the life contexts in which his patients live. This rich and unruly context is dense with beliefs about healing that affect the causal pathways of treatment: if people believe that something works, it often does work. Not good enough, from a hard scientific point of view, which always wants to control for the placebo effect. But from the perspective of a practitioner like Gant, if it works it works, and the fact that belief can make a proposal real is an important thing to know about human life. But, still, Gant differs from many standard medical practitioners on what are the right causal relations among empirical variables. The disagreements he has with mainline medicine are within secular views of human experience. We can imagine conventional tests to settle the differences. The divide that separates critics and proponents of therapeutic touch is different and larger. To the critic, the blind study of Emily Rosa discredits the practice. To the proponent, and to all who claim to have been helped by therapeutic touch, the testing ground is in the practice, not the controlled experiment. The opponents are disagreeing about what counts as a test of the practice.

The metaphysical musings of Ledwith and Ada are another matter. These are the spiritual extremes in therapy that summon an alternative reality for the benefit of the patient. Yet, for the record, when Ledwith visited my seminar on healing practices, he was the only guest speaker who attracted follow-up calls. I discovered later that three students in the seminar visited his office for private consultations in the weeks following his presentation. Obviously the broad terrain of metaphysics that Ledwith invoked represented something that the students wanted and may have needed. Perhaps the altered states of consciousness suggested by all spiritual worlds are the resources that at some stage the students would seek out to assign meanings to their experiences. Ada is a happy combination of the eminently adjusted and the supernatural. She is a contributing member of her community, dispensing healing on a spiritual basis. Both of these individuals are mentally sound and seem quite content. Their metaphysical musings occur in the contexts of the effective therapies they deliver to patients and are drawn up against the personal backgrounds of their sane and agreeable temperaments.

The methodologies of alternative healing have interesting lessons for discussions of the supernatural. One of the considerable distances between scientific and paranormal claims arises from the tensions between experimental controls and the more expansive beliefs of those who accept psychic realities. These tensions also represent some of the more difficult issues in determining whether psychic phenomena are genuine, mainly by raising doubts about the appropriateness of controlled inquiry, and thus one important version of science, as an adjudicator of psychic claims. We might try to relax these tensions, at any point in a discussion of the supernatural, by asking a simple question: Are there rules for evaluating psychic events that are neutral on the differences between experimental and nonexperimental events?

Four come to mind. One, no experience can be dismissed just on the assertion that there is no evidence for its truth. For example, "Aliens are not on Earth because we currently have no evidence for their presence" is not a conclusive dismissal of alien existence. Two, that a belief fails evidentiary and inference tests solely within particular human communities is not a decisive reason to reject it. Human criteria are notoriously variable with time and place, and are (ipso facto) limited to human experience. For example, "Our instruments and/or thinking cannot detect/conceive of alternative life forms on Europa" does not remove the possibility of such life forms from our considerations. Since psychic events by definition exceed conventional human boundaries, it makes no sense to reject the supernatural with proofs confined to any of the current domains of human knowledge at any point in history. Three, in what might be called a balance-of-plausibility test, it is illicit to rely on a poorer or less probable argument to refute a more plausible argument. For example, "Observations of UFOs are due to mass hypnosis" is unacceptable. It dismisses unlikely observations (of UFOs) with what may even be less likely possibilities (spontaneous and chronic mass hypnosis). Note that this third rule cuts both ways. David Hume (a skeptic) suggested the same rule to dismiss religious beliefs: "That no testimony is sufficient to establish a miracle, unless the testimony be of such a kind that its falsehood would be more miraculous than the fact which it endeavors to establish." But rules or tests with a double edge are excellent, applying impartially to both believers and skeptics.

A fourth rule might be called common sense: We must be at least provisionally skeptical of any conclusion that violates indisputable mathematical laws. The reason for this is that mathematics are arguably our most reliable forms of thinking, and while rule two warns against the decisive status of human reasoning, it would be foolish to dismiss our best instruments in the short run. For example, it would be contrary to this fourth rule to claim validity for any single or unrepresentative "run" of responses in a test for psi abilities. The speciousness of unrepresentative patterns can be demonstrated with the responses in the Rhine experiments: early successes leveling out over time to normal distributions. We might expect any controlled test of psi to iterate tests as required by probability rules and ignore the specious decisiveness occasionally indicated by unrepresentative sets of responses. This fourth rule also expels the once common acceptance of optional starting and stopping points for tests of psi (since the researcher who can arbitrarily stop a test can obtain a successful but false outcome representing the favorable distribution of the moment). It is precisely the powers of mathematics that allow us to see through the errors of controlled tests in preparation for the real thing in psychic experiences.

These four rules for exploring psychic experiences are both modest and passive. They establish weak conditions for rejecting arguments with no grounds for accepting arguments. But, still, they are generalizable proposals that allow falsification in inquiry while encouraging innovative beliefs and testing. They offer limited criteria for recognizing poor falsification efforts and help us to avoid a rejection of beliefs that might be plausible with better and more prolonged examinations. They also may improve the test procedures currently used in ESP and PK experiments. Certainly they give us a starter map to proceed intelligently away from formal testing to the more unruly and promising domains of nonexperimental phenomena.

8

A two-part strategy for adjudicating beliefs in psychic experiences can be grafted onto these four conditions. We might regard all human thought as arranged informally in terms of core and peripheral beliefs. Some statements are on the edges of a web of beliefs and can be falsified without significant effects on other statements. A calculation of the number of meteorites in the solar system is an example: any given number can be wrong without requiring revisions in our general understandings of the universe. Other statements seem to be at the core of experience, and their maintenance or dismissal is critical to a wide inventory of understandings. The observation that all humans have a limited span of life on Earth is a fundamental truth about biological reality. If we discovered that the statement is false, and that, say, some persons live forever, basic understandings of human experience would be dramatically altered.

The different requirements for change and maintenance introduced by types of beliefs are common occurrences. At one time in human history malaria was thought to be caused by vapors in the air. Remedies for outbreaks of the disease included firing cannon shots into heavy fog to break up the malevolent vapors. Later discoveries of microorganisms led to the discovery that parasites carried by mosquitoes are the cause of malaria. (Interestingly, the density of mosquito populations can increase with heavy fog.) The shift in causal variables did not radically affect existing frameworks. Fresh evidence and a different theory simply led to a new account of malaria. It has also been held at various times that disease is the product of spiritual degradation, and perhaps possession. The remedy for spiritual problems is prayer, and maybe exorcism. With these conditions in place, a shift to explanations framed in terms of bacteria and viruses is a sea change in how events are conceived and connected. In the language of the day, a new paradigm has dominated a traditional theory. Accepting a germ theory of disease requires a radical displacement of at least some, perhaps dominant, spiritual accounts of experience.

This arrangement of beliefs as differentially embedded in systems of knowing is important in settling on what is at stake in accepting psychic experiences. The web provides a rough measure of the ambitions of psychic beliefs and of their effects on our cherished convictions. The stakes can be measured by what has to be given up if psychic realities *are* real. On this approach to the supernatural, the question of validity is subordinated to another question: What must be abandoned, what must be maintained, if we accept the truth of supernatural experiences?

Some psychic beliefs can be true or false without significant revisions of ordinary reality, while others can only be accepted with a rearrangement of the entire web of our beliefs. I have suggested that ESP may be a simple extension of existing powers, while precognition would require a dismissal of time's arrow (and perhaps lead to a dramatic expansion of quantum phenomena to the macro events of conventional human experience). Canvassing and evaluating beliefs in terms of a conceptual web also allows us to distinguish between improbable and impossible events. The truth of the improbable just repairs the margins of the web, while the truth of what we regard as impossible forces us to consider a rejection of every belief. The far reaches of the imagination are summoned for some possibilities.

For example, that the deceased speak to us is highly improbable, but that we are in truth no more than machines directed for the amusement of a hidden civilization is impossible on virtually every understanding of human life. Trying to see each of these two possibilities as true will demonstrate some profound differences in hypothetical, and alternative, realities. The exercise will also move us toward those issues of human identity that seem to be at the center of beliefs on the possibility of supernatural realities.

The one truth that moves across all versions of the supernatural is that our systems of explanation are numerous, contradictory in some instances, overlapping in strange ways, and difficult to arrange in a proper order. Historical evolutions, and sometimes mutations, in science are testaments to the various ways in which experience is approached and explained. The geocentric theory of the solar system looked as quaint to the Newtonians as Newtonian physics appears in the systems of physics that stretch from relativity to the mysteries of quantum mechanics. Future theories in the natural sciences will surely make our best efforts today in explaining the universe seem primitive by contrast. Newton remarked that he was able to see so far into the physical world because he stood on the shoulders of giants. But all giants eventually recede into the background of history. The next great explanation will surely be of consciousness, and this explanation will require a more precise rendering of mind and body, which is to say of the human person, than any concept available today in either secular or spiritual discourse. This judgment is safe, no matter how heroic are today's champions in deconstructing these concepts.

((Five))

BOUNDARY CROSSINGS

I

The belief that both mind and body are required to define human identity is a routine premise in psychic experiences. The strongest metaphor for this belief is drawn from modern technology. We are, Ledwith tells us, encased in space suits. Allopathic physicians treat the space suit. He is interested in attending to the person in the suit. This metaphor represents the dualism that is at the center of all explanations of the supernatural and seems to include the thought that no causal chain can dissolve the mind by reducing it to the body, because mind is the primary locus of individual identity. We are, in these views, essentially *spiritual* creatures.

In extreme form, dualism maintains that an independent self exists within the body of every person, and that this self is the primary source of the individual's identity. The idea is compelling in many ways. It explains widespread beliefs and feelings that persons are more than just material bodies. It is vital to holistic healing, allowing for the possibility that health is a harmonious arrangement of mind and body. The idea of an animated individual, one with a spirit within the body, also delineates connections with the supernatural. In some religions, for example, the doctrine of dualism leads easily to a belief in the spiritual self living after physical death. For the psychic, however, dualism offers the ultimate payoff: the prospect of parallel experiences, where the essential person, the one true person, can escape the body as an astral form and roam across worlds that exceed conventional realities.

Such travels, reported by large numbers of people, are called out-of-body experiences (OBEs). An OBE is an experience in which an individual "seems to perceive the world from a location outside his (her) physical body." The experiences vary in both detail and scope. Some people claim only to have separated from their bodies briefly to a distance of a few feet, a displacement that nonetheless places the individual in a different viewing location. Others report journeys outside the body to distant locations, including the high reaches of the atmosphere. One particular type of out-of-body experience—the "near-death experience"—takes the person to another level of existence beyond the ordinary world of human experience. Some OBEs include viewings of the body left behind, and occasionally the traveler describes a silver cord connecting the astral body (the projected self) to the physical body. All who claim to have had an OBE obviously must also report an eventual return to the physical self.

Data on the frequency of out-of-body experiences are not always reliable, but several studies with sound sampling methods indicate that the experience is far more common than one might think. In one survey 25 percent of the student respondents and 14 percent of the townspeople answered yes when asked in a questionnaire if they had ever had an out-of-body experience. Another survey, conducted in Iceland, had only an 8 percent affirmative reply to such a question, but a similar survey of university students in Australia elicited a 12 percent positive response. Most surveys, both sound and unsound, range between lows of 8 percent and highs of 95 percent for reports of OBEs. (The average incidence of OBEs in random samples is 14.8 percent.) But even the lower figures indicate that the experience is not some rare or arcane occurrence. An impressive number of people seem to be having OBEs spontaneously, and without necessarily understanding what they are.

2

Julie Gerrard is a personnel administrator for a large corporation in New York City. She works with corporate employees who are relocating, either returning from overseas assignments, or as part of reassignment within the United States or within the local branch of the corporation itself. She was raised a Catholic and went through a period of religious doubt in the late 1960s that she now regards as almost a standard radical skepticism, quite common at the time, that questioned all established religions and institutions in general. In 1992, after the birth of her second child, she developed breast cancer. Suddenly all the questions about the meaning of life and death became very important to her again. It was about this time that she began having out-of-body experiences.

Gerrard believes that she was experiencing three losses in her life when the OBEs began. One, going back to her skeptical youth, was a loss of religion and of God. The second was a loss of love from her husband. The third was the loss of her sexuality through the radical mastectomy she underwent in treating the breast cancer. She believes now that she was in a state of mourning. Slowly, over a period of several years, she realized that she could change her relationship with her husband and redefine her sexuality by accepting the loss of her breast. But she believed that she needed help in restoring a connection to God.

As a youth Gerrard had experienced several episodes when she felt a certain psychic distance from her body. She began seeking to restore the openness to new experiences that she now recalls she had as a young woman. A visit to a priest was not much help. He gave her two books to read, but they stressed the importance of faith. She had rejected faith as an approach to experience back in her skeptical period. She still feels it is "a cop-out, like saying I'll believe this because somebody told me to." Gerrard needs proof, or at least evidence, that God exists.

At one point in her reflections following the illness and surgery, she was convinced that there is no such thing as God, that God is an illusion made up in order for the world to survive, to help people address the terror of death. This conclusion so distressed her that she had to enter therapy. During this time in her life, she was browsing in a bookstore specializing in psychic literature and began talking to a man who claimed to have experienced OBEs. She began meditating in the following days and felt herself open up to the possibility that there might be something more than everyday experience.

Gerrard's out-of-body experiences are unusually vivid. She sees colors and senses atmospheres in extraordinary detail. Her most recent experience was a model of crisp sensations. It occurred late in the afternoon in the month of May. She had been out for hours and returned home feeling all right, but a bit tired. She lay down on her bed and asked her two children, four and seven years old at the time, to play in the other room and let her rest for a little while. "For a change," she reports, "they cooperated." She began a meditation exercise she had been using to relax and quickly reached a state between awareness and sleep. She also began to feel herself sinking down into the bed and then slowly leaving her body.

The experience frightened her at first. She was not sure where she was, and she felt vulnerable to any forces that might be in the area. Also, she felt, as she has always felt in OBEs, out of control a little bit, with some major part of herself not connected to anything physical. So she asked God for protection and guidance.

As soon as she uttered that prayer, she saw a blue light that seemed to start in the center of her forehead. In the center of the blue light was a long line of vivid white light. The blue and white light began to grow in size until she felt like she was a part of it, "a part of the whole light, and it felt very comforting and very safe, joyous, and peaceful, and I was able to relax into the experience."

Then Gerrard felt that she was traveling. She remembers going into a house. People were sleeping in beds, and she was moving over them, above them, looking at the brown quilts they had over them. The wallpaper suggested that the house was very old. Gerrard felt that she was going through the house, through walls, windows, with no barriers at all. She suddenly reached a place in the sunlight. It was over water. Every detail of the scene was sharp. The water was blue. A red and white sailboat was floating on it. Gerrard thought the scene was striking, beautiful.

She then became aware that there was someone with her. She asked the person to identify himself. At that moment she seemed to be back in her bedroom, and the person very gently reached over and kissed her on the cheek with the words "I love you." Then she came back into her body.

The person who was with her during the experience was the man she had met at the bookstore. Later she asked him if he had in fact shared the experience with her. He said no, but did tell her about an out-of-body experience he had once had with her, which she could not recall. So she asked him the crucial question. If they were both supposed to be there in these experiences, why could they not remember jointly?

The man responded with a long and somewhat involved explanation that drew upon quantum theory. The conclusion was that one person can be experiencing something at one time and another person at another time, but really it is all the same time. She found the explanation unconvincing and more than a little unclear. The only conceptual framework she can assign to the experience with confidence is duality: she knows she was doubly conscious, aware of both the travel experience and the experience of being in her bed while her two children played in an adjoining room.

Later she went to a charismatic healing service conducted by a Catholic priest. When the priest placed his hand on her head to "slay the spirit," Gerrard immediately fell to the floor in a blissful state, not fainting exactly but no longer in control of her body. She started to cry as a wave of powerful emotions seemed to erupt from within her. On returning home she sat down on the bed, picked up a book to read, and felt a sense of peace come over her entire body that was so strong she likened it to a "type of body orgasm." This feeling of complete peace lasted for days. She accepted it as proof of the existence of a higher self within all of us. She felt humble. She began again to believe in the possibility of God.

Gerrard's out-of-body experiences have reinforced her beliefs that there are realities beyond human experience. She favors the poetic metaphor of human life as like that of a spider in a web. Imagine, she urges, trying to explain the concept of a room to that spider. Gerrard believes that humans comprehend only a small part of reality. The out-of-body experience tells her that humans can gain limited access to layers of the universe that probably await us after death.

3

What are OBEs? It is not clear. Nineteenth-century interpretations predictably stressed spiritual or mystical possibilities. The spirit or soul of the person was credited with independent powers, among them the ability to leave the body and visit distant locations. Apparitions were sometimes explained as visitations by a spirit wandering outside of its physical body. Some accounts, however, inclined toward materialism, explaining OBEs as pathological hallucinations. A dualism of the body, with a spirit capable of independent travel, was the dominant interpretation, however, and it persisted well into the twentieth century. In 1938 one researcher postulated an "etheric body" which can find release from the "somatic body" that is the natural physical location of the self. Physiological explanations were also suggested (though as minority voices). In that same year (1938) one author proposed that a withdrawal of blood from the brain due to external stimuli could lower blood pressure and induce an OBE.

Since about 1940, and especially from 1970 to the present time, OBEs have been examined systematically from a variety of perspectives. The first of many surveys were taken during these years. These surveys attempted to determine frequency of OBEs in populations and among individuals, details of the experience, how individuals interpret them, how they are correlated to demographic, social, psychological, and physical characteristics, whether they are linked to other psychic or psychological experiences, and so on. The result is a growing body of literature that attempts to fix

OBEs in human experience by collecting reports on what they are, who is having them, and how frequently they occur.

Psychological explanations have dominated the more recent studies of OBEs. One of the more promising interpretations assimilates the experience to imagination skills, usually indicated by vivid dreams (those in which the dreamer becomes aware that she is in a dream and continues to experience the dream as both participant and outsider with knowledge that the experience is not real). Studies have shown that persons who report vivid dreams also tend to report one or more OBEs. The correlation is not especially strong, but it is consistently found, even across cultures. One explanation proposed for this relationship is that some persons simply have skills with vivid images—their thoughts, perceptions, or dreams are unusually vivid for neurological reasons not clearly understood—and OBEs and lucid dreams are cohorts in this particular package of skills. This explanation absorbs OBEs into an understanding of skills that is more acceptable in psychology. Other studies have used such an understanding to suggest that OBEs are not "real" but instead the product of impressive abilities to imagine experiences.

All of the psychological explanations of OBEs regard them as patterns of brain activity in certain conditions, not as experiences in which the person actually leaves the physical body. Three models have been proposed along these lines. One views the OBE as a response to a threatening change in body integrity. A second defines the experience as a cognitive construction of an alternative reality, in effect an altered state of consciousness, that occurs when the body image is destabilized through a disruption in sensory data. The third model, similar in basic form to the first two, regards OBEs as transformations of one type of sensory experience to another due to gradual changes in either cognitive processes or perceptions, or both. Each of these models is helpful to empirical science in allowing for testable statements and in reducing OBEs to psychological and neurological changes.

Many who do research in psychic phenomena, however, continue to entertain the possibility that OBEs are real separations between the person and the person's physical body. The problems of supporting veridical accounts are enormous, however. One is that the physical body is the locus for the powers of perception and thought that make human experience possible. The eye, for example, is a complex organ that is the instrument of sight. Absent the eye—which after all remains behind in the physical body—and sight is impossible. Similar observations can be made of the ear, the skin—precisely those organs of the body that make sensory experience possible—and of course the brain itself. The natural question never adequately answered by those who endorse OBEs as veridical experiences is, How does the astral body see, hear, feel, and think in the absence of those organs that make such experiences possible?

Yet psychic research proceeds with the hypothesis that an OBE is an actual travel experience. Most tests do not produce evidence of separation from the body. Almost all controlled experiments fail to yield any evidence at all that a person is actually in a different location during an out-of-body experience. These conclusions are especially damaging given the ease with which an OBE can be tested: the astral body or person simply has to perceive and later correctly report on prearranged material (symbols, written material, etc.) not seen by the subject before the test. Or, if more ambitious, the spirit simply has to physically affect an objective state—move a chair, a piece of paper, perhaps be seen by others—to prove a presence. Such stories are told and are documented in the OBE literature. But they are mainly anecdotal, impossible to evaluate, and exactly the kind of lore that reinforces the faithful while doing nothing to prove the case to impartial students of OBEs.

Some experiments, however, intrigue followers and detractors alike. One tested the kinetic effects of an astral body. The experiment required placing a subject in an isolated room. He was then asked to leave his body and enter a separate, sealed chamber to identify visual targets. Strain-gauge sensors placed in front of the viewing window of the optical image device registered any mechanical effect in the area of the targets. In 197 trials extending over 20 sessions, the data show that the strain-gauge sensors were significantly more active when hits (correct identifications) were recorded than when there were misses. Something or someone could be said to have been present when the subject was presumably "looking" at the targets. These results were introduced as conforming to the hypothesis that during the experiment the subject was out of his body and somehow in the sealed chamber viewing the targets.

Evaluating this experiment is extremely difficult from any point outside the test conditions. Once the statistical analysis is cleared (and questions have been raised about the significance level of correct guesses), it is not possible to know how effective the controls were. In particular, only someone present during the experiment could determine the baseline sensitivity of the strain-gauge sensors before the trials began. Also, if (as some critics maintain) the success rate of correct calls was close to what would be expected by chance, then one might ask why someone out of his body and present in the chamber could not score significantly higher. The problem of segregating causal chains also recurs. One might argue that ESP explains the correct guesses and that an unconscious exercise of PK triggered the sensors rather than the subject's out-of-body presence.

Still, the experiment is interesting not only because it indicates a veridical OBE, but also because the authors suggest that an OBE may be partial. Some part of the person may externalize, an experience that does not permit the clean and accurate viewing associated with in-body experiences but may be real nevertheless as a graded departure from the physical self.

4

Alex Tanous was the subject who claimed to leave his body in the experiment and view the targets placed in a separate room. Tanous, a psychic who died in July 1990 at the age of sixty-three, reported powers that seemed to extend across natural divisions in the fields of psychic research. Not to put the point too finely, but Tanous was said to have undergone what we might call robust psychic experiences, meaning those that normally occur, or occur most vividly and fully, outside the strict limits of controlled experiments. He was an individual who claimed the ability to foresee the future on occasion (often spontaneously), read the minds of others, affect the material world through his mental powers, heal organic diseases through psychic intervention, and (one of Tanous's main powers) leave his body at will. He also found lost children, helped the police in solving crimes, tracked ghosts, tried to heal the ill, and conducted instructional seminars on psychic skills—in general, Tanous did what psychics do when they exercise their skills in those larger arenas of ordinary life that do not comfortably fit the strict limits of laboratory controls. Yet he was also a willing and frequent participant in a number of controlled experiments at the American Society for Psychical Research (ASPR) in New York City.

A number of the individuals I interviewed observed that researchers who use controlled experiments do not like to use psychics as subjects, for several reasons. One is that psychics are "wildcards." They bring too many resources to the table, with the risk that both negative and positive results from experiments are likely to be skewed away from almost any imaginable norm. These distortions are difficult to interpret and less likely with a random selection of subjects from the general population. A second reason is that the use of known psychics violates a norm endorsed in the early Rhine laboratory: psychic powers are attributes found in the general population, and the most productive ways to study these attributes require test subjects who are ordinary members of human communities, not individuals who are part of the distinguished traditions of shamanism, wizardry, or psi. Third, the psychic by definition possesses abilities that exist outside the parameters of laboratory testing. These abilities challenge the logic and effectiveness of controlled experiments since they are normally exhibited in real-world habitats. The failure of a controlled experiment using a psychic as subject is more easily dismissed as inconsequential than one using a nonpsychic inasmuch as the psychic can claim that the experiment did not tap into his or her powers demonstrated in other venues. Fourth, the psychic is harder to control since he or she possesses powers that in principle can affect the controls that the researcher places on the experiment. Many beliefs in psychic experiences (as I have suggested) require a radical revision of ordinary reality. Once one allows that the laws of physics can be circumvented, all bets are off on experimental controls. Finally, note that the negative attitude of laboratory scientists toward psychics is complemented by the reluctance of psychics to undertake controlled experiments. (They do not like to be proved wrong, one respondent told me.)

This tension between psychics and researchers makes it all the more remarkable that Tanous volunteered for experimental work with such high energy and enthusiasm. He was (by all reports) eager to participate in just about any controlled experiment and regarded psychic studies as eminently scientific at their highest levels. No other psychic may have believed so strongly in science as Tanous did. One result of his enthusiasm was the classic experiment at the ASPR (Osis/McCormick, 1980) that many critics regard as the most palpable and persuasive evidence we have in a controlled setting for an OBE.

But the more dramatic of Tanous's demonstrations occurred in the generous domains of day-to-day life. Six months before John Lennon was killed, Tanous was being interviewed by a reporter from NBC Radio on the general subject of predicting the future. After some questions on how prophecy works, the interviewer offered Tanous the opportunity to make a prediction on anything then and there. Tanous declined, pointing out that he did not make predictions. He claimed to *see* the future, not predict it, and the experience for him was always spontaneous, not producible on demand. At that moment Tanous, thinking that the tape recorder was off, got up from his chair and moved over to the window. He gazed across the street to the Dakota Hotel, and the thought of John Lennon being killed just occurred to him. The thought was a burst or "spill" in his mental state, and included the understanding that the murder would be particularly untimely and affect the whole Earth. The report of the vision is reportedly on tape only because Tanous was unaware that the recorder was still on.

Tanous also claimed to have seen the near assassination of Ronald Reagan. On November 6, 1980, the day after Reagan was elected president, Tanous was participating in an experiment at the American Society for Psychic Research. Suddenly he pushed the button signaling for the experiment to stop. The investigator immediately went into Tanous's room to see what was wrong. Tanous asked if the EEG needle had just jumped off the sheet. "Yes," was the response. Tanous said, "I see a hand with a gun aiming at the president of the United States, a small gun shooting him, and then the president disappears." The investigator asked, "Where is it?" Tanous responded that they had to let him climb mentally to see the scene.

After a pause he reported, "Washington, D.C., and it looks like the inside of a hotel because I see columns." Tanous recalled that the trees were not in blossom yet, so he thought that the time was just before spring. He also saw Reagan with a man dressed in white holding a stethoscope and with a lot of people around him. He concluded his report with the statement, "The president lives." Tanous later explained that he saw those events not as a single thought (as in the Lennon murder), but as a sequence of scenes, "like a movie." This prediction is also reportedly on tape.

Tanous was the child of psychic parents. His father was renowned as a psychic, his mother was known primarily as a healer. Tanous was considered retarded all through his childhood and passed only two subjects in high school. His first awareness of psychic gifts occurred in macabre scenes. When he was very young, seven or eight years old, he shook hands with a man who was perfectly healthy and announced that the man was going to die. Tanous's father was upset by the statement. The man died twenty-four hours later.

Tanous felt the impending deaths of other persons several times in his early life. He shook hands on two occasions with men and told them they should see a doctor. Both were dead within a day. Tanous also claimed to have saved the lives of numerous people with his admonition to see a physician, who then would intervene to heal the affliction Tanous sensed.

After a stint in the service Tanous resolved to go to college. He proved the early judgments on his mental abilities wrong by earning a BA and an MA from Boston College. He also completed an MA in theology from Fordham University. Tanous's family is Roman Catholic, and he himself went to seminary to be a priest. He dropped out after a year, saying that the church could not accommodate his gifts. He was an instructor at the University of Southern Maine for twelve years, teaching courses in parapsychology and expanded consciousness.

Tanous said that he could summon something deep within himself to "read" people and foresee events. He maintained that these powers were always there when he needed them, except in test conditions, where the need is artificial. He acknowledged mistakes and attributed these errors to two things. One, the source of greatest error, was picking up what is in someone else's mind instead of seeing what is there in the world. Disentangling telepathy from clairvoyance is obviously difficult, and confusing the two can lead to the error of what might be called thought reification—taking thoughts as real.

The other error he explained as "my mind doesn't take me through to ends," which seems to mean that he did not extend his insights to the final purposes of the events he was trying to comprehend. For example, he once told a woman who had suffered a miscarriage that she would become pregnant again and carry to term successfully. To her question about the sex of her baby, he "predicted" a boy. She became pregnant. The fetus was male but died in the womb two days before it was to be born. Tanous was unable to explain his failure to see this tragedy. He did, however, recognize dimensions to experience which he could not penetrate, perhaps for higher reasons that are inaccessible. This is of course the standard *ceteris paribus* clause of all spiritual discourse, but Tanous maintained that he had an 85 percent success rate without relying on it.

Neither resistance nor hostility from others affected his powers, Tanous maintained. Otherwise, he pointed out with impeccable logic, police work by psychics would be impossible, since the guilty party resists the efforts of the psychic. Tanous said that he was able to break through the mental opposition of the reluctant party.

Tanous reported that he acquired all of his knowledge about psychic consciousness from the Old and New Testaments. The lessons he learned are not the standard Sunday school interpretations, however. Tanous read in scripture the news that we are gods, in Paul and in Psalms especially. He enjoyed citing the parts of Genesis instructing us that humans were created by God in the likeness of God, and the New Testament messages that God was not content until the division was fused incarnate in the form of Christ. To his mind, then, psychic powers are natural attributes of humans, not supernatural in any sense, because humans are gods.

The stories Tanous related about his psychokinetic powers illustrated his convictions. One story begins with his agent picking him up at the airport in Montreal and driving him to a television station to do a show. At a crucial fork in the highway, someone in another car blew his horn to signal to the agent that her door was open. She immediately opened and closed the door quickly and, this time, completely. But in doing so she missed the turnoff on the right that would have taken them directly to the station. When she realized her mistake, she told Tanous what had happened and added, "We'll never make your television show now." Apparently the next chance to turn around was a considerable distance ahead. Tanous reported that he said, "I have no time to lose," and pulled the car back to the fork.

The agent looked around in amazement and observed, "Alex, we're back at . . ." "Yes," Tanous said, "Now let's go." She turned correctly this time, and they made the show on schedule. The story has a tragic end. The agent recounted the episode on tape later with the added observation that she saw a totally different Tanous in the car. "Three days later," Tanous reported, "she had a heart attack and died from that experience."

Tanous also said he once kept a plane he was on from crashing. It was a commuter flight departing from Bangor, Maine. Tanous said a voice warned him that an accident was going to occur but also urged him to board the plane to save the other passengers. On takeoff the plane did not ascend normally, and the pilot banked to return to the airport. The plane then started falling slowly and was headed for a crevice just short of the runway. Tanous thought, "let's move this plane," and felt his will keep the plane aloft until it was over the runway, where it simply fell straight down. No one was hurt in the accident except Tanous, who suffered a mild shoulder injury and some whiplash effects. But had the plane hit the crevice, everyone could have perished. This story exhibits what most people would label as extraordinary powers. Yet Tanous viewed such events as ordinary demonstrations of the natural powers that humans have and chronically ignore.

Tanous saw reality in both deterministic and holistic terms. No one, he believed, dies before the right time, and no power can change the natural order of events. Like the Stoics, Tanous regarded the universe as governed by a deterministic order that we can resist (and in doing so create our own misery), but never alter. He also believed in the existence of a collective consciousness, a kind of inherited mental stratum that is the public resource for psychic abilities. He urged his students to connect to this universal "mind" and allow their psychic gifts to be nourished by it. Tanous rejected most dualities, especially those distinguishing individuals from each other. He favored the synthesis of self with others and with the world. Where many spiritual perspectives settle for differences—mind-body, self-world, self-other—Tanous recognized the possibility of a seamless web of spiritual connections.

Yet Tanous also allowed for divisions of the self that explain out-of-body experiences. In the ASPR experiment cited earlier, Tanous was in a small room across a hall from the room where visual targets were located. The most remarkable part of the experiment from his point of view was the absence of windows in the box holding the targets and the strain gauges. To see the targets he had to enter a small box in a sealed room. He professed ignorance as to how he did it, but he said that it happened.

He recalled a partitioning of himself into what he later labeled Alex I and Alex II. Alex I remained in the room where the experimenters placed him. This Alex would call out the targets presented, saying, "Upper right, green," and so on. Tanous remembered hearing the experimenters getting excited as he read the targets. But the instrument of his observation was Alex II, who was free to present himself in the box and see the targets.

Tanous also told a story of an even more dramatic OBE that he insisted was both true and utterly spontaneous. It occurred in February 1976. He was in New York City staying at the ASPR (as he usually did on visits to the city). He returned to the Society building after a date and threw himself on the bed to get some sleep. He had to catch an early flight the following morning to Chicago, where he was scheduled for appearances to promote his book, *Beyond Coincidence.*

Suddenly, inexplicably, Tanous found himself physically in Canada knocking on the apartment door of a friend, Elsworth de Merchant, a journalist and physicist who had always been skeptical of the paranormal. The de Merchants' golden retriever, Patty, started barking from inside the house. Tanous was standing on the porch, which shields visitors from the elements somewhat, and he remembers reaching over and tapping on the window when his friend did not appear. At that point Tanous heard his friend's wife say, "Elsworth, somebody is at the door." Tanous recalled that it was 3:30 in the morning.

Elsworth came to the window, glanced out at Tanous, and opened the door. The dog kept barking at Tanous and even tried to bite him, which was unusual since Tanous and Patty had always been on friendly terms. "What are you doing here?" Elsworth asked while trying to restrain Patty. Tanous answered, "Well, I just came to tell you that my book is out and you are in it." "Did you bring a copy?" Elsworth asked. "No" Tanous responded. Elsworth shrugged. "Well, come on in and have a cup of my lousy coffee. Let me put Patty in the other room." Elsworth took Patty away and then came back to the door, but Tanous was gone. Elsworth waited a few minutes, thinking that his friend had gone to get his suitcase or something. Patty started barking again from inside the house. Elsworth could still smell Tanous's aftershave lotion, everything about the scene remained as it was, but Tanous had vanished—no footsteps, no car, nothing. Elsworth went back to bed greatly disturbed. He couldn't sleep. He remained silent the remainder of the morning, to his wife's growing concern. She thought someone had died. At noon he finally told her the story. She was as puzzled as her husband over the event.

Tanous reported the experience in the morning to Carlis Osis, the investigator who conducted many experiments with him. Later in the day, when Tanous had returned to his home in Maine, his secretary told him that Elsworth was desperate to talk to him. Tanous called and, when Elsworth answered, simply said, "I know." Elsworth was berserk by this time, but not so much so that he had let the scientific prospects pass. He had already written a report on the incident and mailed it to the ASPR. Tanous had also written an account before catching his morning plane. The two reports are said to be similar in all important respects. From Tanous's point of view, he had left his body and appeared physically to a friend in a different country. He had externalized in recognizable form and was able to communicate intelligently while out of his body.

The OBE demonstrated to Tanous the truth of survival after death. He had had near-death experiences as a boy. At one point he contracted undulant fever after eating ice cream made from unpasteurized milk. The doctor had packed him in ice to reduce the fever, and Tanous recalled leaving his body and viewing the scene from above. On a later occasion, when he was ten, his appendix ruptured suddenly, and his parents had to rush him to a hospital. Tanous remembered again leaving his body, this time watching as his father carried him into the hospital, and later seeing the medical staff take him into the emergency room for the surgery that eventually saved his life. He recalled a line that his external self broke through, after which he found himself in an immense light and in the company of people he knew. When he returned to his body, he heard some of them say, "We saved him."

Alex Tanous was a person who sought and found connections to others. He usually spoke animatedly, his dark eyes fixed on the listener as his hands moved across the angle of vision to emphasize some point. Tanous's demeanor was elemental and cosmopolitan: accept, he seemed to be saying, and all will be well. Tanous believed that the part of himself that could leave the body was the essential Alex, the being that survives the death of the physical body.

5

Alex Tanous was an unusual and complex individual. When I met him in December 1989, I was filled with my own versions of radical doubt. A few weeks earlier, I had been scanning OBE articles in parapsychology journals looking for some evidence that the researchers had taken even one graduate seminar in methodology. After dismissing dozens of articles as junk, I came across the famous Osis/McCormick study that suggested a partial externalization. A familiar word that is a kind of scatological antithesis of "Bulworth" sprang to my frenzied state of consciousness. I immediately called the ASPR in New York City and got Alex's home phone number in Maine. I called him, told him who I was and about the research I was doing, and he graciously agreed to meet with me when next our paths crossed in New York City. Our paths did cross there in a few weeks, and we spent a morning together in a rewarding discussion. I remember that he scanned me with the same intense concentration that I used to make sense of him. I saw a sincere and fragile individual who believed what he claimed even when his gifts failed him. What he saw in scrutinizing me, I do not know.

I spent the rest of that winter and the spring of 1990 in Madrid. No communication from Alex, even though he had promised to find me a literary agent. I returned from Madrid in May and almost immediately left to chair my politics seminar in London. When I returned in late summer, I wrote Alex the usual let's-catch-up note. The return letter had "Alex Tanous Foundation" on its return address. I knew he was dead before I opened the letter. It was a note from his niece, Alice Kelley, informing me that he had passed on that summer (1990) and asking would I be kind enough to send the Foundation a copy of the interview I had conducted with him the past December. I did, both tape and transcript. Later, I came to understand Alex in different ways. In 1997 I was hired by the Foundation to conduct a number of interviews with individuals who had known Alex Tanous. The purpose of the research was to compile a database for an oral history of Alex's life. The text in this section is drawn up from these interviews, and from Tanous's own work that I have surveyed.

The first thing to say is one of the obvious conclusions anyone would draw in looking at the data: Like most of us, Alex negotiated his life with a variety of shields and mediating devices. These included the familiar distinctions between professional and personal life, and the usual benign compartments that organize relationships among family, friends, acquaintances, professional colleagues, and others. These networks of privacy and access are common fare in any human life, and biographers often try to see through the shields in order to understand the complete person. But Tanous, unlike most of us, also claimed to possess extraordinary psychic powers. These powers inevitably challenge materialist accounts of human experience and, as a consequence, illuminate Tanous's life from a different and uncommon perspective. We are offered large opportunities to study the limits and possibilities of human experience by exploring Tanous's professional life as a psychic. This prospect invites us to understand not just Tanous's personal life, but his identity and standing in the fields of parapsychology and cognate inquiries. The insistent (though not the only) questions are whether Tanous's psychic powers were genuine, and if they were, how he used them.

Tanous was adamant about using the methods of science to test his powers. He was (on all reports) eager to participate in any and all controlled experiments, and believed that the best studies of psychic experiences had to be thoroughly scientific. But notice that two of the events recited by Tanous are demonstrations of powers exhibited spontaneously (the precognition of Lennon's death and the plane crash avoidance). Whether true accounts or not, the validity of these events cannot be tested in controlled experiments. Nor, to turn the point in a different direction, were laboratory conditions the best settings for whatever abilities Alex Tanous had. Karlis Osis, in the interview I conducted with him, said that Alex could not always exhibit his powers in controlled settings because they were more suited for non-laboratory situations.

Alex also employed non-scientific terms in explaining his powers. For example, the divisions of the self that explain out-of-body experiences were part of Alex's orientation to psychic events. In the Osis/McCormick experiment cited earlier, Alex said he divided himself into Alex I and Alex II. Alex I remained in the closed room for subjects. But Alex II moved in the ethereal or alternative reality presupposed in holistic views of the universe and could present himself in the box and see the targets. It is this dimension of reality that Alex explored as the venue for his psychic powers. Alex examined psychic realms with scientific techniques. But he was also a mystic by temperament and religious training.

Were Alex's psychic powers genuine?

If we accept the thought that psychic powers exceed the limitations of controlled experiments, then the question itself must be opened to a wider understanding of evidence. Informal evidence for psychic powers begins with testimony from witnesses. I asked the individuals I interviewed whether they believed that Alex's powers were genuine. The answers clustered near the affirmative side of a scale and almost never went past uncertainty to a point of denial. The eyewitness testimonies of individuals who participated in Alex's seminars are always positive. But even those who work with objective agendas, approaching psychic matters with a healthy immunization of skepticism, are inclined to admit that something was going on with Alex that could not be explained away with materialist accounts of human experience.

Karlis Osis spent the good part of his career setting up controls to isolate and test the variables of psi and other psychic powers. He regarded Alex as the real thing, and the best subject for OBEs that he had ever worked with or seen. He had no reservations about the reality of Alex's powers, and after a number of years of testing pronounced Alex as "gifted with psychic powers." Scott Jones, a career academic and intelligence consultant for the U.S. Government, used Alex in the remote viewing experiments for Army intelligence, the CIA, and the Secret Service. Jones was always careful to warn his superiors *not* to rely on any single source, including the psychic remote viewings, as the only basis for deciding on the use of scarce government assets. But he was impressed with Alex's abilities to discern states of affairs inaccessible to ordinary inspections. (Jones reported that he very much wanted, but did not have the opportunity, to correlate the remote viewing experiments with the physical and emotional states of the psychics, since Alex would respond with increased energy levels when he was on to something.) David Johnson, a close friend who had no particular agenda in the psychic world at the time and who was critical of Alex in other ways, was convinced that Alex's psychic gifts were genuine.

These examples represent the general responses of those interviewed. They constitute the eyewitness testimony that is the best and only evidence for experiences outside the domain of controlled experiments. Yet I think that this evidence obscures some promising opportunities and uncertainties in any evaluation of Alex's psychic powers. Alan Vaughan had no reservations in attesting to the genuine nature of Alex's psychic gifts. But he cited a telling experiment in the interview. (It is an event described by Alex in *Beyond Coincidence*.) Alex conducted sessions with volunteers to see lights on a wall. These lights were the "after images" of illuminated objects that naturally follow when lights in a room are turned off. But Alex thought he could make the images move, which (according to Alan) he did in one case of a sailboat "seen" on the wall. But then Alan reports that he asked Alex to stop trying to influence the volunteers and see what would happen. The result was that no one saw the movement when Alex withdrew his influence. Alan believes that Alex's power in these experiments was to generate a field of consciousness that affected what people saw. The power was over the person, not over the physical objects.

This experiment demonstrates again the problems of causal chains: What is the independent variable bringing about an effect in a psychic event? In this case Alex's mental powers may have been the decisive cause in producing the event. Powers that can influence perceptions and beliefs are considerable powers, not to be denigrated in any way. But they attest to the difficulty of identifying exactly what variables dominate in Alex's obvious array of gifts. He may have been an extraordinary teacher and healer exactly because he could create fields of consciousness within which individuals would see and believe in ways they could not in the absence of this influence. Most people would wish for such powers. But they do suggest different understandings of Alex's psychic powers than those offered by those I interviewed. They also indicate the ambiguities in settling on a satisfactory definition of what we mean by genuine psychic powers.

Then there are the perspectives of believers. Elsworth de Merchant remembers the visit by Alex Tanous in the dead cold of a Canadian night as a true event. Elsworth was a news reporter and a skeptic on the supernatural when he first met Alex. He and Alex had been invited to take part in a New Year's Eve program on a local television station. Elsworth was the end-of-the-year reporter on a show where everyone was holding forth on past and coming events. Alex was scheduled for predictions in the second hour of the program. Elsworth chatted him up for a bit when they went on the air, getting ready (in his words) "to nail him on something" when a note was passed to him that a major traffic accident had just taken place. No details were available. Elsworth thought, "Just the ammunition I need, right on the air. I'll get him." So he turned to Alex. "Dr. Tanous, I have a message from the news room. There's been a nasty accident. Tell us about it." Elsworth reports that Alex just sat there for a second with the "funniest little grin" and then said that a large truck with wood in it has fallen over on a small car near Mars Hill, but nobody is hurt. Everything will turn out alright, Alex assured everyone. When the television show ended, the phones started lighting up in the station. It seems that a radio crew had been tracking the accident and reporting live from the scene. Two women had been trapped in the car but were finally rescued unhurt. Everyone was okay. Elsworth and Alex escaped to a local restaurant to get away from the viewers who wanted to talk to the man who had been right on the money with his psychic seeing and predictions.

Elsworth was still not convinced. But the shared meal at the restaurant that evening and correspondence over the years led to a long friendship that did not depend on Elsworth believing anything about the supernatural. Elsworth was fascinated with Alex, not converted to the paranormal. The two would visit at Elsworth's home for three days of conversation every six months to a year. In between they connected on professional assignments. Every New Year's Eve Elsworth did an interview with Alex to get predictions for the next four years. Then the two would track the predictions through the year and Elsworth would write an article the next year based on what happened. Elsworth says that Alex's predictions would be over 80 percent correct, even allowing for ambiguity in some of the statements.

Elsworth confirmed that the visitation incident occurred in February 1976. Alex had been in New Brunswick the previous fall and had returned in January as a psychic on a murder case. Elsworth remembers that Alex had been very helpful to the police. In February Elsworth had been working all over the province and on that memorable evening had returned home late and retired at 1 A.M. Later during the night Elsworth heard someone knock on his back door. He got up out of bed. Phone calls were not unusual late at night but at that hour a visitor was quite unusual. He figured that a motorist had broken down on the highway. As he approached the back door his golden retriever started to get very excited, growling and carrying on, hair standing up on her neck. Elsworth pushed the curtain back on the door and flipped on the outside flood lights. There was Alex on the porch wearing a turtleneck sweater and a sort of herringbone tweed jacket, smiling "as he usually did, his hair a little longer than I remembered it from the last time I saw him." Elsworth opened the door and said, "Where did you come from?" Alex replied that he was just passing by and thought he "would come in and visit." Elsworth recalls that he was having a little problem with the dog and was just holding the door sort of "at half mast" to keep the dog from getting out. He grabbed the dog by the collar and pulled her away from the door, telling her, "Come, dog, get out of here." He released the dog inside the house and turned back to the door, but there was no one there. It was snowing, but there were no tracks on the porch, the steps, the driveway. There was a distinct smell of a cologne on the porch, English Leather, he thinks. The cologne Elsworth cannot forget because he happens to hate it. He says it plugs up his sinuses. He let the dog out. The animal ran away from the porch very quickly, "kept looking at the porch, barked her head off, and then refused to come back in the house through the back door." Elsworth had to go open the front door to let the dog back in. He says the whole incident seemed be over in seconds.

He was upset and intrigued. He sat down immediately and wrote down what had happened. He mailed the description to Alex in Portland, Maine, the next day. Two days later he received a call from Carlos Osis, the researcher who had used Alex in so many controlled experiments. Osis was at the American Society for Psychic Research, on the Upper West Side of New York City. He asked Elsworth point blank if he had seen Alex lately. Elsworth thought the question was kind of crazy but he answered, yes, I had seen him, but he wasn't there. Then he described the incident to Osis. Osis reported to Elsworth that Alex had been in the ASPR laboratory all night but had told the story of the visit to Osis.

Alex continued to visit Elsworth. On the next visit he stayed three days. Both swam in the pool, toured the countryside. Neither mentioned the incident. The dog and cat wouldn't go near Alex, however. Alex also continued to display his powers. Elsworth recalls that Alex could calm the dog by simply pointing a finger at her nose and staring at her. The dog would stare back, then lie down and go to sleep.

After that last visit, Alex and Elsworth continued to correspond, sending papers and books back and forth. In 1979 Elsworth changed professions. He joined the provincial government as Director of Information, and he and Alex lost touch with each other—except for one further incident. Elsworth had to travel to London on business. In the hotel lobby was a sign: "Parapsychology Workshop tonight, Dr. Alex Tanous." Elsworth and

Alex sat up talking until four o'clock in the morning. He told Elsworth that he was suffering from cancer, that he had had surgery and the cancer was in remission, but that it would get him in the end. He predicted that he would not live much into his 60s. (He died at the age of 63.) When they parted that morning, Elsworth suggested breakfast. Alex agreed, saying that they should call it the last supper. They did have breakfast very early in the morning, since Alex's flight was scheduled for 8:30 A.M. That was the last time they saw each other.

Elsworth is certain that Alex had real psychic powers coupled to a supreme calmness of spirit. To Elsworth, Alex was a compassionate man who believed in the eternal life of the soul and the natural spiritual powers that he was convinced we all have. Alex's followers believe that he had these powers in abundance.

6

Alex Tanous believed in what might be called textbook science. He wanted to display his psychic abilities in laboratory settings, testing them in what he saw as the rigorous conditions of experimental science. It is interesting that Tanous and his cohorts had very little to say about the possibility that psychic experiences might be more effectively explored with different vocabularies and forms of reasoning that are still within the purview of science. These alternatives are worth pursuing. I once asked guests at a dinner party in my home why so many astrophysicists seemed to be preoccupied by God, while all the biologists seemed to be atheists. The biologist at the table, Will Provine, said he could answer the second part of my inquiry. Modern biology, he reminded us, begins with the rejection of a design in nature, and with this rejection comes the rejection of a designer—God. I thought this was a heroic answer (which Provine later elaborated in the interview summarized in chapter 4). Then, later that fall, I visited my younger daughter in Chapel Hill, where she was a freshman at UNC thinking of majoring in physics. I posed the same question to her and asked for an answer to the physics part of my inquiry. "Easy, Dad," she responded. "We refer to God so much in physics because we don't have enough independent variables."

Maybe this second answer explains in part why portions of quantum mechanics, a field where both independent variables and causal sequences seem to be in absentia, continue to invite speculation on the foundations of experience, and on the existence of God somewhere in the mysteries of the micro world. We do know now that the cause-and-effect relationships among macro events taken for granted in Newtonian versions of science do not exhaust reality. If a subatomic particle can travel along all paths and exist in all states simultaneously, then, in some bizarre way, entities can both exist and not exist at the same time in this potential or premeasurement state. But when particles are measured, their wave functions instantaneously collapse into a definite state. Can human understandings of God fit more comfortably with the type of event described in a quantum framework? The speculations seem endless. Robert John Russell, a theologian who was once a physicist, believes that the radical indeterminacy of the subatomic world allows God to act without violating the laws of physics. On this view miracles occur not as a contravention of natural laws, but in their absence (where God has free will).

The possibility of action at a distance among subatomic particles also offers an alternative in understanding psychic experiences: if the paranormal cannot succeed under the controls of cause-and-effect conditions in the laboratory, then causality itself might be opened for inspection, and perhaps even abandoned on occasion. Uncontrolled evidence for psychic events gathered in informal situations also might be taken more seriously. It is possible, after all, that the dissenters are right in saying that psychic phenomena may not be entirely suitable for the test conditions of ordinary science. Psychic events may be a family member of those strange and intriguing occurrences that quantum theories assert for the micro worlds of subatomic particles.

A revised strategy for assessing psychic beliefs would include a more generous view of science. Scientific reasoning may be the most closely inspected thinking of the twentieth century. It has been deconstructed, examined in isolated sections, reintegrated to working levels, elaborated, criticized, celebrated, dismissed, maintained. The premises, logics, and forms of scientific inquiry seem to serve as a background to be retained or abandoned as one examines varieties of reasoning in different social contexts. Also, contemporary science offers an enlightenment account of its own history and logic; and like all enlightenment accounts, the storybook version of science seems to rule out rival disciplines, including magic, alchemy, and metaphysics in general by elevating falsification to a dominance in inquiry.

But science, even as a programmatic effort to falsify, is complicated by the ways in which theory influences experience. Theory and data do not seem to be separate tiers. The two appear together as intimate partners in rational inquiry. At an ordinary level, we usually "see" what we expect to see. The influence of expectations on observations is also found at the highest levels of theory, not simply as a contaminating device but as a means to make experience intelligible. Michel Foucault cites the case of Pomme, an eighteenth-century physician who seemed to "see" membranous tissue on the human body "like pieces of damp parchment" that medical observers only a century later dismissed as pure fantasy. The fantastic tissues were dissolved by the later development of a more precise vocabulary permitting the visible forms of modern medicine to emerge.

In the weeks after Carl Sagan died in 1997, a number of television programs ran interviews that had been conducted with him earlier. One, on the Charlie Rose show, began with the host observing that his guest, Sagan, had once defined faith as belief without benefit of evidence. And it was on this definition that Sagan, the scientist, had rejected religion, since faith is contrary to the central role of evidence in scientific inquiry. Yet Rose also recalled the famous Sagan argument that disbelief in extraterrestrial life is arrogant even though (as Sagan knew) there is not a scintilla of evidence that such life exists. Why, asked Rose, could not Sagan have belief without evidence in God if he had belief without evidence in extraterrestrial life?

The question was never answered satisfactorily by Sagan, but it does point to the varying ways that unexamined belief and available evidence interact across fields. Sagan may have been an atheist because God did not accord with his background understandings of reality. He may have accepted extraterrestrial life because such life complemented and extended his accepted structure of reality. Intuition and faith may have combined to lead Sagan away from religion toward science, and in science toward beliefs that had no evidentiary base at the time that he accepted them. The beliefs in both movements depend on convictions about the way the world is ordered, even though this order is a construct of faith.

One reason that human knowing is dependent on background expectations is that we must have some things in place, without examination, in order that we may prove other things. If these place markers are missing, unambiguous connections among events are simply ignored. Contiguity is one such place marker in Western thought. For example: even the strongest correlations between patterns of sun flares and fluctuations in the stock market must be dismissed in Western societies because these cultures have no mechanism to explain such connections. Contiguity is missing: nothing connects the two phenomena. But in a sun culture that elevates the activity on our home star to a privileged standing in human affairs, such correlations might be clean and even perfect demonstrations of causal activity. There is no proof for either set of expectations. They each follow the background beliefs in how reality is ordered.

The influences of background expectations on research is well documented in the history of science. Sometimes even the very best scientists fall into the trap of seeing what they come prepared to see. Charles Darwin systematically collected specimens during his five-year journey on the *Beagle*. The Galapagos Islands were the richest areas of evidence for his later theories of evolution because of their geographic heterogeneity and isolation from larger land masses. This fortuitous geographical arrangement allowed the same species to vary with environmental differences. The one British resident on the Islands, loosely in charge of an Ecuadorian penal colony, remarked to Darwin that he could tell which of the Islands any given tortoise came from by examining the shell of the creature. Darwin in his own notes remarked that variation in species of birds was correlated with different Islands. These observations alone spoke to the impossibility of maintaining the theory of the immutability of species, a theory which was one of the linchpin theses in biology and religion at that time. But Darwin completely missed the significance of these findings, to the point of mixing up some of the collections of specimens from the different Islands (which later, in England, caused him much consternation when he finally understood the importance of this variation for evolutionary theory). He saw but could not understand at first the meaning or significance of the data he had discovered. The facts were conceptually distant from the dominant theoretical and cultural expectations of Darwin's historical time and culture.

More recent examples illustrate the interpretive dependence of data on theory even in the most precise scientific experiments. The American physicists at Bell Telephone Laboratories in New Jersey who inadvertently picked up surplus noise when testing a microwave detector in 1965 were able eventually to make sense of the unexpected data only with the use of theories about the universe. The theories consisted of assumptions about the identical (or uniform) nature of the universe from any observation point in it, and the statement that light from the early stages of the universe should be red-shifted as a result of the expansion of the universe. These theoretical assumptions allowed the physicists to conclude that they had picked up light from the very early stages of the universe. The definition, or meaning, of their experimental data was provided by speculative theories. Absent the theories, and the data—the surplus noise—would have been inexplicable (or explained by alternative theories).

The longstanding resistance of scientific communities to the possibility that UFOs are real can be explained in part by background beliefs. The thought that alien forms of life visit our planet is contrary to all known physical theories, which seem to limit intergalactic travel by the natural distances among stars and the absolute ceiling on rapid travel set by the speed of light. But the possibility of forms of travel not governed by the limit fixed with the speed of light, or travel that is not itself physical, has not been an alluring thought for those dominated by conventional science. In 1968 a two-year investigation by scientists (backed by the U.S. Air Force and the CIA) dismissed UFOs and rejected any further study of the possibility that such sightings are real. Yet a panel of nine scientists supported by Rockefeller money concluded in the summer of 1998 that there is "compelling physical evidence" that UFOs are not figments of our imagination, but some set of real events that we do not understand. The panel, led by Stanford University physicist Peter Sturrock, called for serious investigation of UFO phenomena on the basis of the evidence they examined. The findings resulted from a four-day discussion in Tarrytown, New York, followed by a three-day meeting in San Francisco. The scientists did not see any violation of natural laws or convincing evidence for extraterrestrial intelligence. They did see unexplained physical evidence inviting serious study (which they regarded as more promising than eyewitness accounts). The panel also reported that scientific communities might acquire valuable knowledge if the fear of ridicule could be overcome in investigating the topic. The reasonable translation: be open-minded about odd and anomalous events and prepared to examine and change basic concepts used in explaining experience.

The point accepted by all scientists today is that we encounter experience, even that gained from scientific observations, by means of concepts, abstract languages that condition our visions and provide the mechanisms needed to make experience intelligible. There are no facts without theories (though there are theories without facts). A fact is a statement that the world is a certain way as ordered by the best theories of the time. Theory and data occasionally do not fit. Anomalies can occur, which roughly are experiences that cannot be accommodated by theory. Sometimes anomalous experiences cause a shift, perhaps minor, at times substantial and rapid, so that we are required to have a new arrangement of concepts to account for reality. But the reality we encounter is set by the filters of languages, and the formal uses of evidence—in argument, critical tests that falsify, auxiliary hypotheses that retain—occur always within a complex framework of theory and observation. Both levels of science must be attended to in explorations of the supernatural, not just the part of science that touches the empirical world. The abstract levels of science are sometimes the more important resources in explaining psychic experiences, for they represent in some way the neurological resources of the human brain. Studying these levels of science is a way of studying our own limitations and powers.

<h1 style="text-align:center">7</h1>

The tensions between the experimental science favored by Tanous and the looser arrangements of much ongoing science recalls the narrow tests of the Rhine laboratory. The memories of those who were part of that historical scene is testimony to the emphasis on controlled testing. Sally Feather is the next-to-oldest of the Rhines's four children. She was born in 1930, less than three years after her parents arrived on the Duke University campus to begin their lifelong efforts to test psychic abilities with controlled experiments. Her childhood memories are filled with the work her parents did in the newly established paranormal laboratory, much of which, she recalls, "spilled over around the house." The house was often full of visitors who her parents described to her as "important," and all the laboratory people would come over every Saturday. The Rhine family home had a big back yard. Her mother would cook, and her father would play softball with his colleagues. In early 1941, with the war years on the horizon, the Rhine family moved to a house on Lake Junaluska to escape the heat of the no-air-conditioning world of North Carolina. Feather remembers that things were so tight and exciting. Then the war began, and the young men disappeared into military service. Feather was a teenager by then. She began working in the laboratory, checking data at first. This was a time long before computers or calculators, and so the work had to be done by hand. One of the experimenters got very upset when she found a mistake. He was someone who did not think that he could make a mistake, but he did, and a teenager caught it.

Feather recalls the protracted and even endless conversations about disentangling the causal chains in psychic experiences. Her parents and

McDougall were prepared to see the exercise of psychic powers as veridical, but impossible to test in the typical ways that they were manifested in life experiences. This problem of fitting the experiences to the laboratory was the main reason for cutting back on the number of phenomena tested, even after acknowledging that many non-testable experiences were probably real, and concentrating on the manageable expressions of ESP in the card testing experiments. At first her parents were stymied over which methods to use in testing the paranormal, an uncertainty that was resolved with the design of the Zener cards. The Rhines tested children in orphanages first, then the students that Banks had in his classes at Duke. Even at the beginning, Feather reports, some individuals did much better than others, and these students were initially singled out for further testing, including examinations of the psychological and physical conditions that might occasion the display of talent.

The early years of this testing were very informal. There was no actual laboratory until 1935, five years after the start of the tests. But from the beginning the Rhines were the primary experimenters. McDougall was chair of the new psychology department, and according to Feather, his time and energy were devoted to building this academic unit. He was not physically present much around the laboratory, but he was her father's intellectual mentor, and Banks did report to him. Feather remembers him vaguely as a large man with a hearing aid. She also recalls her father telling her (she thinks she was six or seven years old at the time) that McDougall was the most famous, the most important man she would ever meet. He died painfully in 1938, after a long battle with lung cancer. Feather believes that McDougall was the only psychologist in the world at that time who had the stature to supervise research into the paranormal.

In 1947 Feather went away to college, to the same school her parents had attended, the College of Wooster in Ohio. She majored in biology, knowing by her junior year that she wanted to return to Durham and work in parapsychology. One of her psychology professors at Wooster had admonished her with the skeptical grail of vocational inquiries: "You don't believe in that, do you?" Well, yes, she did, with a belief that was augmented when her father visited the campus for a talk. (Feather's husband, whom she met at Wooster, told her that she was the only student on campus with a famous parent.) Later, when she returned to the Duke laboratory, Feather began working with animals, trying to determine if they had ESP. Then she married and moved away from parapsychology for awhile, earning a PhD in clinical psychology at Duke University. She still thought that she might use the doctorate to do experimental work in parapsychology. The parapsychology lab had moved off the campus by then, and so Feather found herself doing experiments one year at the para-psychology lab and then the next year moving a few hundred yards onto the campus to do standard experimental work in Duke's psychology department. But she went through a divorce, and by then had small children to support, so she began working in traditional fields of psychology with "a 9-to-5 job" for which she "didn't have to think so much." She describes research into parapsychology with a combination of realism and melancholy: "the salaries are poor, the jobs are few—it's a tough field."

In 1993 Feather returned to Durham and parapsychology with a new husband. She built a house right on the space where her parents' home was located, and she and her husband joined the board of directors of the newly named Rhine Center. In this position Feather can inspect the high-tech use of computers to test psi powers, and she can reflect on the history of the Rhine laboratory. She remembers cases of cheating in the experiments, of workers so eager to find psychic abilities that they manipulated the data. But she also remembers a father who was the most careful researcher she has ever met in any field, and the most skeptical in never taking anything at face value. Feather describes her father rather ironically as a behaviorist, no less, in the field of parapsychology, meaning that he dismissed talk of mind in favor of strict descriptions of observable behavior. On the whole she still regards the controls in the laboratory as being as tight as any she has found in laboratories during the years before computers. Now the possibilities of fraud are minimal given that so many tests are double-blind and run directly on computers, and that cameras record the isolated subjects during tests.

All along the research paths developed by her parents was the awareness, Feather reports, of the parallel universe of spontaneous psychic experiences that could not be formally tested. Sometimes this awareness was brought home by the special subjects, the gifted individuals who seemed genuine in their own settings but could not perform on demand in a laboratory. Eileen Garrett would get some good, some mixed results in the laboratory, but Feather admits that, on the whole, the laboratory was designed to test for attributes in the general public, not explore the gifted individual outside formal testing. Her father's 1934 monograph, *Extra-Sensory Perception,* documented the testing of several individuals who scored extraordinarily high. But shortly after that early period, researchers stopped looking for individuals. Patterns of ability were the targets of the research.

The irony for Feather in the entire history of the Rhine experiments is that her father may well have the distinction of being the most controversial of all American psychologists. She says it is a designation he would not have wanted. He is in her memories a distinctly nonconfrontational person, a gentle, sweet, kind person who wanted to be a minister. He never expected to have the kind of effects or reputation that he had and has. But she recalls that he died the perennial optimist, believing to the end that what he had done was important, and that it would make a difference.

The relaxed and open atmosphere in the laboratory is attested to by another survivor. Dorothy Pope was hired in 1938 for clerical and administrative work shortly after graduating from Brown University with a Phi Beta Kappa ring. She told me in our interview that at the time she had twin daughters, her marriage was quickly folding, and she was unhappy in the clerical work she was doing in Providence, New Hampshire. So she wrote a letter to the Rhines telling them all about her education (math and Latin, which finally led to an English major) and her work "and all that crap." It worked. She was hired and immediately began displaying her talents in every assignment the Rhines gave her. She became assistant editor of the *Journal of Parapsychology*, retiring from that position in 1982, but was still with the laboratory at the time of our interview in 1998.

Pope remembers in particular the discussion sessions. Rhine would gather the researchers and staff around a large, long table whenever a new procedure or method was to be given a preliminary trial. Everyone would talk the new proposal through, and there were usually first-rate conversations with "lots of fun, you know, all of us in there together and a lot of hilarity and that kind of stuff." She remembers being impressed with the freedom that Rhine gave to everyone. Even the youngest person on the staff could critique the proposals. Since most of the people at these meetings had doctorates or were working on them, the discussions were at the highest levels. Pope also remembers that the researchers were concerned with motivation. They were, after all, taking an individual out of his natural environment and "shoving him into a laboratory with conditions that had to be observed on account of safety and interpretation and that kind of thing." So the researchers would try to make the subject comfortable and happy, sometimes even giving little rewards (hence the reward of $100 to Hubert Pearce for each correct identification of a Zener card). But the openness of Rhine to criticism, to alternative methodologies, was a consistent theme at the laboratory.

One of the more sensitive memoirs written in any century is Louisa Rhine's *Something Hidden*. She tells us at the opening of the book that the "all-engrossing" professional question in her and her husband's lives was this: "[D]oes the human being possess any inherent feature detectable by objective scientific method that is not physical and which could give a basis for religion?" She recognizes this query as "the ancient question of mechanism versus vitalism" that has historically separated science from religion. These two disciplines, Rhine continues, employ "quite different methods" in addressing this question. For the Rhines, the question was always best answered "not by faith and authority, the method of religion, but by the method of experimental science."

Yet the investigations that the Rhines undertook began with ambitious topics that were unreasonably contentious and very difficult to confine to the laboratory. McDougall turned out to be a Lamarckian sympathizer. The first task that he assigned to Rhine was testing a hypothesis that trace amounts of individual experience are inherited. Rhine dutifully set up experiments with rats to see if anything might be retained from Lamarck's approach to biology. Louisa Rhine reports that a slight decrease in errors across generations of rats suggested some inheritance of learning experiences. Then the researchers examined whether the human personality survives the death of the body. This research took Rhine back to the activities of mediums and their claims to communicate with the dead. Examinations of telepathy followed. The later problems of disentangling the causal chains also occurred at this early stage. Is the medium hearing the dead or reading the minds of others still living?

To his credit, Rhine was usually the most skeptical member of any research team. Finally, in the fall of 1930, a colleague in the psychology department at Duke, K. E. Zener, helped Rhine design the cards he then used for decades in testing for ESP. It was not easy. Funding was difficult, and the campus was not entirely supportive. When research money came in, it was often directed toward "sexier" problems than the plodding accumulation of statistical data on "seeing" cards without employing the usual senses. Eileen Garrett, for example, and her benefactor, a Mrs. Bolton, were prepared to give a generous amount of money to Rhine and his colleagues for research into survival after death. Rhine actually pursued reports of a ghost in a haunted house to placate Mrs. Bolton. He later described to Louisa "how foolish he had felt when, alone in that little one-room building, he had repeatedly talked aloud to the ghost." All researchers have taken on embarrassing assignments at one time or another to secure needed funds, but Rhine's experiences must be at some distant extreme on the humiliation chart.

Rhine's later discoveries of inaccuracies and dishonesty in the controlled experiments were heartbreaking by comparison, however. Louisa reports the criticisms and their effects on her husband in *Something Hidden*. Almost immediately after the first monograph on the experiments was published in 1934, the people most sympathetic to psychic matters turned out to be among the more vociferous critics. The methodology of the experiments was questioned, and in 1938 it was revealed by Dael Wolfle (who had been alerted by B. F. Skinner) that the Zener cards were flawed. In 1937 and 1938, a spate of critical articles appeared in the *Journal of Parapsychology*, and some actually savaged the experiments. But nothing compared to the discovery of chronic and widespread dishonesty by one of the main researchers, who had reported some of the most significant findings. Rhine made this discovery just as he was about to present his research to the 1938 national meeting of the American Psychology Association. Rhine was devastated by the revelation.

The scientific boundaries of the research programs in the parapsychology lab were never as tight as one would have hoped, however, even when they worked properly. Rhine seemed always pulled between the need for rigor in his work and his lifelong fascination with the powers of consciousness to extend beyond the conventional limits of nature *and* the laboratory. He was ready at least on occasion for the fringe experiment. Read part of a letter Rhine wrote to Timothy Leary in 1961: "Some of our people are eager to get started on psylocibin experiments and if you have enough of the drug for a short experimental project, I hope you will bring it along." Is it too much to wonder what has happened to the Zener cards at this point?

But the best insight into the Rhine experiments may have been provided by Rhine himself. In a letter to the editor of the *Chronicle* published on December 6, 1996, Peter Klopper, a professor in the Department of Zoology at Duke University, recalls his stint as a research assistant in the parapsychology lab: "When I pointed out to Rhine that he couldn't ignore the rounds that didn't give him the desired result without invalidating the statistical tests he was employing, he replied, 'the abilities of a clairvoyant are highly fragile: They come and go, so there is no reason to include data from trials where they are not present.'"

One wants to say, yes, exactly the point. But then one has abandoned experimental trials for the more complex and rewarding trials represented by real human experiences of alternative realities and altered states of consciousness. Certainly the distinctions between religion and science become far more subtle and shaded than the concepts on which the Rhine laboratory was designed. Also, human connections—the fears and loves described by healers, for example—are now at last more promising candidates for enlightenment on psychic matters. And we may see more clearly what the seers and religious figures throughout history have tried to tell us: the supernatural cannot be collapsed to the paranormal. Experiences "beyond nature" may be understood as more real, and thus more normal, exactly as they are explored beyond the formal restrictions of laboratory experiments.

((Six))

SPIRITUAL LANDSCAPES

I

One universal datum in human limitations and powers is the inevitability of death for all of us. The significance of this datum exceeds the boundaries of any laboratory, for the certainty that life always ends in death is one of the more plausible *and* nonexperimental explanations for beliefs in a spiritual reality. We may accept another realm of existence because we cannot accept a material end to life. The strong negative emotions invested in death are universal and indicated in the frequency with which it is the subject of disturbing hallucinations and dreams. The many narratives and philosophies that define human death as a transitional stop in a journey to an existence after death can alleviate these fears with the prospect that dying is not the end of individual consciousness. In *War and Peace,* Tolstoy draws on a familiar metaphor in presenting death as a beginning. Prince Andre dreams that he dies, and at the moment of his death in the dream he awakens from his sleep with the understanding that death is an awakening. Popular art is even more rewarding in its sentimentality. In an opening scene in the film *City of Angels* (a remake of a true classic, *Wings of Desire*), an angel leads a small girl down the hallway of the hospital where she has just died. When she asks him where they are going, he replies, "Home."

No literatures, however, provide physical evidence for a life after death. Narratives may suggest that we continue to live in some form after the death of the body, but these stories always move through and alongside the secular and scientific views that no one has returned from the land of the dead to offer definitive proof of another existence. When claims for the survival of physical death are accepted in spiritual communities, the implications are often extraordinary. These implications are especially profound for religious movements. The conviction that Jesus Christ was resurrected after dying has been a core belief in the development of Christianity.

Now, at the end of the twentieth century, reports from individuals who have visited what they believe is a reality after death are being filed and examined in medical settings. These near-death experiences (NDEs) are an unexpected union of the supernatural and science: they are typically presented as spiritual events crafted from Western technology. Individuals who have had no cardiac and pulmonary functions for up to an hour, who are "dead" on criteria used for centuries, can now be retrieved successfully by medical techniques. Score one for science, zero for death. But death has played an unanticipated trump card. Many survivors of near-death experiences describe a spiritual region that we are presumably to enter when we die. For the first time in history, research into death has subjects who have died (in traditional terms) and come back to tell what they have seen.

The sights are extraordinary by any standards, and easily the most dramatic version of a self capable of leaving and returning to the body. The descriptions of this uncharted reality follow a narrative of travel and spiritual redemption and have been cataloged in works like Raymond Moody's *Life after Life*. The individual often recalls being declared dead by those nearby. At this point he feels outside of his physical body and is often able to view his body and the efforts being made to resuscitate him without being able to communicate with anyone in the world left behind. Then he hears an uncomfortable noise—ringing or buzzing—and enters a long dark tunnel. An intense feeling of peace, of bliss even, soon descends on the person. Figures come near, loved ones who have died. A being of light—warm, comforting—appears and leads the individual through an evaluative review of his life almost scene by scene.

At some point the individual realizes with considerable reluctance that the moment of death is not at hand, that he must return to life to complete some unfinished assignment. He rejoins his body and resumes living. The memory of the near-death experience often remains with him, and typically changes him permanently. He become more reflective, less concerned with life's trivia, and no longer fears death.

The near-death experience is a frequent but not universal experience for those who have come close to death. Surveys differ in both quality and results, but data secured through a variety of sampling methods suggest that more than a third of those who almost die have some type of near-death experience. A Gallup Poll taken in 1982 revealed that roughly eight million American adults and some unknown number of children have had near-death experiences. More recent studies report that 35 to 45 percent of people who have almost died report such experiences. Details vary, but the reports are remarkably similar, and consistent with a structure that has strong generalizing powers across cultures (though the interpretations, and even the descriptions, of the experiences are often a function of culture or the individual's beliefs). One of the more intriguing discoveries is that the early stages of a near-death experience are more commonly reported than the later stages, which would seem to be consistent with the expectation that more people survive less serious brushes with death than more prolonged periods without vital functions.

There is little doubt that NDEs are complex mergers of physical and psychological/sociological experiences that may or may not indicate a spiritual dimension. Controlled experiments suggest the NDE can be artificially induced with chemical stimulants that affect brain function. Allan Kellehear has argued that the near-death experience (which he prefers to label "experiences near death") is a form of crisis experience similar to other crises, like "bereavement or in being lost in the desert or at sea." Physical and psycho-social explanations of NDEs are important. They situate the experience in neurology and in cultural contexts. Without these forms of explanation, we could not see the experience as a human response within and to events. For example, assimilating the NDE to any loss-and-survival experience allows us to regard and evaluate the experience as a coping mechanism for the individual who is in crisis. But left open by all parallel or reductionist explanations are equally important issues of meaning and validity: Do the experiences indicate a life after death? and How can we go about answering that question?

2

Helen Thornton is a more or less typical case study. She did not "die" and so did not have to be resuscitated. But she did have a partial near-death experience when her medical team almost lost her after cancer surgery. The cancer had been a surprise. Thornton had gone in for her biannual gynecological exam with no signs that something might be wrong. Her doctor gave no indication after the exam that she might have a problem. Later that week she called his office to get the results of her pap smear. His assistant, a young woman new to the job and obviously without adequate instructions, hesitated. The doctor was busy. Thornton shot over a quick question—Were the results positive or negative? The assistant answered, positive. That means I could have cancer, Thornton said. Yes, the assistant agreed, that means you have cancer. After hanging up the phone Thornton was so shaken she could not move. The time between that moment and the later hysterectomy still seems unreal to her. All during the week before the surgery she was convinced that she was going to die.

Her near-death experience occurred in the recovery room after the surgery. She was still unconscious from the drugs used to sedate her during surgery. At some point, however, she realized she was moving through an aluminum-like tunnel, like those she had seen in the funhouse at the fair. The tunnel was very bright. At the end of it she saw her son, who had died when he was only fifteen months old from complications following surgery for hydrocephalus. He was calling to her, saying, "Mom," and holding out his hand. In life he had seemed to Thornton always to have his head bandaged, which Thornton thought made him look chronically sad. But now his head was fine, its size normal, and she remembered thinking that he was healthy and fit. "He was reaching his hand out to me, but the light was in my eyes so bright that I could never see all of his face. It was like I was swimming, and he was saying, 'Mom, Mom,' and reaching for me, and I was reaching out trying to get him. I thought that he was trying to apologize to me. I said, 'Please don't ever be sorry, because I was so glad I had you.' I kept looking at this light, and I was thinking I wish the light would go out. . . . It scared me it was so bright. But I also wanted to go to him. It was like I was trying to reach his hand."

Then Thornton felt herself turn, and she was looking down on her own body on a table. Several doctors and nurses were working on her. They were all dressed in green and talking very softly behind surgical masks. The scene seemed far away.

Thornton felt that they were trying to mix and inject into her body a quantity of fluids to keep her body wet enough to prevent her from leaving permanently. The fluids appeared in different colors amidst the needles and bags and tubes. She thought the doctors were trying to perform a trick: mix just the right amount of this green with that red, and so on, and inject the mixture into her body to get her back. It was a kind of fight or contest. She knew that if she got too dry, she would leave for good.

Her body looked ugly to her. The abdominal area was hideous with the recently sutured incisions. She had on no lipstick, her mouth was open, her eyes closed. She could see her right hand opening and closing, the same clasping motion being made by her son at the end of the bright tunnel. She wanted the medical people to stop treating her so that she could join her son. She wanted to put her hand down and say, "Just stop."

She does not remember returning to her physical body. She recalls only opening her eyes and seeing her cousin, a registered nurse who was present in the recovery room, asking her, "What is your name?" Thornton answered, "Don't you know me? Did I die?" Everyone laughed, and the episode was over. Later Thornton found out that she had almost died in the recovery room from wild fluctuations in her electrolyte balance.

Thornton no longer fears death, though if pressed for an answer she admits to not being sure what her experience was all about. She leans toward a survival hypothesis and believes she had contact with an existence that follows death. But she also acknowledges that the experience could have been an imaginary episode triggered by drugs. That is the unsolvable conflict for her—either explanation fits the experience.

3

William Sutter concedes that his near-death experience probably was a type of hallucination brought on by drugs in surgery, though the vividness of the scenes he remembers still makes him wonder if perhaps he didn't briefly enter another reality. His surgery was facial. He had broken his nose and went in to have the bone set and a deviated septum corrected. The doctor gave Sutter cocaine, which is a standard drug to control bleeding in nose surgery. At some point in the surgery, with Sutter awake and alert, the cocaine started wearing off. The pain quickly became unbearable so the doctor gave him more cocaine. When the new dose entered his body he suddenly began hyperventilating. The doctor became agitated along with him. He had a patient unstable in the middle of surgery.

Sutter remembers everyone trying to calm him down. One nurse urged, "Just think of the most pleasant thing you can." Sutter loves to swim. He began imagining times when he was in the Pacific Ocean off the coast of California, when he was young and swimming with his wife and their small children. His daughter, seventeen at the time of the surgery, used to cling to his neck as a toddler when Sutter would swim across the water to the sand bar at the far edge of the cove. Sutter began imagining the scene—his daughter holding onto his neck, his four-year-old son paddling alongside in his life jacket, the sun, the smell of the salt water—it suddenly was real. He was there, in one of those moments in his life when he was relaxed, content.

Suddenly he lost control again and began crying, sobbing out of control. The nurse, alarmed, asked him what was wrong. "The happiest time in my life," he remembers blurting out, "and it is gone, my children are grown now, and my wife and I are separated." He began hyperventilating again and lost consciousness.

The next thing he remembers is being out of his body, somewhere near the ceiling, gazing at a busy scene below. He could see himself on a bed or table and a nurse kneeling on his chest trying to stop the hyperventilation. The nurse's voice drifted up to the ceiling. She was saying, "OK, you can breathe when I count to a certain number, not before."

Sutter felt exceedingly calm up in the corner of the ceiling watching this activity. He turned his head slightly and saw a tunnel with a bright light at the end of it. He thought, "I'm going to die," and began wondering if he would see Greg, the grandfather whom he had loved so much. Then he wondered about his grandmother, who had died at the age of thirty-five, forty-five years before Greg died. He remembers worrying briefly about the discrepancy in their death ages and then realizing that spirits have no ages. He felt calm, in a mood of acceptance.

It was the conversation among the medical people below that brought him back down. The doctor asked one of the nurses to call his wife in to help calm him, stabilize his condition. The nurse answered that his wife was not in the hospital, but his daughter was in the waiting room. He remembers thinking, "Oh, no. Jody needs me. I really have to snap out of this." Jody was the daughter in the hospital, the child who was still fragile from Sutter's point of view. She was the one who needed his attention and care. This thought brought him back to his physical body, where he began controlling his breathing by responding to the nurse's count.

The frightening part of the experience for Sutter now is the realization that dying is easy. We can just give up and pass over unless there is some reason to be here, something to be done that no one else can do. If he hadn't felt a sense of need at the moment when he saw the tunnel and the light, he is convinced he would have died during the surgery.

4

If near-death experiences reveal a life after death, then nothing can be more puzzling about the experiences than null cases. How can we explain those instances in which the individual recalls nothing of the experience of almost dying?

Frank Butler came close to dying after surgery. He was in a minor automobile accident. Someone "rear-ended" his car, leaving him with back pain that got worse over the weeks and months following the accident. His doctor prescribed limited activity, then complete bed rest for two weeks. Nothing helped. The pain reached the point where Butler couldn't sit, stand, or even lie down without distress. So his doctor finally sent him to the hospital for a procedure in which dye is injected into the back to gain a complete X ray of the vertebrae. The results confirmed a herniated disc. The memorable event for Butler during this examination was a seemingly casual comment made by one of the nurses giving him an EKG. "Did you know you have an extra beat?" the nurse asked. Butler didn't know and thought nothing of it until his later troubles began.

The back surgery was uneventful and successful. Butler felt great in the days immediately following the operation. He was free of pain for the first time in months and optimistic about a complete recovery. Then, on the third day after surgery, he felt bad for some reason. He told the nurse he was feeling a bit punk and had a little pain in his chest. She sent some doctors up to see him. They took an EKG and said everything was fine.

The following morning he again told the nurse he did not feel well. A couple of cardiologists were summoned. They took another EKG and had Butler taken downstairs to one of the treatment rooms. He remembers lying there waiting and the doctors coming in and telling him that he had suffered a mild heart attack. Butler couldn't believe it. There had been no heart problems of any sort in his family. Then they took him up to an intensive care unit. On the way, he arrested.

Butler was unconscious for most of the next several days. When he went into cardiac arrest the first time, electrical stimulation was needed to restart his heart. In the next twenty-four hours, he arrested eight times. When they put a temporary pacemaker in, he arrested. One time he regained consciousness, sat up, and promptly pulled the respirator tube out of his mouth. The last thing he remembers before arresting that time was the doctor rushing in at 4:00 A.M. and calling him a son of a bitch. Every time he moved, it seemed, he would go into cardiac arrest.

Once, when the medical team thought they had Butler stabilized, they transported him out of intensive care to do an echocardiogram. Butler's wife and children were in the lounge on the same floor as the intensive care room. In this particular hospital, the staff shouts "six charley" three times when a patient is in distress. Butler's family heard the shouts, and his wife turned to the children and said, "That can't be Dad because they still have him upstairs." Her daughter went to check. It was Butler. They had brought him back to intensive care, and he had arrested again. This one lasted for forty-five minutes.

It was during this long arrest that a doctor came out and told Butler's family that he probably was not going to make it. He said they had never had a patient who had arrested so frequently and, now, for so long, who had survived. He told Butler's wife that they were going to continue CPR, but they were not optimistic. He also admitted that they did not know why Butler kept arresting in spite of all their best efforts to control his condition.

Butler's heart function stabilized when the doctors immobilized his body. After resuscitating him from the prolonged arrest, they injected him with pavulon, a drug that paralyzes the body. Butler could not move a muscle. They kept him on pavulon with a morphine drip for three days. Every time he regained consciousness they explained to him why he was paralyzed, counseling him to relax and ride it out. He did not arrest again. Finally they took him off the pavulon, and he gradually regained normal movements. His heart function continued to be strong. After three weeks recovering in the hospital, he was discharged, and he went home for a full recovery. The only lasting effects of his ordeal are minor problems with short-term memory.

There was one final scare, however. Before Butler had gone into the hospital for the back surgery, he had made his wife and doctor promise that there would be no blood transfusions ("unless," Butler told his wife, "from your sister, who definitely does not fool around"). He feared AIDS—rationally, at the time. But when he was in the hospital arresting time and again, the doctors were withdrawing blood frequently to monitor his blood gases. At one point in the ordeal the doctors told his wife he had to have a transfusion. She objected, reminding them of the commitment. Butler's doctor put up his hands. There was no choice, he told her. Butler was given the transfusion, though no one told him about it while he recovered.

Later, when he went back to the hospital for the final catheterization of his heart, Butler reported to his doctor that he had been losing a lot of weight lately. The doctor nodded and said that they were going to give him a test for HIV because of the blood transfusion. Butler turned to his wife ("If looks could kill," Mrs. Butler recalls), then looked at and through his doctor. "And you're worried about me smoking?" he asked. Three days later Butler was out on the golf course playing when his son came out and announced that the HIV test was negative. Butler was so relieved he kissed his playing partner sitting next to him in the golf cart. "Please," his partner remarked, "I'm not clean." Butler gets checked for AIDS every six months. Four years later he is still free of the disease and its syndrome.

Frank Butler was dead (on traditional understandings) for forty-five minutes in an intensive care room at a hospital. He saw nothing during this experience—no tunnel, no light, no accompanying spirits, no sense of himself outside of his body, no existence beyond the ordinary world. Everyone has asked him about the experience, beginning with the nurses in the hospital right after he regained consciousness. He has thought about making up stories—that he saw God and she is black, wears a single gold earring, and smokes pot, or that he saw all of his deceased friends down there somewhere shoveling coal into an enormous oven. But the truth is that the experience for him was like going to bed at night and waking up in the morning after a deep sleep without dreams. It was simply a complete void.

Butler is happy to be alive. He retired from his accounting position in a national business a few years after the experience and now assists his wife in her job. She is the manager of a local golf course and restaurant. He does the accounting, for which his boss pays him nothing. He is puzzled that we can live all this time and then there is just a void at the end of life. But he finds equally implausible the possibility of life after death. Like one skeptical friend observed in a play on a Yogi Berra aphorism: "When it's over, it's over."

A short time ago Butler was playing golf and hooked his drive on the tenth hole into the adjoining fairway. He followed the flight of the ball and noticed a man sitting quite still in a golf cart as the ball sailed over his head. Then the man just fell out onto the grass. Butler and his son rushed over and began giving the man CPR, his son administering oxygen mouth-to-mouth. The man regained consciousness. An ambulance arrived and took him to the hospital, where he died twenty-four hours later after being resuscitated three times following cardiac arrests. Butler gave the man his best effort. But as he irreverently observes, "The thing is, I shot a fifty on the front nine, and then a forty-three on the back nine after it happened." He shakes his head, laughing softly. Death remains for him a natural occurrence with no second acts.

What is to be made of these experiences? One is tempted toward the irreverent: Nothing—and everything. Both scientific and spiritual inter-pretations fit comfortably with the data. The brain's coping mechanisms in coming to terms with death may conjure the most soothing hallucinations to comfort a reflective self going out of existence. These mechanisms may lie so deep within the physiology of the brain that they are universal across cultures. But spiritual interpretations fit equally well. The near-death experience may be proof of an existence after death in a reality completely unlike ordinary experience.

But Frank Butler does present an interesting and unresolved issue for all veridical interpretations of the near-death experience. After hearing the account of an utter void from a good and sensible man, one is curious, spiritually, about the selection criteria for those who are to have a life after death, and, scientifically, about the physiological requirements to have those experiences, or at least memories, of another existence that so many others relate after nearly dying.

5

What happens when we die?

A number of physiological changes mark the onset of death. These changes can be precisely noted when death is a gradual decline and final cessation of vital functions. Respiration slows and stops. Cardiac activity often changes erratically, sometimes speeding up and then slowing down. At some point it ceases entirely. The brain, deprived of oxygen and blood, slowly expires. Body temperature drops. Secondary functions, like hair and fingernail growth, continue but eventually stop. Decomposition begins almost immediately. The body is no longer a homeostatic unit, taking and producing energy in a self-regulating manner. It has lost its powers to maintain its own equilibrium and begins to disintegrate. Slowly it becomes a part of the biological setting in which it once moved easily and autonomously. The person has become an object, a thing, a body that soon will not exist in any recognizable form.

Death is sometimes more easily understood in contrast to life. Classical Greek has separate words for being alive, living, and living well. Human life, just being alive, is satisfied when the human organism can function biologically, meaning that it performs certain spontaneous and continuous activities that integrate and generally maintain biological functions such as circulation, elimination, digestion, metabolic actions in general, movement. Karen Ann Quinlan was alive in this minimal sense. Living, however, requires mentation, the performance of cognitive activities. The

Greeks regarded the rational life as the distinctive and most important of human activities. Living well is a more complicated species of human activity, requiring an orderly and well-defined system of values carried out in daily life. It is sometimes said that living poorly is close to death, but such observations are metaphorical uses of language.

Death can even be broken down to distinct linguistic categories: a definition of death, criteria to indicate the definition in experience, and tests for the criteria. Someone (or stuff) that is dead is in a state of complete and permanent cessation of those vital functions that maintain the organism as a whole. The whole organism, meaning each and every part, may not have ceased functioning, for secondary functions do continue after death; and a wide variety of secondary functions (hearing, sight, movement, for example) can stop while the organism is still alive. The cessation of vital functions, however, means that the organism as a whole is dead and all other functions will shortly cease.

The criteria for death are widely recognized. The absence of cardiac, pulmonary, and brain activity over time indicates that the individual is dead. These are the three vital functions needed for life. Tests for those criteria have varied, however. The traditional cinematic gesture of placing a mirror under the nose and mouth to check respiratory function is now out of fashion. Even the use of a stethoscope to determine heart function is no longer definitive. Modern technology has provided sophisticated devices to monitor vital signs, so that physicians today can measure blood gases, respiratory rates, oxygen ingestion, subtle cardiac movements, and the waves generated by an active brain. Determining that an individual is dead is usually a precise and simple exercise today, though the exact nanosecond of death may be impossible to fix when death occurs in incremental stages of decline.

The tests for death are sometimes controversial. Reliability can be an issue, especially in the use of EEG tests to determine brain death. (There have been dramatic instances of partial and sometimes full neurological recovery from brain conditions that produced a flat EEG reading.) Modern technology encourages the thought that the cessation of cardiac and pulmonary functions may only be a temporary experience as well, reversible with effort. Also, tests are not always clearly fitted to the criteria for death. Cortical inactivity can sometimes occur with an active brain stem. Is the brain still functioning when it can only maintain cardiac and pulmonary functions, not thought? Still, it can be too easily forgotten that disputes over tests do not undermine the clear and paradigmatic sense of death that even children understand easily. The corpse dug up after three months in the grave is a dead body, and the definition, criteria, and tests that allow us to make such an identification are widely acknowledged. We know what it is for the organism to be dead, even as we may disagree over the full scope of those practices that define and determine death.

It is not always clear, however, exactly what dies in the event of a death. An individual dies, that much is clear. If the individual is seen as a person (in social relations with others in a community) or an agent (with autonomous powers), then brain death may be accurately regarded as death. But there are also problems here. The individual may in all important respects be dead, be extinguished, even when the brain is alive. Victims of severe strokes, for example, may be unrecognizable as the person everyone knew before the calamity. In some extreme conditions, advanced Alzheimer's disease comes to mind, the person may not even be there in any reasonable sense, even though the brain is alive. If, however, the individual is seen as an arrangement of parts, not completely identifiable with any one part (including the brain), then brain death is not enough. The death of the brain may yet leave some residue of the individual, represented in the bodily form that allows others to identify the individual. We know and love not the neurological brain, after all, but its embodiment along with other recognizable features—a look, something in the eyes, some life force we sense, a particular way the body is arranged, the history of a person's acts and words.

Nevertheless, the brain is the most vital instrument of the self, the one part of the body where the main features of the individual seem to be located. Putting a brain in a vat seems to relocate the individual, even though the body is left behind. The proviso that the individual is in some way the organism as a whole is eminently plausible. How can human identity be confined to a part of the body? But it seems equally strange to deny that the brain is the primary instrument for expressing identity. Reductions in the capacity of the brain seem to reduce the whole person in a way that bodily reductions do not; and enhancements of brain capacity (as with Charly in Daniel Keyes's *Flowers for Algernon*) can produce a different individual.

One sign of the brain's importance is suggested in commonplace resolutions to disputes over whether a person is dead. The use of spontaneous activity as a test of vital functions, and so of life, can no longer be applied to cardiac and pulmonary functions. Individuals can have pacemakers and be on respirators permanently. They are alive so long as the brain functions. If the whole brain dies, then healthcare specialists will almost unani-

mously regard the individual as a neomort, a dead body, even when artificially maintained with cardiac and respiratory support systems. One can
imagine, in some future time, neurological pacemakers that send electrical
charges into the brain to maintain its active state. No one could doubt
that an individual so stimulated would be capable of living as a person or
agent. The brain seems to be (and is) the center of human identity and
life.

If we stipulate that a person is dead if the brain and all other vital
functions are not active, and have not been active for a period of time
sufficient to guarantee that the inactivity is irreversible, then the closest
approximation of death is what courts of law call a permanent vegetative
state. This is a condition with no cortical activity but with an active brain
stem that can maintain cardiac and respiratory activity. The next closest
cut is irreversible coma. Here the individual is permanently unconscious
due to brain damage, but some cortical activity is occurring. Both of these
conditions must count as being merely alive since neither permits mentation. After these two states, a number of conditions are connected to death
in intimate ways. Individuals who are dying (death is imminent) or terminally ill (death will follow from an existent condition, but is not imminent)
need not be impaired neurologically. An individual in these conditions is
on a slope toward inevitable death, but is conscious and can function as
an agent or person.

Certain cautions are needed here. One is that we are all on some slope
toward inevitable death. But the differences between a healthy individual
who will die at some point in the future (because human, and thus not
eternal) and a dying or terminally ill individual are considerable. The dying
or ill individual can be a candidate for euthanasia. Not so the healthy
individual. Death is an appropriate consideration in the life of the ill individual, but not a vital reflection for the healthy individual. Mainly, however, the condition of the dying or terminally ill individual is defective in
the most essential way. The healthy individual, by contrast, is in a state
that functions effectively in terms of the natural laws governing the human
organism.

The confusion over the states leading to death is primarily in the differences between death and irreversible coma. Some equate the two, on the
grounds that the equivalence avoids diverting medical resources to hopeless
cases, permits the timely use of organs for transplantation, and is in the
best interests of the patient in avoiding a prolonged senseless condition.
The last is certainly an important consideration. But equivalence only es-

tablishes reasons for allowing irreversibly comatose individuals to die, not reasons to say that they are dead already. The tendency to equate the two states is assisted by the use of medical technologies that can maintain artificially the activities of some vital functions even while others are inactive. The unconscious brain may still be housed in a body kept functioning by cardio-pulmonary support systems. But the obvious death of a comatose person when life-support mechanisms are shut off indicates that irreversible coma and death are separate conditions. If, however, the brain is dead, with no activity in any of its parts, it is impossible to consider the mechanically-supported individual as anything but dead.

The main indisputable feature of death is that the individual is extinguished in the empirical world. All the senses of an individual—biological being, agent, person—are lost in death. The individual no longer exists in ordinary reality. In this sense death is the final event in life, and if survival occurs it is not found in empirical existence.

{

6

Dying is by definition a mysterious experience. The meaning of death cannot be fully absorbed since it contains the prospect that consciousness will end, or at least be radically transformed. Hospice workers tend to the needs of the dying with comfort care. This care is a communal effort to mediate pain and discomfort and provide some understanding of death to those who are terminally ill. For many a version of dualism is eminently comforting since it suggests that death attends to the body. The soul or spirit lives on after death. At a nursing home once, where I had gone as a volunteer to provide information to residents on how to fill out advance directives (which specify one's preference for types of care at the time of dying), an elderly man blurted out a question for me: "When you die, do you go to heaven?" To my lasting regret I gave him the answer only academics seem able to offer shamelessly: "The answer varies with different religious beliefs." I left the home filled with sadness that I had not seized the moment with the only answer he wanted: yes.

The near-death experience is intriguing because it seems to provide us with proof for that "yes." It invites us to turn away from materialism and reconsider with new evidence those traditions that accept an existence after death. No culture believes that individuals live forever in their empirical forms. Biology compels us to witness aging, illness, and accidents, quick and prolonged death, so we know a natural and final decline, or a sudden ending, to human life is unavoidable. So far as we know, no one escapes death. In this sense all humans are equal, an unwelcome leveler that would nonetheless be more intolerable if some escaped while others were forced to accept it.

The issue is not survival in the empirical world, but whether individuals survive death in some other dimension. Can the person, the conscious self, continue to exist after the vital functions have ceased all activity? To a materialist, the answer must be no. Persons may be integrated units of life, arrangements of organs sufficiently complex to permit consciousness to emerge from constituent parts. But in a materialist view the body, the total physical endowment of the living being, is the instrument or medium that expresses personhood. Take away the body, and the person does not exist. Death, according to a physicalist view, must end life for the individual in all imaginable forms.

It is important to remember that near-death experiences are not death experiences. Metabolic processes, including brain activity, may no longer be measurable in an individual who is having a near-death experience, but the individuals who "return" from these vivid experiences have not suffered from irreversible comas, or extensive brain damage that renders them capable only of merely living, and certainly not brain death. Physicians assume the brains of their patients are alive and functioning within normal parameters throughout the near-death experience, though often sedated with drugs. Put bluntly, NDE individuals have not died. No one who has actually died has ever returned to relate the experience in terms that can satisfy even relaxed notions of scientific proof of an existence after death. Experiences of a reality outside the boundaries of the empirical world are by definition not falsifiable. Faith is still the traditional resource for accepting life after death.

Nevertheless, the frequency and uniformity of near-death experiences suggest a type of survival after death that brackets, and perhaps falsifies, a purely material view of individuals. The arguments in favor of survival have traditionally relied on an understanding of the individual in dualistic terms. The body does not survive death. It is interred and disintegrates biologically. But a variety of philosophical and commonsense approaches to experience maintain that the self is somehow more, or at least different, than the body. In religious terms, individuals are unique instantiations of the divine. Each individual *is* a soul. In secular philosophies, the self is often defined by consciousness or sentience, which can be extinguished while the body still lives. These beliefs accord with at least some intuitions. Reflection often yields a sense of self which is not simply physical material, but something else not easily defined.

Yet equally persuasive philosophies remind us that the self may be no more than a collective arrangement of physical parts. The brain is a heterogenous set of items. Changes in this neurological structure can alter the self. Any of the traditional criteria used to define the self, including the core proposition that individuals have a concept of themselves as continuing entities over time, are vulnerable to neurological changes. Drugs, surgery, and natural changes in the brain can all interrupt the continuity of the self and even compromise the sense of self as a conscious, reflective creature.

Perhaps each of us is no more than a group of disparate biological items organized by the brain, with the consequence that individuals are in graded states of being in existence. Like a club or association, human identity may depend on a certain numerical threshold of parts and activities. But no definitive point short of death may exist to say that *now* an individual *is* when the brain is so, and is *not* when the brain functions less robustly, or, more to the point, slips to some lower state of activity. Are the Karen Ann Quinlans persons? Like Hal, the sentient computer in the movie *2001,* individuals may be forced slowly out of existence by declining cognitive powers. This possibility suggests an intimate and entirely dependent relationship of the self on neurological resources, with the conclusion that death—complete and final brain death—extinguishes the identity and existence of individuals.

This much is certain: To the degree that a mechanistic view of the universe is maintained, one in which individuals are discrete physical units located in space and time, and where the laws of motion and decay govern these units, survival is unthinkable. Individuals are born, exist in life, and die. They do not exist after death in a mechanistic universe, for they have lost their place in space-time through the death and decay of the physical instrument—their bodies—that afforded them an existence.

An alternative take on reality, the universe viewed in holistic terms, is more generous in allowing a life after death. Those subscribing to this view often use field theory in physics to generate a conception of the world that permits individual survival. Field theory regards events as interpretable only if they are placed within a larger context. Like notes in a musical score, the meaning of the individual unit depends upon its location in some collective arrangement. This collective arrangement has the conceptual power to define events from a variety of perspectives, most of which are formed from the use of different contexts. Thus light is either a wave or a particle depending on the theoretical frame brought to bear on the event. Units on this understanding do not go out of existence when undergoing changes, but simply are defined within different domains of theory. Wood becomes smoke when burned, but the change in form is simply a relocation in theoretical perspectives. Time itself is viewed as no more than a construct that governs the identification of events. Past, present, and future can all be domains existing on a holistic map of reality.

On such a holistic view of the universe, individuals do not go out of existence. They are constituted by energy and matter, and death is simply a rearrangement, a change from one domain in a conceptual map to another. This view of the universe as a cosmos extending beyond sensory reality is in accord with psychic understandings of experience. In psychic reality the individual is part of the cosmos, an entry in a comprehensive pattern that can be only partially apprehended by humans. There is neither time nor space in this larger reality, since these are constructs that the brain uses to order data and make experience intelligible. Death is a reabsorption of the individual into this cosmos.

The tantalizing prospect of a merger with extended being is that the experience can be sensed while individuals are still members of ordinary reality, which means that psychic phenomena are presentations of the different rules and principles of a possible higher reality within the context of sensory experience. Those who believe in psi and PK know that there is some reality outside the normal range of human experience. Those who have had mystical experiences encounter this extension in more direct form. The individual senses, *sees* the oneness or unity of the universe, experiences a reality without the dualities created by the constructs of space and time. The experience is inevitably ecstatic and dominated by a feeling of utter harmony. If death is a fusion of self with this transcendent reality, then there is not only an existence after death, but the existence is more real, more true, than anything found in ordinary reality.

The problem is that the reality apprehended in mystical experience illuminates the illusory qualities of ordinary reality. One illusion is the existence of individuals. The appearance of discrete, countable individuals occupying positions in space-time is just that from the perspective of mystical experiences—an appearance. Individual identity, that separateness of self that so inclines us to believe in immortality, is an illusion in the wider context of the cosmos. Given this enlightenment, it is not clear what survives death, or at a prior level, what there is in human experience to survive death. The mystical experience intrigues because it is an individual experience, and the individual who has the experience then returns to the biological state of the self. But if this discrete biological individual is an illusion, and if a more comprehensive reality demonstrates that individuals do not, and cannot, exist in any genuine holistic perspective, then the individual does not survive death (and technically speaking does not even survive life).

The lure of near-death experiences is that individual survival seems to be demonstrated, or at least suggested. The puzzlement is where and how individuals survive if the universe is a unity without distinctions. Perhaps the light toward which near-death survivors are drawn is the radiance of annihilation, a point at which individuals cease to be individuals—and rejoice at the experience. This possibility gives a somewhat different meaning to life after death than that accepted by most believers in eternal salvation.

7

The more important consideration is whether NDEs present an opportunity to close the distance between scientific and spiritual explanations. The brain (this much is beyond dispute) must be involved in all states of consciousness and unconsciousness. The NDE, whatever it is, occurs when the brain is still alive and so in a state that can in principle be documented. The most exacting representations of brain activity are found with the techniques of neuroscience. A recent experiment has suggested the chemical changes in the brain that occur in near-death experiences. Karl Jansen has induced what he claims are near-death experiences with the dissociative drug ketamine. He reports that all of the features of a NDE can be reproduced in controlled experiments with an injection of the drug.

On the surface Jansen's experiments are remarkable introductions of hard science to what many regard as a spiritual manifestation of a reality after death. There are limitations. The presentation of the experiments contains no information on the number or type of subjects, no data are offered on frequencies or intensities of responses to the injected drug. Jansen also admits that there are as yet no experiments inducing the NDE in those who have had the spontaneous experience. The exception, according to Jansen, is himself. He claims to have had a number of spontaneous NDEs and also injected himself with ketamine (an unusual practice in a controlled experiment). Not surprisingly, Jansen pronounces himself satisfied that the "NDEs and ketamine experiences were clearly the same type of altered state of consciousness."

But the experiments succeed in spite of limitations, in part because the NDE has always been amenable to controlled tests (though not, obviously, simulations). First, the NDE has been structured by those doing research on the phenomenon. The ineffable and formless nature of many mystical experiences, barriers to experimental science, are not part of the descriptions of NDEs. Second, it is also convenient that NDEs often occur in hospital settings, meaning that the conditions of an NDE constitute reliable data even as the reports by subjects have been impossible to confirm or falsify in conventional ways. The two most solid scientific pillars of NDE reports, however, are their frequency and uniformity. People of almost all ages all over the world report the experiences, and the reports have unfolded as narratives that converge toward a common structure. Given these helpful foundations it should not be surprising that those doing research in neuroscience have attempted to thicken the structure of NDEs by locating an evidentiary baseline in controlled experiments. The remarkable part of these experiments is that those who have noncontrolled, spontaneous NDEs believe that the experience is real, not an artifact of the brain like hallucinations, and it is precisely this conviction that the controlled experiments are challenging.

The outcomes of the controlled experiments seem to follow conventional physiological laws. For example, Jansen has administered ketamine to test subjects by two methods: intravenous and intramuscular injections. He reports that the near-death experience results from both methods but (as might be expected) the intravenous injection produces a more rapid response that is yet less enduring than intramuscular injections. All induced NDEs reproduce the structure of the experience for the subjects: feeling peace and contentment, sensing detachment from the body, entering a transitional world of darkness (the tunnel experience), emerging into bright light, and (provisionally) entering the light. The chemical effects of ketamine on the brain provide for Jansen the physiological causes of NDEs. Unlike other chemicals that act as tranquilizers on brain functions but are not hallucinogens (endorphins, for example), or cause the brain to conjure other types of hallucinations (LSD), ketamine seems to have a specific effect on brain functions that triggers the NDE. The precipitating neurological conditions of spontaneous NDEs (such as low oxygen and blood flow in the brain) apparently release a flood of glutamates, and this results in a dramatic increase in ketamine-like brain chemicals that bind to certain receptors to protect cells from the toxic effects of increased gluta-mate. Jansen believes that it is the ketamine binding that produces the altered state of consciousness in the near-death experience. His subjects in the experiments, their brains responding to the exogenous ketamine, feel the peace, enter the darkness, move to the light, and as an extraordinary pièce de résistance, are convinced after the ketamine wears off that the experience has been . . . real.

Jansen has a different fix on reality and NDEs. He argues that the simu-lated NDE indicates that the experience is an altered state of consciousness. On this there can be no dispute. But Jansen takes this conclusion to an-other, more ambitious level. He asserts (without much in the way of argu-ment) that the fact of neurological correlates for the subjective NDE means that "'mind' results from neuronal activity." He employs, in short, what appears to be property dualism. Oddly he seems disinclined to reduce mind to brain, though the quotes Jansen places around 'mind' and the tenor of the article presenting the work, suggest that the mental is biological, or even worse, epiphenomenal, entirely dependent on brain, and that the brain is the primary variable in explaining the near-death experience. Also, he observes that it is impossible "[w]ithin a scientific paradigm . . . 'that the spirit rises out of the body leaving the brain behind.'" The experiments, in other words, cannot address the spiritual claims for the NDE, and the spiritual experience (if it exists) is outside the domain of scientific inquiry.

The question is whether the two species of explanation are so sharply distinct. The spiritual approach to the near-death experience cannot deny neurological conditions and correlates. The brain is clearly the instrument by means of which we have all experiences, including the NDE. So it is not surprising that there is brain activity corresponding to an NDE. Nor should it be a surprise to discover that brain-based experiences can be replicated within the laboratory with the introduction of stimulants. Noth-ing in these claims and the experiments undermines the validity of a spiri-tual interpretation of the NDE. It is also eminently reasonable to see the brain as an instrument to gain access to alternative realities. It may be that we undergo certain physical changes in the transition to another life, and the right stimulation from drugs and probes can mimic and perhaps even initiate the process. The laboratory reproductions appear to undermine a spiritual interpretation or explanation only if we accept an extreme version of dualism that assigns ontological standing only to what purport to be physical variables.

But the distinction between mental and physical isn't clear even in the realm of the human body. Some events undermine the view that the self is entirely physical. The dominant physical theory of the person is a simple and unambitious materialism in which the brain is the biological locus of the person, and the body the vehicle for feelings and thought. The final stage of life in this view must occur with biological death. Another physical theory is possible, however. One may argue for a kind of biological holism in which the self is distributed throughout the body. In this view of the person, any division of self, whether brain and body or mind and body, is a distortion of the true corporeal nature of the self. There is no separate spirit to survive death. But some sense of the person may survive biological death if parts of the body survive. The alternative to both of these versions of a physical self is of course represented in the mind-body dualism accepted by survivors of near-death experiences. Here the person is divided into spirit and body, and there are no problems in assigning primary standing, and life after biological death, to the mind (or spirit, soul).

Consider the anecdotal case of Claire Sylvia. Sylvia, a forty-seven-year-old former professional dancer suffering from primary pulmonary hypertension, received a heart-lung transplant. The identity of the donor was not disclosed to her (which was hospital policy). Five months after the operation, Sylvia began dreaming of a young man, tall and thin, who was named Tim and had a surname that began with the letter *L*. She also developed tastes and traits that disturbed her and puzzled her friends and family. She began drinking beer and eating junk food, including chicken nuggets, and walking (her friends told her) with the gait of a confident and aggressive male. She felt that a new and distinct soul was present in her body, sharing her life and infusing her with a new masculine energy.

Years later Sylvia found out that the organ donor was a young man named Tim with a surname that began with the letter *L*. A visit to his family turned up the additional facts that he did love beer and junk food, particularly chicken nuggets, and was a restless and energetic youth who had died in a motorcycle accident. Sylvia was convinced that the young man's soul had gotten stuck in her body after his traumatic death. She consulted therapists, accepted and explored her dreams, and did what she considered the work needed to release Tim's spirit. After the release, her old habits and needs returned, and she feels integrated as a single entity now, "neither the old Claire nor the new Tim, but some combination of the two."

Sylvia's experiences, like so many anomalous events, can be explained in several ways. Two of these explanations are within material assumptions about the self and human experience. One is that the dreams and physical sensations, and the changes in Sylvia's movements, can be attributed to the chemicals that are given to all transplant patients. These medications include steroids that can produce masculine features and movements, and also unusual appetites. With this explanation, many of the mysterious results of the transplant are present and accounted for in terms of standard physical causes. This is the account that a mainstream natural scientist would prefer since it rests on accepted data and established theory. It is also the explanation that regards the cognitive and emotive self as confined primarily to the brain.

Biological holism, however, maintains that the self is the entire complement of physical systems constituting the entire body. One implication of this view is that all parts of the body may acquire memory in life, including the cells that make up all tissue and bone matter. When any part of the body is transplanted to another person, at least some of these memories may be transported as well. To put the point in clean and succinct form, Sylvia may have acquired some of the memory and perhaps the cognitive "stuff" of her donor.

This second explanation still relies on physical causes, but without the support of any clinical data or accepted theory in medicine. There is evidence, however, that indicates the presence of memory in some parts of the body. We do after all acquire muscle knowledge that stays with us even with lack of practice (like the coordination for riding a bicycle). Many athletes and doctors refer to body memory and often attribute soreness after a workout to the use of muscles that have not been "taught" to carry out new demands. The spectacle of "phantom limbs" seems to be a case of body memory gone haywire. The body can recall an amputated limb so strongly that pain is somehow felt in the missing member. The thesis of cell memory, however, is more ambitious. It suggests but does not prove that a transplanted organ can bring memories that the host must deal with as a conscious presence.

A third explanation moves us away from the physical domains that contain the first two. One might explain Sylvia's experiences as she does, with the acceptance that the young man's soul entered her body with the transplantation of his heart and lungs. Sylvia writes that in one early vivid dream, she and Tim "kiss. And as we kiss, I inhale him into me. It feels like the deepest breath I've ever taken, and I know that Tim will be with me forever." Sylvia wakes up knowing that the young man in this dream is her donor and that his spirit and personality are in her.

This explanation requires a movement of spiritual entities that is not countenanced by material explanations. One must believe that individuals are souls in bodies and that the soul leaves the body at death to begin some type of journey (which can on occasion be interrupted, sometimes because the soul stays for a time with the body left behind). The only generalizable evidence for this view that can fit rational explanations, and not just articles of faith, consists of the reports of near-death survivors (and these stories—as we have seen—can be interpreted in different ways). But the view does provide an explanation for Sylvia's experience and the one set of facts that the two material explanations cannot explain: how Sylvia knew the first name and last letter of the surname, and the physical characteristics of her donor.

Cases like those of Claire Sylvia, and the competing explanations that purport to account for them, invite an answer to the question of human identity that is at the center of life after death in particular, and supernatural experiences in general. In basic form, the question is whether humans are the kind of creatures who can transcend the conventional limits of physical bodies by redefining and perhaps rejecting dualisms of all types. Can we exist as spirits, without the body, or are we corporeal creatures in our entireties, needing the physical frames we call bodies to sustain our continued existence?

8

The Spiritualist Association of London is located in an impressive block of attached homes in Belgrave Square. Everyone entering the building by conventional means passes through a revolving door into a lobby, where two receptionists sit behind a high desk. The sessions with mediums take place in small rooms that one reaches by passing through a corridor and then turning right to walk down a narrow hall. On this June afternoon I am sitting in room seven waiting for Peter Walker, who has agreed to give me an interview on what mediums do and how they do it. The controlling assumption of the Association (communicated to me in my initial phone call to the organization) is that there is no such thing as death. People simply pass over to the other side, where they can be reached by the mediums.

The room I am in would be called nondescript by any discerning soul. The walls are painted a light green and are bare except for a painting of two clasped hands extending upward in what can only be called supplication. A single window is open to a brick wall at the back of the room. One small table and three modest chairs are at center right. I notice that only the medium's chair has arm rests. There is a tape recorder on the table. The first thing I do on entering the room is gently place this house recorder on the floor and set up my Sony recorder. On the left edge of the table is a typed note: "If you are dissatisfied with your sitting you must tell the medium within the first ten minutes. You will be escorted to reception for either a refund or replacement with another medium of your choice as soon as that medium is available." A Notice to the Sitters is posted behind the single door into the room. It consists of four numbered statements: "1. Every sitting is in the nature of an experiment. 2. It is not possible for a medium to give specific evidence required by the sitter. 3. A medium's work is to try to provide evidence of survival, and not to predict the future. 4. Refunds can only be given if the medium is told personally, before leaving the building."

I have just finished jotting down these two cautionary tales when Walker enters the room at precisely the appointed time. He is a middle-aged Englishman with an affable and confident manner. He takes his seat behind the table and, when I ask, says that the door should be shut and locked. I do this and sit down to ask my questions, but not before calling him Peter Taylor twice (a cohort medium or spirit?). I start with my standard inquiry (since Walker's profession is not a standard vocational choice): "How did you come to be a medium?"

Walker answers with a response that I have come to accept as the standard opening in psychic narratives (which makes it more rather than less persuasive): As a child, nine years old, he recalls, Walker began seeing things that others did not see. He saw a spirit. Actually, he was greedy. He didn't see just a spirit or two. He saw a whole town full of spirits. More. He *felt* as well as saw this assemblage of ethereal creatures, and this feeling was one of warmth and the security of an entire community. After this experience, he went back to the place where he saw this town full of spirits, only to find that there was no town there at all.

Walker's mother insisted that he join her at a local Spiritualist Church. He remembers the experience as better than the bingo that had distinguished his former church. But he still could not completely identify with any religion because of what he kept seeing. He decided to take formal training to learn how to use the real spiritualism that was all around him. Nothing happened in the instructional sessions for about three months. Then, during one novice reading he was doing with a male client, another man suddenly stood next to Walker. The visitor was stark naked, and the reason for his nakedness was quickly evident: to confirm his identity. It seems that he had a tattoo on his private parts that only his mother and brother knew about (apart from his fifty or so girlfriends). The brother was the client receiving the reading from Walker. The client was impressed. He told Walker that his brother had died in a car crash in Cyprus, and no one had ever brought him back before. It was a first for Walker. But since then, he reports, he has conducted thousands of sittings where the dead have returned to communicate with the living. He believes that clairvoyants begin telling people about themselves as a way of treating their own difficulties. They work through their own insecurities by acting as an instruments, telephones, he believes, for others. When he thinks back on his life he concludes he was searching for God and ended up being a medium.

Walker does not regard himself as a religious person. He believes that he has pursued the Christian ethic in his life but does not believe that religion is the answer to spiritual questions. In Walker's case he claims that he was having exactly those contacts with spiritual worlds that he found described in religious books. He regards himself as a kind of reverse psychotherapist. Instead of asking questions, he just provides answers: the dead appear before him in sessions with his clients and tell him about the clients' lives. Walker just reports what these spirits tell him. The reports include information on love lives, jobs past and present, and of most value to the clients—the future. Walker believes that the dead simply pass through a door, and the only difference between them and the living is that they cannot come back through the door. But they can return as spirits to give information and help to the living. Their most important contribution is to provide understanding.

The understanding comes to the living in the form of intuitions, premonitions, hunches. Walker believes that these feelings are often communications from spirits. He also believes that at night during sleep the spirit leaves the body and mingles with its relatives and friends, and guides who have passed over. These conversations enter the subconscious to influence decisions during the times that the individual is awake. We have lived many previous lives, according to Walker, and the life we lead now is one that we have chosen for ourselves. We choose our families and friends, and if they appear as unusually unpleasant, we must remember that the choice might have been inspired by a desire to learn certain lessons while here in this life.

Once Walker gave a message to a client about one of the client's friends. The friend was not very well. The client said, Oh, you know Jack. No, Walker told her, I do not know him, but I do know that he is dying of cancer. She said, Yes, it is very sad, really. Walker told her that Jack would die at three minutes past three in the morning on June 19. This conversation took place in March. The woman asked, Why are you telling me this? Walker answered that he didn't know, that he just knew he was told to tell her. They talked again later. Walker told her that Jack was all right now. No, the woman replied, he is the same. Walker said, No, I mean that he's ready; his sister Elsie is with him. Walker then explained to his client that the transition between this life and the next is painless, literally. On the evening of June 18, they spoke again. The woman said, You're wrong, he's getting better. The doctors are very pleased. No, Walker replied, he's calmer, more at peace. She said, No, he's getting better. Walker said, Fine. The following day the woman rang Walker up and told him very rudely that the man had died at three minutes past three in the morning on the nineteenth. Walker could not resist saying, I told you so.

Walker regards the near-death experience as an anomaly. Actual death, for Walker, is an experience replete with guides to help the dying person travel over to the other side. The near-death experience, by contrast, is isolated. There is almost no one there to greet the traveler, no familiar figures coming through the spirit world to meet the "dying" person (except for the lone figure reported by those who have the experience) because the person is not due to go yet. Walker is sanguine about the delirium that the terminally ill go through, even when induced by drugs. Unlike Provine he regards end-state delirium as meliorative (in helping the dying avoid pain and suffering) and instrumental in assisting the dying person to see visitors from the spirit world. These visitors, usually dead friends or relatives, reassure the dying by telling them that death is an easy transition, like walking through a door or changing clothes. The one difference is that when you do step through that door, you are given a new body, which you don't get with the near-death experience. Walker believes the near-death experience is probably very similar to what the medium sees: a vivid look into the spirit world without entering it.

Reincarnation is the fate of those who have passed over. For Walker the spirit world is unlike temporal existence. There can be no coercion, no lying (spirits see through one another), and no time. Some spirits will reincarnate immediately, some remain in the spirit world for what on Earth would be many years. The question is why anyone reincarnates. The answer for Walker is that we are all on the pathway back to God "because we are God's inner making." The point to reincarnation is to move further along that pathway by settling moral debts from previous lives. This point helps make sense of wretched lives. Spirits will select a handicapped life, for example, in order to balance an earlier life of advantage. Suffering on this view makes sense in terms of the larger equilibrium of learning, and the effort to become more spiritual by having experiences across many lives.

There is also what I call the Merlin effect moving through the spirit world. Merlin, in the myth, was said to able to tell the future because he was living backward through time. The future for mere mortals was his past and thus eminently knowable. Since the spirits live in a timeless realm, they can and do provide information to us on the temporal future. Walker believes that we all have a certain level of ability to gain access to the spirit world. But most, he says, do not develop that ability. He claims that he and other genuine psychics have taken the ability to high levels, and these levels permit knowledge of the future through contact with spirits. Walker does predict, and more often, he says, than most psychics. He has also predicted events without the knowledge of the person at the center of the prediction. These predictions, which control for suggestibility, have also come true he reports.

At this point in the session I have enough for my research needs. I tell Walker to regard me as a client for the remaining ten minutes of the session. I ask for predictions. He agrees and begins with my children. "You have three children?" I have two. "A boy and a girl?" Two girls. "Well, the eldest must be stronger. There's a very strong personality." He then proceeds to describe my two daughters at length, getting almost everything wrong except the predictions (which, of course, only time can falsify or maintain). Then he turns directly to me and tells me that I will die in my sleep. I ask the obvious: "When?" He answers: "I'm not telling you." Then he does something that at the time I found stunning. He zeroes in on the fact that one side of my family suffers from mental deterioration as they age, a kind of dementia that indeed has caused me some concern as I get older. His assurance is crisp and to the point. He touches his own forehead and says, "You will keep it up here, my friend, until the dying breath, that sharpness." Then he adds another datum. "You take a bit of a nap in the afternoon given the opportunity." He looks at me. "When you pass, it may not be at night."

After a final exchange of views on the afterlife, I thank Walker for an enlightening session.

What can we make of these types of sessions (that occur every day, all over the world)? The obvious is probably the least interesting: errors are as frequent as accuracy when observations are matched with actual information. The interesting exercise is decoding the *apparent* true statements. The one statement that galvanized my attention was the dementia observation and prediction. The man nailed down my one worry about growing old. But when I ran the prediction by my daughters, they were (as the younger said) "underwhelmed." They pointed out that I had presented myself as a professor on a research project, the author of several books. *Of course* I would reasonably fear a diminution of intellect as I age. Still, Walker caught the problem afflicting only the one side of my family and saw it as confined to only one side. I was impressed, but not convinced.

9

The Tibetan Book of the Dead (or, in Tibetan culture, the *Bardo Thödrol*) is a practical guide for the human death process that is widely read throughout the world. Scholars of Buddhism remind us that the English translation of the title is misleading. Death in Buddhist thought is a transition between states of being, and the book is a set of instructions to help us prepare for and negotiate our way through this state. A more accurate title would include a vocabulary of "understanding the in-between." The guiding character of the book is formed on an acceptance of the practical truth that human death is a passage through several stages involving states of the mind and body, and that the prudent individual is one who has prepared well for this journey.

For Buddhists there is an art to dying, and it must be acquired through careful preparation for death. The *Book* outlines five types of ordinary preparation. The first is informational, which is simply the acquisition of knowledge about what death is and what one might expect. The second is the cultivation of one's abilities to imagine the states of being that follow death. This second preparation requires a familiarity with the prominent texts in one's religion and a use of the imagination to conjure the (positive) visions of the settings for existence after death. Third, one must ethically prepare for death. The main ethical practices in Buddhism are generosity, sensitivity to others, and tolerance. These practices are life-affirming. Luciano Pavarotti once told a story about a time in his life when he was suffering from mild but chronic depression. Then he found himself on a plane from New York that encountered trouble in approaching Milan one foggy December night in 1975. The plane crashed on landing at the airport. Pavarotti survived unscathed but, in his words, "It was as though God had grabbed me by the neck and said, 'You are so indifferent about life? Here, take a look at death and tell me how you like that!' If that was His plan, it worked." Pavarotti threw himself back into his life and work with gusto, renewing his love of life and others. One could say that he was engaged again in an ethical preparation for death by living well and fully.

The fourth preparation is meditation. There are many types of meditation, both in and out of Buddhist thought. The most well known is the meditation that brings calmness. Buddhism urges that the one meditating assume a relaxed position with the legs crossed. Regular breathing is important. Concentrating on a meditation object helps focus thought. One begins to monitor one's own mind. Control of emotions and reactions follows. Insight meditation is the next higher goal. Here the calm and focused mind concentrates on itself, on the body and mind of the one meditating. The result of mindfulness is a discovery: there is no fixed and palpable self, no "real" self that meets the criteria of Western notions of individual identity. This discovery is the point of enlightenment. It opens the "self" to a heightened awareness of domains not restricted to the Cartesian "I" of modern Western philosophy. The next type of meditation is therapeutic. Here reflection shapes thoughts toward the positive and away from the negative. Imaginative meditations are the fifth type. These reflections conjure the unexpected and prepare the individual for a wide variety of possibilities. The sixth and final type of meditation combines spiritual reflections with the needs and logic of ordinary life to help the person infuse daily activities with contemplation. The recitation of a mantra is common in this type of meditation.

The *Book* also describes extraordinary preparations for death. These consist of preliminary exoteric enlightenment teachings, the development of a relationship with a qualified teacher, practices that accelerate personal evolution, the crafting of abilities to visualize, the heightening of creative abilities, and a mastery of the perfection stage, wherein the journey of death is rehearsed and may even begin. These preparations are designed to instill the person with a wisdom that extends far beyond the goals of ordinary preparations, and that at some stage may allow an escape from the boundaries of the self. The perfection stage involves a domination of what Buddhists call the subtle consciousness and leads to a transcendence of the space-time frames in which the body exists. Death itself can be simulated with a temporary cessation of respiration. It is a stage available only to those who have mastered higher orders of Buddhist teachings and discipline.

The art of dying is developed on an acceptance of Tibetan attitudes toward death. The *Book* takes for granted that death is no more than a journey to a waiting room on the way to a future life. It is never seen as an annihilation or the instant nothingness of existentialist thought (there is no uncertainty about this in Tibetan beliefs). Death is a conscious and involuntary movement to a transitional stage that all humans enter and then leave to begin the next stage of life. It is not altogether pleasant to die on this understanding of death. Yama, the God of Death, makes judgements about individuals after they die, and their assignments to the next level of existence may be undesirable in all respects. But death is inevitable and the most powerful force for consolidating life in a meaningful manner for individuals who continue to exist through and after the death experience. In a sense *The Book of the Dead* is a hard and deep inspection of our own mental regions, of human limitations and powers, that concludes with practical directives on death. It is a text that prepares us for the transition that death represents, from this existence to another existence still enriched by life.

Jung regarded *The Book of the Dead* as a presentation of the foundations of the psyche that reveals to the dead "the ultimate and highest truth, that even the gods are the radiance and reflection of our own souls." Jung recognizes inherited psychic characteristics, "such as predispositions to disease, traits of character, special gifts, and so forth," but he also proposes inherited forms, "universal dispositions of the mind," that, like Plato's forms or the modern understanding of neurological structures, organize the contents of the mind. These forms are typical images, which Jung has called "archetypes." He sees *The Book of the Dead* as presenting these forms to the dead. Since the forms are pre-rational and essentially visual, the vast sight show arranged as stages in the dead's journey is "karmic illusion"—a dream state not governed by the organized intentions of the conscious mind. But to say that the *Book* is an expression of the archetypes of consciousness is not, for Jung, to regard the account as "just" psychological.

The archetypes constitute the collective unconscious and so are not confined to any individual mind. The reality of *The Book of the Dead* is of course a psychic reality. In the skeptical culture of the West this means that the world described in its contents is not "real." But to a believer the *Book* describes the state encountered by those who die. Jung's notion that this state represents the contents of the mind can be seen as a natural extension of the foundations of consciousness to an afterlife.

10

My mother died on a Saturday. I had attended a Syracuse University football game in the early afternoon and afterward walked over to my office on campus to check messages on our home phone before going out to dinner with my wife. The only message was a hysterical call from Wendy, the woman my brother and I had hired to take care of our aging parents in the family home on Summerland Key in Florida. Wendy was crying and saying that my mother seemed to be dying, and she didn't know how to care for her. I called her immediately and reminded her of the instructions that we had all signed off on years earlier: comfort care, no heroic resuscitation. Then I called my brother and told him that it appeared that the woman who had borne and raised us was dying.

That day is a blur of cold decisions and overwhelming emotions. I was on the phone making dozens of calls, to her internist, to the hospital, to family and friends, again and again to my father, all aimed at bringing loved ones into the circle of death and grieving and ensuring that no aggressive medical technician would place my mother on a ventilator. She was eighty-three years old, dying of Alzheimer's disease, had been unable for months to recognize with any consistency her own husband, and there was no point to heroic measures to prolong a life that had lost the person who lived it. Cold and right decisions on the phone. Crying between every call. I told my younger daughter in one call that I couldn't believe the intensity of the emotions I was experiencing. Wasn't this death supposed to be a blessing? "But Dad," she told me, "this is your mother. What exactly did you expect?"

Late that evening I sat alone at the breakfast bar that divides our kitchen and dining room. The phone was silent, and I was watching the pendulum in the clock on top of the coffee table in the living room, watching it move back and forth. It was then that I felt my mother pass on. A series of her memories entered my mind, from her childhood in the early part of the century in Key West through to her adulthood and old age, like the gentle flipping of moving photographs bathed in a sweet yellow light. The pendulum swinging in the background. She brushed my consciousness on the journey to something else. One thought came into my head as she passed through me: dying is the most natural thing that we do. It is so easy to die. I phoned Summerland Key. The caretaker told me that the nurse practitioner we had called to attend to my mother had just come out of her room. My mother was dead. I went back to making phone calls to tell people the news and set up arrangements for the funeral. And every time I put the phone down, tears flowed down my face.

Is there a spirit somewhere in this story? Just before my mother died, my brother and I had visited our parents to see them and check the arrangements for their care. My mother needed help with everything by then. My brother and I bathed her, cleaned her, fed her. Her brain was so ravaged by the disease that she had lost control of both physical and mental functions. Yet one night, when I was sitting with her feeding her dinner, and she was sitting in the chair that overlooked the blue and green waters of the Keys, she came back. I could make her laugh with funny sayings, she made jokes back to me, and she told me that she could see her mother and several sisters (all dead). Such a return is not possible. There is no way that a person whose brain is virtually destroyed by Alzheimer's can return like that. Yet there she was, lucid, affectionate, funny. Two months later she was dead, the spirit I saw that day released for another journey.

The spiritual state of mind is at issue here. It is marked by a willingness to be vulnerable (to let experience break our hearts), a capacity to shift from temporal to "holy" time (in sensing the eternal in experience), to be prayerful, to touch and affect the other, and to respect ritual. These features of spirituality require the presence of a mind, or spirit, in the human body. Spiritual states of mind are special forms of meditation that focus on metaphysical questions: the purpose of life, the meaning of existence, the question (raised earlier by Leibniz, then again by Heidegger) that Frederick Copleston said philosophy cannot answer—why something instead of nothing? In these areas the spirit takes precedence over the body, and the reality conjured or found is never reducible to material things without substantial loss of meaning. [The doctrine of dualism may be strongest in those areas that seem to require a spiritual approach to experience, including the events of death, dying, and redemption]

((Seven))

MYSTICAL EXPERIENCES: SELF AND REALITY

I

The strongest beliefs in the powers of consciousness to detach from the body and enter a distinct realm of experience have a long history in mystical traditions. These beliefs are crafted on a recognition that the human body is a limited resource to sense and know things. In the unlikely event that this is news, enter in the record that our perceptions and thoughts do not engage experience in any complete or direct way. We seem to need instruments of mediation to structure and comprehend experience. The basic mediating instruments in the modern world, with all imperfections intact, are the senses represented in languages. Mysticism represents the impulse to abandon the instruments, to break through to something permanent and universal, something "real" on the other side. The image of "crossing over" to another side is powerful. William Blake, in a frequently quoted statement, said, "If the doors of perception were cleansed everything would appear to man as it is, infinite." Mystical experiences offer the prospect of a direct (though momentary) viewing of reality by a self that has escaped the limitations of the body.

The boundaries and contours of the self are opened in mystical experiences to what can only be called dramatic possibilities. From some perspectives mystical experiences are ordinary: they are so commonplace that they are taken for granted. We all sense routine shifts in consciousness that invite union with larger experiences and require holistic perspectives on events and other persons. Both ordinary and extraordinary empathy is a union with another, a welcome loss of self in seeing and sensing experience from the point of view of someone else. The power of empathy was claimed by Jung for many of his intuitive connections to the inner lives of his patients. There is little doubt, however, that the full mystical experience is on another order of magnitude. There is wide documentation for a complete loss of self. The descriptions are often modeled as sequences (paradoxically enough) that outline what its adherents describe as a process in which the self enters and becomes one with the true real world.

The first step in the mystical countdown is an expectation, shared by participants, that the experience is possible. A complicated architecture of background beliefs prepares individuals for both the shift in consciousness and the meaning of the experience. This first step, however, is bypassed when individuals have mystical experiences that they do not expect and have not even welcomed into their lives. Second is the experience itself, consisting of a brief but almost unbearably intense state of mind during which the individual is thought to engage a different, genuine reality, or attain a higher spiritual identity. The third stage is the period of time after the trance, when the individual has regained normal consciousness and is able (with others) to reflect on the experience and interpret it for his own life and the lives of other participants.

No one is sure what neurological resources make mystical experiences possible, or exactly what the brain does or undergoes during the peak moments in the mystical event. But the social interpretation of the experience is remarkably consistent across different beliefs and practices. At the core of all mystical experiences is an abandonment of the discrete empirical self. The individual is thought to merge with some larger whole. The transcendent moment produces insights into reality that mundane experience cannot provide. Like near-death, a mystical experience typically reconfigures the dimensions of reality for the participant. Persons often report that nothing is the same, though they do not always agree on what that judgment means.

The object of union is not the same in all mystical experiences. Sometimes the individual is said to fuse with God, or with a spirit representing a dimension of God. At other times the union is with a universal or divine principle (the One in Buddhism). Secular mystical experiences fold the identity of the individual into everything, all of reality. But in all cases the individual, the isolated self of ordinary life, is believed to have merged with a more comprehensive state of being, even if that merger is brief and unrepeatable.

The full mystical episode is both awesome and inviting. It is usually described as a peak experience, a sequence of ecstatic moments when the brain knows reality directly, without any mediating instruments. Both rational processes and sensory data are suspended in some way. One *sees* (and knows) immediately and exactly. The totality of the experience extinguishes doubt. Some students of mysticism label these moments as types of "zero experience," suggesting that a baseline has been reached where it is impossible to go any further in that type of experience. The defining belief is that one has experienced absolute reality.

Those who explain mystical experience identify one overriding purpose that is common to the devoted. They aim to discover a unity that is without distinctions, where all differences are exposed as illusions, including self and object and the separation of humans from God. The mystical experience is also understood as self-validating, desirable regardless of the consequences that follow the experience. A reverse validation occurs: the transcendent moment of a mystical experience itself discloses value and meaning for ordinary reality.

Mystical experiences can occur spontaneously. The legend of Saul's conversion on a trip to Damascus suggests that the mystical episode can even be coercively thrust on individuals and compel the most radical changes in individual identity (Saul becoming Paul). But most mystical experiences occur as a result of preparation over extended periods of time. In general the novitiate systematically denies the body and enhances the mind through ritual and study. Then conditions are put in place to trigger the mystical episode. [Mysticism, like all human experiences, occurs in a network of beliefs that simultaneously make the experience possible and ascribe meaning to its occurrence.]

2

Since any assessment of mystical experiences is likely to be influenced by one's prior sense of the real, it may be helpful to ask about the understandings of the self and reality that inform mysticism. What conditions of human experience are required for mysticism to be intelligible?

Unfortunately the best thinking on the subject has yielded a variety of contradictory views, making the identification of benchmark conditions difficult. Strong and influential theories have not only presented arguments that proof of an external world is impossible, but that the self is also an illusion (or at least difficult to prove). Then there are equally cogent realist theories asserting (in almost simplistic fashion) that reality is a Euclidean world of objects populated by conscious subjects.

Western culture is filled with conjectures. Bishop Berkeley maintained that all visual objects are in the mind. Thoughts exist, but the stone in the road cannot be said to be an object independent of thoughts. David Hume doubted the existence of a self apart from perceptions. Sense impressions are real, the person is not. Berkeley's view reduces objects to mind, Hume defines mind as perceived objects. Uncertainty on so robust a scale, where one can doubt the existence of both the self and an external world, occasions Descartes' reflections in the *Meditations*. These reflections finally lead to the acceptance of a benevolent and truthful God as the only guarantee that the self and an objective world exist. The modern scientific realities that provide comfort to materialists are products of a form of reasoning that excludes all spiritual presences.

The holism found in certain Eastern traditions offers a different direction, away from both God and science toward a fusion of all differences in experience. In these traditions can be found the quest for a reality that collapses the distinctions between self and reality taken for granted in Western cultures. The goal of Zen enlightenment, for example, is a relinquishing of the self, a "letting go" that extinguishes both body and mind so that pure being, absolute reality, can appear. A unity is sought that has no space for distinctions of any sort, whether self-object, mind-body, reality-God, human-God, perception-object, thought-object. There is simply a seamless One that eliminates even the differences between thought and thinker that allows individual understandings of unity. This absolute unity requires a logic outside of language, a transcendence of the necessary modalities and sequences of human thinking. Reality *is,* with no dualities at all. Like Husserl's reductionism, reflection on perception and the self (or ego) seeks an unmediated experience that can absorb the self.

Let the words of those who say that they have had mystical experiences guide us in our attempt to understand a holistic reality.

"One night when I was about twelve, it happened for the first time. I was falling asleep, when the whole world turned into one: one entity, one indivisible certainty. No euphoria, no colors, just a deadeningly sure oneness at which I was at the center—as everything else just this, and nothing else. For a fraction of a minute perhaps, I saw nothing, felt nothing, but was that oneness, empty of content and feeling." (Agehananda Bharati)

"But as I turned and was about to take a seat by the fire, I received a mighty baptism of the Holy Ghost. Without any expectation of it, without ever having the thought in my mind that there was any such thing for me, without any recollection that I had ever heard the thing mentioned by any person in the world, the Holy Spirit descended upon me in a manner that seemed to go through me, body and soul. I could feel the impression, like a wave of electricity, going through and through me. Indeed it seemed to come in waves and waves of liquid love; for I could not express it in any other way. It seemed like the very breath of God. I can recollect distinctly that it seemed to fan me, like immense wings." (Charles Finney)

"My eyes closed, I suddenly perceived inwardly a long cloudbank in an azure sky. A brilliant sun rose above the clouds until it was clear of them; as it rose, it seemed to grow brighter and brighter and I sank deeper and deeper into an intense rapture, a sheer intensity of feeling and concentration excluding all else, even joy. Then, after a timeless moment, the sun gradually began to fade and I gradually became more aware of my surroundings; I began to talk to my wife about what happened. I recall that as the sun faded, more detail appeared. I saw small objects, like planets or planes, circling the sun briefly. Then finally it was lost from view but seared indelibly on my memory. The experience was so powerful that for over an hour afterward I could not do anything, not even read; I just sat in a chair quietly recovering strength and mental orientation." (Robert Ellwood)

The observant reader will notice that these three experiences differ from one another in remarkable ways. Bharati felt that his own identity was merged with a cosmic reality of some sort. Finney and Ellwood encountered some additional dimension to reality that transformed their perspectives (momentarily, permanently) while allowing them to hold on to their identities. For about a year before his experience, Bharati had been reading Hindu literature (the Upanishadic dictum of oneness and various literatures on this subject) but can hardly be said to have prepared spiritually for the event. Finney was thinking hard about salvation (his own primarily) and practically willed himself into the experience on the critical day. Ellwood, a graduate student in history of religions at the time, was trying to enter into a type of religious trance when his mystical episode occurred. Bharati saw nothing, and felt oneness. Finney encountered one divine figure and sensed a second. Ellwood saw a natural scene filled with what he took to be religious significance.

The effects and interpretations of the mystical experience also differ in striking ways among these three individuals. Ellwood accepted the experience as a message or symbol of obvious religious significance for his life. Finney believed he had encountered the primary representative of God, Jesus Christ, and was appropriately taken to new levels of belief. Bharati consistently believed that mystical experiences have neither ontological nor moral implications. He maintained that they are simply natural experiences that can (and do) mean almost anything.

It follows from these (and other) variations on mystical experience that the amendments mysticism requires of ordinary reality also differ considerably. For Ellwood and Finney, the demarcation between ordinary reality and some ultimate reality can be crossed in the mystical episode. They each claimed to see, or at least to glimpse, a reality beyond sense experience. This alternative reality is viewed by both Ellwood and Finney as outside the laws governing ordinary reality and the source of meaning for human experience. Bharati's experience momentarily extinguished the self, collapsing the commonplace distinction between subject and object. But such revision for Bharati is provisional only, good for the duration of the mystical experience but not for one moment beyond it. Bharati also dismisses the thought that the "reality" experienced in mystical episodes has the power to fix meaning on human experience. For Bharati mystical experiences have value in and of themselves, but do not confer significance on any other part of human experience, and certainly do not revise the structure of ordinary reality.

3

Are mystical experiences genuine?

The structure and sequence of events in mystical experiences cannot exclude individuals who fake an occurrence by going through the motions. Still, a fake does not invalidate the real thing, and in some important sense every fake depends on the existence of the genuine item against which the false is defined, evaluated, and rejected. The problem is that no one can be sure what exactly occurs in a mystical experience, and so it is difficult to say whether any given experience is authentic. But questions of authenticity may miss the key point obscured in all detective work, which is that the authenticity of any particular event is not crucial. Studies of mysticism are undertaken in part to settle exactly what is meant by such experiences when they do occur, not whether they are occurring or not at some particular moment. There is also the consideration of motive. There is finally not much in the way of material gain as an incentive for faking a mystical experience, and (to put it bluntly) little to gain in sorting out the genuine article from the pretender. The experience, whatever it is, occurs for some people. That much cannot be doubted even when one allows for the charlatan who presents empty experiences as the real thing. A shift in inquiry may be helpful. The issue may not be whether mystical experiences are authentic (whatever that means), but what they tell us about alternative realities, if anything.

We do know some things with reasonable certainty. There is good evidence that those who do in fact have what they think are mystical experiences enter a different level of consciousness, even though it is not certain where any particular episode is located on a scale leading to the gold standard of the zero experience. There is also anecdotal evidence that some individuals have experiences involving a fusion with some type of holistic phenomena, and these experiences are of a sort not easily explained within the expectations of ordinary seeing and knowing. But the problems for experimental science of inferring a falsifiable anything from mystical experiences are legion. They begin with the fact that the experiences are often spontaneous, even though usually preceded by spiritual or intellectual preparation. A spontaneous experience does not readily occur in controlled test conditions. It is also difficult to observe, without intrusive controls, the physical or mental transformations in an individual having a mystical experience. Nor, of course, are the claims for a fusion of subject and object, or the intervention of an external reality, usually expressible in terms that would allow falsification. Consider, on this point, Finney's belief that the Holy Ghost baptized him. What conceivable evidence could sustain or falsify this belief? Any "evidence" would be defined by the highly personal and emotionally charged experience that Finney had. To introduce such data to a rigorous inquiry is impossible since its significance is entirely a matter of adopting or refusing the religious mantle that Finney enthusiastically embraced.

But, again, the limits of controlled experiments must be appreciated. Like artistic achievement, mystical experiences may be realizations of an ability that cannot be produced in controlled settings, and one that varies greatly from person to person. Also, testimony on the experiences themselves is widespread and particularly vivid, and the absence of hard data means little if mystical events are qualitative and contextual. Mystical experiences may be recurrent phenomena that indicate the scope of human experience. Approaches other than formal tests are surely worth exploring given the elusiveness of the variables and the importance of the beliefs.

The testimony on mystical events seems to converge toward a particular structure. Though Messrs. Bharati, Finney, and Ellwood had different experiences, in some important ways the experiences approximate a single form: the recognition of a different reality, and the subordination and (ideally) fusion of individual identity with that reality. Both Finney and Ellwood maintained their identities throughout the experience, but they also felt the supernatural reality penetrate their respective selves. Note the language of the baptism Finney received as seeming "to go through me, body and soul," or Ellwood perceiving "inwardly a long cloudbank in an azure sky" followed by a "brilliant sun"—in both cases the objective reality has entered and controlled the psychic space within.

But what do the experiences signify? Two possibilities occur, neither undercutting a minimal account of ordinary reality. One is that mysticism signifies nothing beyond a sign that the human brain is capable of—mystical experiences. This possibility accords with Bharati's views. Studies of the brain suggest that consciousness is an elastic state permitting a variety of experiences, some involving temporary suspensions of ordinary reality, that yet are merely subjective with no implications for any reality. The general acknowledgment that drugs can trigger mystical experiences neither supports nor denies this first possibility, since one could simply argue that access to a different reality is provided by certain drugs.

The second possibility is ontological. Mystical experiences may be a signal that ordinary reality is only a limited and transient domain of the real, and that there is considerably more to things than conventional sensory experience and reflection provide. There is nothing in this second view that is inconsistent with either current scientific views or ordinary reality. Try the following thought experiment. Suppose that there is a different or more comprehensive reality, and that humans have access to this reality in ways not fully understood but clearly not entirely susceptible to formal testing. Say that the brain can receive and process information from stimuli not perceived in conventional ways, and that these stimuli originate in a reality beyond that seen by the conventional eye or dreamed of in conventional physical theory. More: that this reality is in fact the source of meaning for human experience, and, finally, that under certain conditions, the human mind (brain, sensory system, etc.) can gain conscious entrance to this reality in what are labeled mystical experiences.

Science cannot dismiss such an account of things, nor is there any need for such an account to dismiss science. Beliefs in an external reality occupy a conceptual area having little to do with scientific programs. True, the extension of these beliefs to the empirical domains of science do encounter, and sometimes contradict, scientific accounts. Witness efforts to dismiss evolution on the basis of a creationism said to be revealed in a privileged viewing of God's plans. But the ontological beliefs in themselves need not contradict an empirical account of the realities that science addresses and explains. No scientific account of empirical reality would have to be abandoned or radically changed if the boundaries of reality were extended beyond that which can be perceived directly or indirectly by the conventional range of the senses. Science, finally, attends to a reality bounded by the powers of scientific methods to reveal it. Only if this reality is accorded privileged or universal status does it clash with mysticism. Mysticism exceeds the conventional boundaries of science without having to refute scientific accounts of a material reality.

The limitations of science in examining psychic experiences is nowhere so vividly displayed as in the recent scientific research concerned to find out exactly what happens in the brain when individuals enter an altered state of consciousness. One set of recent experiments may have located the region of the brain involved in mystical experiences. A research psychologist, Michael Persinger, claims to have induced mystical or religious experiences in subjects by stimulating the temporal lobe with magnetic forces. If true then mystical experiences of a certain type might be replicable in a formal setting. At the very least these experimental sessions suggest that we do have resources in our brains that, under certain conditions, transform the universe (for the experiencing subject) into a kind of cosmic unity, often infused with God's presence. These experiments raise interesting questions about the survival value of the temporal lobe sections that allow mystical experiences, and how natural selection influenced the evolution of the requisite neurological powers. But of course the sessions do not falsify mystical experiences, or reduce them to brute physiological variables. They simply tell us that the experiences are possible, and that they can be tracked to "real" events in the brain.

Another recent study has explored the neurological correlates of shamanism. Shamanism is a world-wide system of healing that has a pedigree of more than twenty-five thousand years. The shaman does his work by entering a trance, which grants him access to alternative realities. These realities guide the healing process of prayer and sacrifice that restore the health of the petitioner. The critical feature of the trance is the journey of the shaman's soul to and through the spiritual world, for it is there that the soul engages in dialogue to find the right healing therapies.

What happens in the brain when the shaman is in the ecstatic state that is supposed to release the soul for its journeys? The neurology of meditation is documented in medical literatures. Numerous studies have demonstrated that the brain generates increased alpha and theta waves during a variety of meditative states. The data on shaman trances are nonexistent, and any conclusions are almost purely speculative, but certain EEG changes in controlled experiments may be reasonably extended to actual shaman experiences. One paper that attempted to consolidate the existing literatures hypothesizes links between the shamanic conversion "call" and the altered states of consciousness in shaman sessions with seizure-like electrical activity of the temporal lobe, either minor or epileptic in nature. Research has also postulated a correlation between voltage activity in the hippocampal-septal area. Other studies of the brain in a variety of stressful situations suggest that certain rituals in shaman practices could also produce a release of endorphins. These identifications of neurological correlates are not the products of field work. The anthropological literatures are filled with excellent descriptions and explanations of shamanism, but there are no realistic possibilities of wiring the brains of a shaman in the field to gain EEG data in medias res. All of the work currently found on the neurological correlates of shamanism is a set of extrapolations from other studies to shaman practices.

But even if data could be secured, it is not clear what it would signify for altered consciousness. Suppose there are definite neurological correlates of various types of shaman practices. What would this mean for the authenticity or meaning of the experience? For the believer the data would only be a sign that the brain of the shaman is active in certain ways when his soul is traveling through the spirit world. The skeptic would look at the data and conclude—what? Presumably that the brain of the shaman is active in certain ways when *he claims that* his soul is traveling through the spirit world. Both believer and skeptic must conclude that the brain can produce altered states of consciousness. There also can be nothing in the data to deny that the human brain, when in certain conditions of EEG activity, enters a spiritual reality, nor anything to support that proposition.

Mysticism, in its traditional guise, is a species of psychic phenomena in claiming to produce knowledge in unconventional ways. Like all inquiries into psychic experiences, studies of mysticism rely on the testimony of participants whose reliability is in part established by the extraordinary nature of their experiences (suggesting more rather than less accuracy of recall). The mystical experience can be dismissed only on the basis of alternative explanations that are even less credible (e.g., spontaneous hypnotism that produces converging experiences across cultures), or by classifying the participants as mentally defective (when no evidence supports such judgments). And the rules or laws that might explain the episodes simply do not exist in any satisfactory form.

But notice that the compatibility of mystical experiences with the best and most imaginative efforts in science does nothing to establish the ontological significance of mysticism either. Just as mystical beliefs cannot be falsified, so they cannot be supported either *as ontological beliefs*. That individuals have mystical experiences can hardly be doubted. What those experiences mean, whether they are patterns of subjective perception and knowing or actual entrance into a more comprehensive reality, cannot be settled outside the reality of faith. Notice also, however, that either possibility—subjective, ontological—expands the self beyond the discrete boundaries of secular thought. Whether individual sensibilities are simply robust enough to construct a unity through expanded perceptions, or individual capabilities can provide entry into a larger reality, still the self has exceeded conventional limits.

4

David Hoisington is working on his doctorate in rehabilitation counseling. His dissertation is on the meanings and processes of advanced empathy in counseling. His first profession, for which he prepared with a bachelor's degree, was geology. As a child and young man, he was what other members of his family called a really sensitive male. He remembers this perspective as an attitude that was not entirely flattering since in his household (and others) it was not very manly to be sensitive. This sensitivity took what Hoisington still regards as a spiritual turn when he was a married undergraduate at the University of Vermont.

He and Sarah, his wife, had just moved into their first apartment. It was a basement apartment with one small window and one modest bathroom. During one of the first nights in the apartment, he and Sarah suddenly woke up at the same time and looked across the room to a corner formed by the wall containing the window and the one enclosing the bathroom. A ball of blue light had appeared in this vacant corner, and it was illuminating the entire room. The blue light just filled the room. Hoisington reports that he would have chalked it up to an illusion of some sort except for the unnerving fact that his wife was also seeing the light. He says he was not frightened so much as shocked. He was studying geology at the time, and was a "down-to-earth person," he reports (with apologies for the pun).

Now he was experiencing something for which he had no satisfactory explanation. There was no light coming into the room (even through the one small window). Neither he nor his wife were substance users, and so the experience could not be a drug-induced co-hallucination. For Hoisington the event was as simple and complicated as a boundary-changing experience.

Sarah was remarkably sanguine. She told David that the blue light was probably a spiritual message for him. A couple of days later she asked him if she could try something. The proposal was as interesting as it was surprising to David: she wanted to do some guided and progressive relaxation techniques with him. The aim was to lead him to an out-of-body experience. He cautiously requested assurances that there would be no problems with any of this. His wife answered no, it would be perfectly normal, he would be fine, he couldn't hurt himself. So he agreed to try, adding that it sounded interesting (which might be considered the standard answer a husband gives to a new wife). The experience turned out to be just that, taking David to this little white light in a dark space, through a tunnel, and then outside, where he was looking down at himself just lying there on the bed. He remembers saying very distinctly to himself, What the hell are you doing out here? and then in a flash (like the snap of fingers) he was back in his body looking at the world like he usually did. Later, in conversations, he found out from his wife that she had done some seances and other medium practices before they met, but she had given it up because it was too negative.

The vision of the blue light and the out-of-body experience abruptly changed David's whole sense of reality, its parameters and the inventory of its contents, and his understanding of who he is. He began to explore his spiritual nature, which was the beginning of a journey away from the hard empiricism represented by geology. His sensitive nature at last had a point and a purpose. It also provided a different framework for understanding his experiences. Some understandings were new perspectives on earlier beliefs. He had served in combat in Viet Nam before going to college. Almost everyone in his platoon died in the war except him. He felt protected in some way. Not only did he not die, but he was consistently *not* in the place where the fighting would occur. The platoon was in six battles, and six times the enemy attacked directly opposite from the hill he was on. On one occasion the platoon leader took everyone off the mountain except for him, ordering David to stay in place and guard one whole side of the mountain while the rest of the platoon went to the other side to engage in combat. He did not know what was going on. It was the first time that he actually felt something else was involved in his life. The vision of the blue light and his OBE extended this inchoate sense of the spiritual. He eventually accepted the spiritual as a complete meaning for his entire life, from past through present and future.

After college he searched for work and eventually landed a job as a geologist with an oil company, but he also began exploring psychic experiences. He became proficient with tarot cards and practiced palmistry. From 1971 until 1979 he performed both seriously and for entertainment (though never commercially) almost everywhere—on trains, buses, and planes, in bars, hotel lobbies, private homes, and offices. In 1979 he became disillusioned with these parlor activities, in large part because he felt they were dependent on props and so limited what he believed he could do. From 1979 to 1983 he conducted what he called at the time psychic readings. He became known for his insights, so much so that people began flying in for readings. His clients were a heterogeneous lot. One was a specialist who treated UFO abductees. The reading lasted until 4 A.M. and was oddly reciprocal as David and his client traded stories of vivid supernatural experiences. During this time David also tried psychometrics, which is the art or skill of perceiving events from holding objects. For example, one woman gave him a ring, and he was able to tell her that it was from a boyfriend of six years ago. He also was able to sense sports sneakers and could then tell her that the boyfriend was a basketball player, and so on. On another occasion he saw that a man would have three accidents, with each one worse than the last, unless he seriously changed his manner of living. After the three accidents, the man came to David for advice and direction.

In 1983 he traded careers, giving up a ritzy and lucrative job with the oil company to take a $7,000-a-year position in a school system. He wanted to do something in the area of human services. It was an expectedly difficult transition, but Sarah was consistently supportive. He describes her as his wife, lover, and best friend. (They had been married for twenty-six years at the time of this interview.) With her encouragement, he began cultivating his spiritual powers. At this time, without warning or effort, he started having clairvoyant dreams. These dreams he describes as flash dreams. He reports that they have many of the features of regular dreams in allowing the dreamer to wander into something and then back out into something else. They are, in a word, *dreamy*. But a flash dream for David "starts boom and then ends boom." They are extremely vivid, rich in character and circumstances—the dreamer cannot distinguish them from what we call real life—and they begin and end suddenly. They are also uncanny predictions of future experiences.

In one flash dream, David was in a small car going up a hill and somehow his vision became blocked. He could not see the road. Then he saw the large back end of a truck that he was approaching very quickly. He tried to put on the brakes but couldn't stop the car. The car was out of control, and he crashed into the truck. Then he saw the color brown and woke up in an overwrought state. He felt the intense emotion he had learned to associate with trauma victims. One year later almost to the day, he was driving a small sports car up a hill in the Rocky Mountains. It was early morning, very sunny, and the driving was a little slushy because there had been snow and some ice the night before. David drove over the crest of a hill, where his view was blocked by the slope of the road. Immediately on the down slope there was a large brown truck stopped in the middle of the road. He slammed on the brakes and discovered that the sunlight had not yet thawed the back side of the mountain, and the road was covered with ice. He watched himself go right into the back of the truck, exactly as in the dream. He was not seriously hurt but was emotionally distraught at the near tragic event represented by an intersection of dream and waking reality.

He also has had several flash dreams of plane crashes. One was a crash in Texas during a heavy fog. In his dream he was on the plane walking along the aisle. He remembers that the pilot spoke in a southern drawl, and that they were having great difficulty seeing. The pilots kept complaining that they could not see where they were going or what they were doing. David remembers they were wearing grey uniforms. He also remembers seeing some numbers on the plane and trying to make them out. He knew this time he was in a dream, and he wanted to see the numbers so he could do something to prevent the crash when he awoke. But he could not get outside the plane to see the numbers. A couple of days later, a plane that had taken off in Florida crashed in Texas because of poor visibility. After this dream David decided he did not want to see these things and so willed himself not to have any more of the flash dreams.

Instead he decided to develop a counseling service. His goal was to connect to people spiritually and try with this internal understanding to discover and assist them in securing their well-being. The one event he reports as a precedent for counseling happened when he was in Georgia, working as a geologist and still giving psychic readings. One of his acquaintances asked him to come over and talk to a woman who was in trouble. He went to the woman's trailer, sat down with her at the dinette table between the kitchen and the door, and began a practice he had carried over from his days as a palmist: he asked her to place her hands in his. As soon as they joined hands, the entire room changed. David could see the woman sitting over on the sofa in the trailer's dining room under a framed print on the wall, and standing in the doorway was her husband. He was very angry, yelling at her. Her head was down, and she was not speaking. The man walked past David, slamming the door as he left the trailer. David pulled his hands away, and the scene returned to normal. No trace of a husband, and the woman was still at the dinette table. He rubbed his hands together and could feel something like electricity going through them. He had no idea what was going on but had enough common sense to ask the obvious question: Are you having trouble with your marriage? he asked the woman. She started crying, and they ended up talking about her marriage and what she could do about it. David began realizing that the images he seemed able to conjure by physical contact could be powerful forces in counseling. It was the beginning of a practice he would later call advanced empathy.

In his counseling David tries to go beyond the traditional efforts of the analyst to understand the patient. He tries to *be* the patient, to enter the imagery of the patients in such a way that he can have experiences as they have them without "getting myself in the way." He still has problems with his own self, his identity, interrupting an immersion in the lifeworld of the other. But his goal is a type of limited mysticism in the particular confines of counseling: to see and experience what the other experiences by momentarily becoming the other (an open state of oneness with the other rather than the cosmos). This reduction of the self to the other is of course transitional. Its duration is typically that of the brief spiritual joining of selves that he experienced with the woman in the trailer, an empathic seeing that disclosed in almost theatrical terms a troubled marriage. Put in basic terms, David tries to become the other for a brief time for therapeutic purposes. He believes that this empathy, what an economist would call "extended sympathy," is eminently useful in counseling. It is an empathy advanced by a kind of telepathy, and he attempts to achieve it whenever he thinks it is needed in his counseling sessions.

Occasionally he has a client who cannot talk about the problems that must be addressed for the counseling to be successful. Once he worked with a young woman who had been raped. She could not tell anybody about the experience. It was not that she resisted talking about the experience. She wanted to talk but was simply unable to do so. David did not use hand contact in this case (which he has discovered can make some people nervous). Instead he employed a set of relaxation exercises that he had used successfully in a variety of circumstances. In the course of these particular exercises, he reports that he uncovered a very intense and powerful image. This time the empathic moment extended to fifteen or twenty minutes because he ended up experiencing the young woman's rape. He says he felt the bruised lips and stomach, all the emotions and feelings that went into the experience, and then actually experienced the rape as it happened—"what the room looked like, what the person looked liked, the lighting conditions, everything." As it was happening David began talking about the experience, speaking about what was happening. It was a transformational experience for the woman. She was able to have the event heard, have it be known, and then was able to move past that mental block and successfully talk about it in the therapy session. It was a kind of literal transfer of experience to the therapist as a way of finding relief from a traumatic event.

In the last several years, David also has begun doing physical healing through spiritual interventions. In one case a man came into his practice with a cane and an admission that his lower back was simply terrible. David routinely selects an appropriate spiritual image to negotiate healing. In this case he chose the Holy Spirit because the man was a devout Christian. (In other cases he has used the Buddha, Native American images, or whatever fits the client's beliefs.) David again used the relaxation techniques that have served him well since his first OBE. While doing this, David urges the client to trust in the process, to believe in a connection to (in this instance) the Holy Spirit. Then, in this session, he just placed one of his hands on the man's chest, the other on his back, and he could feel the moment at which the man let go. The man's whole body shuddered, and David could feel this flow, a something that was happening between them, and then it was over. The man stood up and walked out carrying the cane on his arm.

Another healing occurred during a Buddhist retreat. At these retreats, a robust amount of time is spent in meditation. David could not help noticing one man who was bent over and having obvious difficulties getting into and maintaining the Lotus position for the expected two to three hours of meditation. Later, on a break when David was walking in the garden, he noticed the man sitting on the stone wall at the edge of the small field of roses. He went over to the man, and they started the causal conversations that fill these settings. David remarked that meditation is tough on the back. The man agreed with a painful grimace. So David asked him if he would allow him to touch his back. The man said yes. David recalls that he himself was in a state of "extreme readiness" from the two hours of just completed meditation. The man was sitting at his side. He immediately placed a hand on the man's chest, the other on his back, and urged the man to breathe deeply. David watched him as the shudder went through his body. The man seemed to move into a relaxed state and drop away from his problem. David turned in front of him and "face to face" asked him how he felt. The man answered "wonderful, the best I have felt in my entire life." David told him to continue sitting on the stone wall and concentrate on this place, "your place of well-being." The man did not experience any back problems during the remaining days of the retreat.

David Hoisington does not have any compelling explanations for his spiritual experiences. He cannot even provide the obligatory distinctions between healing from spiritual causes and the placebo effect. His view of reality is not concerned with these distinctions. The *real* to him is a product of interactions between the self and experience, and it may be variable with each person. He believes that he is a servant of higher powers, here to provide help for others and to see through the illusions that disguise the true spiritual nature of existence. He also knows that the distinctions of secular reality, including those among persons in human experience, are thin membranes that allow access across domains of experience, and between self and other. He brings these convictions directly into his counseling practices.

5

In the spring term of 1997, I taught a course on healing practices. In this seminar we explored a variety of approaches to health and healing, from more-or-less standard allopathic techniques to forms of complementary and alternative medicine, finally making our way to spiritual healing. One of the members of the course was John Delgrosso, a student at that time in respiratory therapy at the Health Science Center who had an interesting story to tell about his own miraculous (from his point of view) healing. I invited him to share the story with the class after I heard it from him, and he agreed to relate his experiences during the last meeting of the course. I had invited a reverend from the Church of the Infinite Light to instruct us on spiritual healing at this last meeting. (I introduced Reverend Joan Lee erroneously to the class on that day as from the Church of the *Eternal* Light, and, when she immediately corrected me, I invited her, with some mischief, to draw a distinction for the class between infinite and eternal light in her introductory remarks. She did, with reasonable effectiveness.) Later in the session, she demonstrated a form of spiritual healing, an exercise she performed in Syracuse University's Maxwell School, the leading school of public affairs and social science in the country. I told a friend later that I had never been so grateful for tenure.

The memorable moment during that last meeting came at the very beginning of Reverend Lee's talk. She opened by scanning the room and remarking that the students all had beautiful auras (which of course she could see clearly). Then she stopped at John Delgrosso. After a brief silence she reported that this particular student had a very unusual and complex aura, quite different from any she had seen. I said, "Stop," and asked the obvious question: "Do you two know each other?" No, they did not. The Reverend had picked out the one student in the class who had experienced a religious event that changed his life. Later in the meeting John told his story to the class.

John Delgrosso is one of five children from a middle-class Catholic family. Both his parents are immigrants from Benevento, a town some two hours by car outside of Naples, Italy. His father's family had a stable, rural life organized around a small farm. But John's father, like so many others, left his homeland while still young to find fortune and happiness in America. He worked for a time in New York and, when he had accumulated enough capital, returned to Italy in 1968 to marry John's mother in an arranged marriage. He brought his sixteen-year-old bride to live with him in Carmel, New York, which still passed for the New World in their part of Italy.

John's father is a masonry contractor who taught his sons the virtues of hard work with the hands and body. But the family learned early that the virtues of diligence cannot avoid life's tragedies. In 1983 they lost their oldest son in a swimming accident. The loss was unbearable at first. John could not even sleep in his bedroom, since it was the room he had shared with his older brother. The family decided to start over by buying some land in a different area of Putnam County and building a new home. They worked together on the house, and this shared effort drew the family together again, as did the birth two years later of another son, who became the loved youngest child in their tight-knit Italian family. They were happy again.

John helped his sister and mother in raising his younger brother, went to school, worked on a farm part time, and assisted his father on construction projects on weekends. His parents stressed the importance of school since they didn't want him "to work like an animal, as his father did." John was very active in his teenage years, working long hours at various jobs but finding time to play sports of all types, especially ice hockey and baseball. He remembers playing game after game with an abandon that expressed his conviction that he was indestructible, even immortal. He seemed always to be outside in those years, cutting down trees, building forts, skiing, hunting deer, fishing. He never spent time on indoor diversions like video games or computers. Nature, in all of its manifestations, was his chosen dominion.

When he was sixteen years old, at the end of the summer before his junior year in high school, he was beginning to think about a future represented by SATs and college choices. But the future was still a residual variable in his thoughts. The controlling experiences of that year were defined by what he now remembers as his elegant physical prowess: the time in his life when he definitely felt the best, the strongest and healthiest, when he was filled with the special energy that seems to be the truest artifact of youth. He had helped his dad build a large antique-looking building that summer. John had worked as a laborer on the project, slowly acquiring the skills of brick laying, working so hard and long that his father gave him a week off at the end of the summer. A week off before school began. A week to do whatever he wanted to do. John began some serious riding on his dirt bike. He and his friend Brian used to take their bikes up a trail by John's house that was known as Logwood. It was an old logging trail that cut through the woods for about one-half mile. Heavy rains would flood the trails, bringing up the bedrock, and this particular trail was filled with rocks, some quite large. John admits that Logwood was not the best place to ride a dirt bike, but the "cops would end up chasing us if we used the roads." So he and Brian rode this hard trail again and again during that magic week off.

On Saturday of that week, John decided to take his four-wheeler out and leave the dirt bike at home. He remembers his mother out in the front yard on that afternoon working in the rose garden, his little brother out back feeding the chickens that they kept around the house, and then his mom hollering at him to be home early because the family had a birthday party to go to that night. He went down Logwood with his four-wheeler, where he met some other boys, friends from school. Two of these boys were riding dirt bikes from the 1960s and '70s, "pieces of junk" as John recalls, and he remembers making fun of their bikes as he rode the side trail that went down to the lake. The lake is private, secluded, with mon-eyed property and expensive summer homes. John began riding the four-wheeler around, disturbing what was otherwise a tranquil afternoon, and one of the owners told John that he was going get hurt and that he would call the police if he didn't leave immediately with his vehicle. John was "just, like, whatever," and promptly drove down to the lake and rode around in two feet of water, submerging the muffler, getting soaked in what turned out to be the last shower he was to have in six months. He then drove back up to the main trail and met a new kid with a brand new dirt bike that was supposed to be upgraded, faster than other bikes. The new boy, Anthony, invited John to try out the bike. He had heard about John's skills with dirt bikes, and he was curious to know how his bike rated. So John and Anthony exchanged machines. John began driving a different bike with no real understanding of its power.

Immediately John began screaming up and down the trail with the new power bike, his adrenaline rushing up to fresh levels as he pushed himself to the edge of his skills. He even invented a new jump. He found a ledge on the side of the trail, about six feet high, which he would drive up to at high speed and then simply go into the air about ten feet up, landing some twenty feet away. There were trees on both sides of the landing area, a rock wall on either side, and rocks all over that part of the trail. But he didn't care. He was basically flying, and pushing himself and a souped-up bike to new limits. At the end of one jump, John saw Anthony standing near the path. Let's switch, he called out, I've got to get home. As if in a bad movie, John said the cinematic words—one more ride and we'll call it quits.

On that last jump, everything was going fine. Then just before take-off, the throttle stuck. "The thing was wide open," and he lost control completely. He remembers seeing the other boys on his left watching in horror, one with a "holy shit" look on his face as the bike came down on one of the rock walls. John came over the handle bars on impact, realizing at that second that he was wearing no helmet, seeing the neon green Kawasaki from the angle of its fender as the bike came over him, and then at last knowing that he was going to die. He hit his head on the rocks "really hard," and at that exact point felt a complete loss of sensation, his arms flapping like alien appendages in front of him. He could not move and found it hard to breathe. Yes, he had the quick memory scan of his family and life flash in front of him, and then the sad and catalytic realization that he had lost everything in a single instant.

The two boys with the old bikes ran off crying, and Brian seemed to be in shock. A man fishing in the lake had seen the accident and came on shore to help. Someone called an ambulance. The medical team had to trek in a quarter of a mile to retrieve John. They carefully rolled him onto a stretcher, stabilized him, and then located a small truck that they used to drive him to the waiting ambulance. In the ambulance the medical team tried to comfort him by describing the injury as whiplash. John asked them not turn on the siren because he didn't want to make a scene, but they said they had to. They drove away from the wooded area and accelerated through the streets of John's village, siren wailing, toward the Putnam County Hospital, a small hospital that does not get many trauma cases. At the same time, the father of one of the boys at the scene brought John's four-wheeler to his home and told his parents what had happened.

In the hospital emergency room, John veered between an inquisitive state, asking everyone who came over to his bed whether he would ever walk again, and a state of exquisite drowsiness in which he wanted nothing more than to be left alone so that he could sleep. The first family member John saw was his father, who was crying out loud. John had not seen him do that since his older brother's funeral. John remembers just apologizing again and again to his father, who kept telling him not to apologize. He asked where his mom was. His father told him that she was in church praying for him. Later John was told that many of his friends had gathered outside the emergency room and were praying there for him. Suddenly a man appeared at John's bedside dressed in a suit, pink shirt, suspenders, and a bow tie. He was smiling, really smiling, and seemingly happy, John now recalls. He was the neurosurgeon called in from Westchester County on a Saturday afternoon. He ran some tests and told John's parents that X rays showed that the C4 vertebrae was severely compressed. Being able to walk again from this injury was not likely, he said. The medical team placed a metal traction device called Gardner-Wells tongs on the sides of his head. An orthopedic surgeon in the Bronx was consulted. After examining John, he recommended surgery on John's neck. In the first surgery, the doctors inserted a bone graft. In the recovery room, his mother, "in her broken English," told him that they had taken a bone from his hip and put it in his neck. After he got over the thought that the surgeons were crazy, he came to understand that they had fused his damaged vertebrae. During recovery the nursing staff helped him sit up to begin the movements that would prevent muscle atrophy. The graft dislodged. He was returned to the operating room for more surgery, this time successful. It was after this second surgery that John's mother saw what looked to her like an angel sitting on top of her son's head when they took him down the hall on a stretcher to the recovery room. Then the days of waiting began, with John paralyzed in a hospital bed, being visited by friends and siblings, his parents by his side.

Images began dominating his thoughts and his dreams. Once Brian and his sister came in to see him at 6 A.M., before school on a weekday. John told them, *seeing* these scenes in his thoughts, that he would be out hunting, fishing, skiing, and running again. John could feel himself at one magic moment in the conversation actually skiing down a particular slope. The snow was incredible. He could feel the goggles he was wearing and the heat of the sun at the same time that he was feeling the snow as he went down the path with Brian. John says now that he can only vaguely remember Brian's reaction to the description of that scene, and he doesn't think that it was good. At another time, he remembered a place down by the creek near his home where he and Brian would go fishing on summer nights. John started dreaming about the place. He could feel the cool summer air and the moisture off the stream, could hear the water come out of the woods winding down in front of them. It was so real to him. Then he would wake up and be unable even to lift a hand to his face. Later, after the second surgery on his neck, these images receded for a time, replaced by pain. All he can remember about the time after the last surgery was his throat hurting with "an incredible, incredible pain." He thinks that the source of the pain was the fact that a tracheal tube had been in his throat for seven hours, and of course the oxygen from the respirator had dried out the tissues in his throat. His entire body ached long after the surgery was over, and he remembers experiencing prolonged hunger and thirst in intensive care before the nursing staff could give him nourishment. He started a basic exercise: staring at the clock for days and then weeks on end. One nurse, her name was Denise, would talk to him, help him with his physical therapy, pray with him and for him. Later, when the paralysis did indeed seem to be permanent, he asked his parents to just let him die, or better, shoot him. It was a very bad time for John Delgrosso and anyone who loved him.

He began praying, asking out loud for God to help him. A nurse in the intensive care unit gave him a relic, what was supposed to be a piece of St. Elizabeth's shroud inside a metal container. The relic had been given to the nurse's son when he had suffered a head injury. The story about the sacred object was that each person was to pass it on to someone else after its spiritual effects were completed. John's mother pinned it to the halo device on his head that was designed to keep the neck immobile. On one of the days after the relic was in place, the attending physician told John's mother to stop crying because for the first time John had been able to move his little toe slightly on command. The images began returning to John's thoughts. A nurse had explained to him that his injury was like a hammer blow to a utility cord: the intricate wiring was crimped, stuck, swollen. When the swelling goes down, she said, the wires will fall back into their natural arrangements, and the electricity can flow again. John began working with this image, willing the wires in his spinal cord to recovery. He would have sessions in which his concentration was complete, his mental energies focused entirely on jolting the hardwiring of his system back into service. His mother told him two doves had been on his window sill in his room since he had entered the hospital. He imagined them waiting for something to happen.

One night John started having vivid dreams that turned out to be prophetic. In the first dream he was at the accident site and saw a man sitting on a rock. The man was dressed in a white robe and sandals and had his head down. For some reason John could not look directly at the man. He could talk to him, but it was impossible to look into his face. He knew that he was seeing Christ. John asked him whether he would ever walk again, though he remembers that he was walking in the dream. The figure got up and told John to follow him. "When we get to the end of this path," he said, "we'll see." John began walking with him. It was a struggle to keep up. The man would look back from time to time and smile. John would keep walking. This dream began repeating itself. Every night John would find himself walking behind Christ, trying with great difficulty to keep up with the pace the figure in front of him was setting. One night during the dream, John and the Christ figure reached the end of the trail. The message was clear. The figure turned to him and told him that he was going to walk again.

That next day, almost one month after the accident, John entered a state of intense concentration. His mother was seated at his bedside. He remembers now that it had rained for two days, and his mother had told him again that the doves were still there on his window sill. He summoned the memory of the dream of the night before, and then he entered a prayerful state in which he was uncertain if he was awake or in a trance, his eyes closed, teeth clenched, all of his will directed toward healing his injured spinal cord. Suddenly he felt a burst of electricity, almost like someone was shocking him with a live electrical cord, and he saw what he describes as a blinding light, so bright that it had gold inside of it. The jolt from the flash of energy threw him off the bed and caused the metal halo to dig into his skull, tearing his skin so deeply that he has a scar to this day on his scalp. A nurse came running into his room to get him back on the bed. No one knew what had happened. In the confusion of the next several minutes John started to move his fingers and thumb, then his hand, and then he began twisting his arm and flexing his ankle, and he could rotate his left leg from side to side. It was apparent that he had in that instant begun what many on the medical staff still regard as a miraculous recovery from the accident that had paralyzed him.

The orthopedic surgeon who had operated on John has a scientific temperament and tends to see his skills as primarily technical. He repairs the body's structures. He tried to explain the mystery occurrence in terms of data from paraplegics who had almost been electrocuted accidentally. They did seem to regain some movement after these accidents, perhaps because the neurological system reacted to the electricity. He was as happy as anyone in John's family that something like this had happened to restore the physical powers of one of his patients. But he had no idea where the electrical energy had come from to trigger the event. He did know that it was time for John to start rehabilitation for injuries that now were clearly healing.

The rehab center, in Rockland County, New York, was scary from John's point of view. The people there were all recovering from disasters. Some were victims of shootings, one had fallen out of a moving truck, many were in wheelchairs, all seemed to be victims of some split-second event that had destroyed their lives and families. John became a very quiet and serious patient, working to regain mobility. He began moving most of his limbs, started to walk again, and slowly regained the use of his entire body. His left side came back first, so that he found himself writing with his left hand for a time, even though he is naturally right-handed. When the right side of his body regained strength and mobility, he discovered that he was ambidextrous. Five months after entering rehabilitation he was able to resume his studies at school. The adjustment to a normal life was expectedly hard, but he found that he had acquired some permanent gifts that were missing in the old life. He was now more reflective, able to appreciate and muse on simple natural things like leaves on trees, the wind blowing in his face. He continued to progress and eventually went off to college on schedule. He was certain that he wanted to be a member of one of the healthcare professions.

In 1993 he was home from college for the summer and attended his sister's high school graduation. The event had the usual party atmosphere, except that there was a thunderstorm outside the auditorium where the festivities were being held. John had a strange feeling throughout the entire evening. The next day he was talking to Brian and found out that there had been a serious road accident that night. Some of the students had been drinking and driving, with tragic results. Two had been killed and several others seriously injured. His sister, whom he had not seen since the previous night, told him that her best friend was in a coma from the accident. John offered to go to the hospital with his sister to help in any way he could.

The hospital was a scene of devastation. The lobby was filled with family and friends, all wandering about with bewildered looks on their faces. John began urging everyone to have faith and pray, just believe that their daughter, their friend, would recover. The cognitive side of his consciousness was telling him as he spoke that these words were risky, that the young woman might not recover. But he found himself reassuring everyone as they asked him about the coma, the injuries to the girl's face, the pain she was experiencing. John kept talking about faith, trust in God, with an attitude and voice that sounded to him like a preacher and was obviously shocking to his own close friends who were at the hospital. But he kept talking and preaching, telling each person to stay strong, hang in there together, and, most of all, to keep talking to the young woman. She's not awake, John told the assembled family and friends, but she can probably hear you and especially feel your presence.

At some point John went home. He kept thinking that there was something he could do to help, but he didn't know what. The situation was beginning to look like a case for him, one in which he should somehow get involved. Late that night he awoke from a deep sleep remembering the relic. He woke up his mother and told her that they should pass on the sacred object to the girl. She agreed. The next day John went to the hospital and placed the relic on the young woman, telling the family its story. A few days later John went to a family party and heard that the girl in the coma had died. John did not, could not believe the story. He immediately called one of his friends and found out that the story was false, the young woman was still alive. He decided to visit the hospital on the way home. It was a Saturday night, and all her family was in the intensive care room with her. The security guard wouldn't let him in because of the number of people already in the room. But then, for some reason, they made an exception for him. He entered the room. Maybe ten to twelve people were already in the room, most standing at the end of the bed talking to each other. John walked over to the head of the bed and stood very close to the young woman. He remembers having this warm feeling, a feeling that something good was about to happen, and he began speaking to her very softly, telling her to be strong, that she had to make it, that anything is possible. He held her hand and told her, "God is with you." At that point she opened her eyes, straightened her body a bit, and said, "Thank you." John did not immediately realize what had happened, but the girl's parents were stunned. Those were the first words their daughter had spoken since the accident. John felt that he was going to pass out as everyone in the room started to run around with excitement. John's sister was there, and she came running down to him as he left the hospital. She kept saying, "Holy shit," again and again, and, "I can't believe this. That was a true miracle."

John told his mother what had happened when he got home, and she responded with the quiet reserve of parental love, which is to say that all miracles are commonplace events within the domains of our children's talents. She told her son this: "Do you remember what happened to you? You've been touched by God." John responded by going to his room and drinking several beers while smoking a couple of cigarettes. His mother was astounded. She told him he should be giving thanks, not drinking. He told her that she didn't understand. He went to sleep that night with the strangest yet most comforting feelings of his life. He had another dream of Christ, who told him that he was here on Earth for a purpose, and that he would change people's lives. He woke up several times to pace around the house. His mother, changing the metaphysical reference, asked him what the hell was wrong with him. There was nothing to understand, she told him, just learn to accept the gift that you have. He tried to do just that from that point on.

A Manichaean sense of reality broke through these reveries, however. A week later John started having dreams about malevolent creatures. He dreamed of scenes with sinister laughter coming from all directions in his bedroom, and he had the feeling that he was being electrocuted and burned with fire at the same time. The dreams were vivid enough that he could not always distinguish them from reality. He would wake up screaming, and his mother would come running in. It was a very fearful time for him. His mother counseled him to stand up to these creatures he was seeing and hearing. Later, while at Brian's house, he saw a fire suddenly circle him as he left the front door. Then, as quickly as they began, the malevolent scenes stopped. John began writing about his experiences in a journal.

The young woman who was in a coma recovered completely and went on to college. John sees her casually from time to time. At the time of this writing, he is a respiratory therapist at Rochester General Hospital. He does not seek out candidates for his own type of spiritual healing, but he is ready to offer strength and guidance if the need arises. He continues to be a Catholic but does not regard himself as especially religious in a formal sense. He does, however, consider himself a healer.

6

One of the oldest paths to alternative, even transcendent, realities is that special form of meditation known as prayer. The use of prayer to change or maintain the temporal world is distinct from the effects of prayer gained through the suggestibility of those for whom one prays. Prayer that helps create a positive attitude toward experience is effective in health and healing, for example, but this effectiveness is a variation on the placebo effect. The efficacy of prayer as a force on experience must be demonstrated independent of the beliefs of those affected by prayer. There are some problems here. Beliefs are crucial to religious practices. If this is doubted, imagine a congregation of atheists receiving Holy Communion. It would be both grotesque and spurious: the practice of Communion cannot be valid in the absence of the belief that the wafer is the body of Christ. Prayer is similarly framed by religious beliefs. Yet belief in the efficacy of prayer can bring about the results that prayer aims to achieve. Nothing more may be happening than mind (read: attitude or belief) affecting body.

Most double-blind empirical studies of prayer that attempt to eliminate the placebo effect focus on healing. In one study, "Positive Therapeutic Effects of Intercessory Prayer in a Coronary Care Unit Population," efforts were made to determine the therapeutic effects of intercessory prayer (IP) to the Judeo-Christian God on patients in a coronary care unit (CCU).

Patients in the CCU at San Francisco General Hospital were randomly assigned to a prayer group or control group over a ten-month period in 1982–83. The first set of patients received IP from participating Christians praying outside the hospital. The control group did not. The conclusions of the study were that the control group required more ventilatory assistance, antibiotics, and diuretics than patients in the IP group.

In an earlier study, "The Objective Efficacy of Prayer," forty-eight patients "suffering from chronic stationary or progressively deteriorating psychological or rheumatic disease in two out-patient clinics at the London Hospital" were studied. Six prayer groups were formed, "five organized by the Guild of Health and one by the Friends' Spiritual Healing Fellowship." Other prayer groups scattered throughout Great Britain were also included in the study. These groups were assigned patients to pray for with no contact between the one praying and the patient. The prayers were variations on silent meditation, with short sentences (often from the Bible) used in conjunction with a state of mind open to God. A mental image of the particular patient assigned to the meditator was brought forward in the thoughts of the one praying "in the context of the love and wholeness of God." A paired partner among the patients, similar in relevant ways including pathology, was not a target for prayer. Changes in the paired patients were monitored as the main variables of the study.

No advantage to either set of patients was found within the six months of the study. But there was a clinical improvement in the treated group (those patients who were prayed for) when compared to the control group (those for whom no prayers were made) in a period of one year or more. Improvements in the treated group were 31 percent, in the control group 13 percent. There was no way in the study to determine if the prayers had continued beyond the time limits announced for the study, and so it was impossible to rule out the efficacy of prayer over a longer run than the study imposed, either from sustained prayer or from a kind of prolonged effect of prayer. Also, the traditional conditions of prayer require collaboration among those who pray and those who are the subjects of prayer. The absence of any access to the patients by the prayer groups may have caused individuals to slack off in their prayers or may have vitiated the factors that make prayer effective. The weak initial results from prayer in this controlled study can be explained again in terms of the differences between experimental science and traditional ways of conducting spiritual practices.

A larger question is what we expect from prayer. A prayer finally is a species of magic within religion, an attempt to alter or maintain the natural world through words that invoke divine beings. This type of effort exceeds the boundaries of traditional mysticism. Nondual philosophies offer many resources for psychic beliefs and practices. The denial of time in favor of permanent being suggests possible access to "future" events. The fundamental unity of mental states promises entrance into the thoughts of others. The denial of subject-object dualism may even be taken as a partial explanation of psychokinesis. But the affinities between psychic practices and nondualism are limited. Prayer is the sure indicator that the two approaches point in different directions. The underlying logic of psychic practices, represented in prayer, aims at individual mastery of the natural world in escaping out from under the laws that govern human experience. Nondual philosophies urge a surrender to reality, and an eventual elimination of individual powers and even separateness. Seen in this perspective psychic and magical powers are arrogant, for they assign special insights and abilities to individuals standing apart from the natural world. Mysticism is passive by contrast and filled with humility.

Augustine employed the concept of time to bifurcate existence along two domains: the temporal worlds that humans occupy, where time is the framework which organizes experience into a past, present, and future, and the eternal dimension of God's existence. The Western notion of time as a continuum on which the present is a point moving toward the future and away from the past adequately represents the temporal frame of human experience. Eternal reality is timeless. The instrument for Augustine that allows humans to know eternal reality is prayer, which is a studied reflection that is in some sense timeless. In the spiritual experience of prayer the human mind has some contact with the stillness of eternity, and so the mind of God. Prayer in this receptive form of experience may be the highest form of human contact with the universe, which mysticism invites us to enter, in an accepting rather than a modifying spirit, and at a considerable distance from the experimental tests of the scientific temperament.

7

To many psychics, the standard scientific map is useless at the very beginnings of one's travels through life. Sally Aderton provides yet another narrative for beliefs in supernatural experiences. She is a healer and spiritual teacher, and is known in the profession as a knowing sensitive, which she sees as the most evolved of psychic states. She uses intuition to gain direct knowledge of her clients' needs, which she believes allows her to be even more present with people. She regards her ability to know as a heightened sense of our "normal" senses. She believes that we are all psychic and have a simple access to what is real. She creates rituals and processes for people to work through, and the range of her techniques includes regressions through a mirror, breath work, counseling, career planning, business decisions, meditation, and more. She helps the client find the right procedure for healing, and then sends them away to heal themselves.

Aderton believes that she came to this planet with a purpose. She saw her first spirit guide when she was about eight years old. On waking up from nightmares, she would see this little beacon of light, a set of concentric circles of white, red, black, and green light. Her minister called the beacon an apparition. Aderton would focus on this apparition, which she called a clown face, and it would help her think of running outside or riding her bicycle or being in the garden—things that made her well. Then she would not worry so much about what was in the closet or what was under her bed. At the age of twenty-five, Aderton had her first guided meditation. A teacher led the class she was in through a visualization tour. In their imaginations, the students were to walk away from a place that they considered their sanctuary, a library or study, for example, and walk into the hallway where they would meet a spirit guide. Aderton went through the exercise and saw the familiar concentric circles of light waiting for her. It was her spirit guide, which she knew had been with her throughout her life. She claims that the guide is still with her, and that her name is Aslyn.

Aderton knows that Aslyn is planning on being her first child. When she got upset a few years ago about not yet having a child, Aslyn told her to get over it, that the planet is not ready for her to be born, and she is not ready for the planet. But Aderton continues to look for the connections promised by love. She says that Christ was one of her first spiritual teachers. She was interviewed on a cable show once in San Francisco where she did actual channeling work while they were on the air. Someone called in and asked Aderton if she had a close and personal relationship with Christ. She answered yes, though with the qualification that it was not the kind of relationship that the viewer would want her to have or that the viewer would define as right. The caller was livid. He said he could not wait to be standing at the Pearly Gates with St. Peter to turn her away, and called her a witch. She does not see this attitude as very Christian, which she regards as a practice of unconditional acceptance and love.

In Aderton's belief system, there is no real separation among persons. Part of the illusion in human experience is that we are separate beings here on Earth. The illusion is created by allowing the physical world to determine what is of value. We begin to believe that the world of the spirit is unattainable, imperceptible, confusing, mythical. For Aderton reality is the spiritual world, which is permanent. It is the physical world that is illusory and transient. She told me that she has frequently moved into that state of collective consciousness which maintains no separations among individuals. She says she usually does not go there without being invited because she is still the good moral Methodist of her youth, and it would be bad manners to enter any domain without an invitation. She teaches and believes in "psychic etiquette." But she admits that sometimes she enters the holistic world unintentionally. She just finds herself there.

One indication that she is in or on the edges of the spiritual world is that her thoughts and the thoughts of others begin to merge. A short time ago she was walking with her friend Dez through the streets of downtown Telluride. She knew that Dez wanted to take her to a particular gallery to show her some jewelry, so she uttered Dez's thoughts before her friend could speak them—"Oh, Dez, we have to go to this gallery"—which naturally spooked her friend considerably. Another time, running late after a lengthy dental appointment, she was rushing to make a flight back to Chicago. She took a taxi to her apartment, where she was rushing to change her clothes and pack her bag before the driver who was to take her to the airport arrived. She was distraught, crying, and missing the man in Switzerland who was then her fiancé when the phone rang. She answered, thinking it was her driver, but it was her fiancé. He had a bad feeling about her and so postponed a session with a client to call. "Are you all right?" he asked. To Aderton this kind of thought sharing is testimony to the holistic universe we all occupy. We share each other's thoughts because we are not separate beings but one being. The etheric body is just a vehicle for the spirits that we are in reality.

In my interview with Aderton, I asked her where she expected to be in twenty years. A grandmother, she said. She sees herself as continuing to teach, write, and lecture, and by then she believes that she will have visited every continent on Earth. She hopes that one of her siblings will live close to her in the future. Aderton believes that the future is not one of ascension, of going up to heaven, but of realizing heaven here on Earth. She knows we have the power to realize this and hopes to help open people up to that possibility.

((Eight))

ON KNOWING AND NOT KNOWING

I

The long history chronicling what we know and how we know typically relies on perfect or unbounded knowledge as the gold standard for knowing. The most common version of this standard is the omniscient observer. To see how this model works, imagine a person who knows everything and then measure how close (or far) one's own knowledge is from that standard. Then try to get closer to the omniscience one has imagined. In its most ambitious form, the omniscient observer is God. This ideal of perfect knowledge is the goal that is impossible to reach, yet has consistently been used (from Plato through Hume and into contemporary theory) to identify the path to understanding the world in which we live. In many ways this standard of knowing has guided the appetites of modern science to construct a single theory of everything and in this way (in Hawking's concluding phrase in *A Brief History of Time*) "truly know the mind of God."

The closest rival in human experience to the acquisitive ideal of perfect knowledge is the mirror image of the restriction represented by forbidden knowledge. In many religions the source of forbidden knowledge also represents the ideal of perfect knowing: God. In chapter 2 of Genesis in the Bible, the Lord God commands Adam not to eat of the tree of knowledge of good and evil. The temptation of the serpent is more seductive than God's command, however, when the serpent promises Eve that eating the fruit of the forbidden tree opens one's eyes "and you shall be as Gods, knowing good and evil." Adam and Eve eat the fruit and acquire the forbidden knowledge. God expels them from paradise, telling Adam that he has become like the gods in knowing good and evil, and so must be sent out "lest perhaps he put forth his hand, and take also of the tree of life, and eat, and live forever." The biblical account of human experience begins with a banishment drawn up from the acquisition of forbidden knowledge.

Perfect knowledge, the knowledge that God has, cannot be acquired in this story without a sanction that keeps humans from becoming gods.

Some form of forbidden knowledge is a commonplace in human communities. Plato recognized that acquiring knowledge can sometimes be painful in demanding an inquiry into one's cherished opinions. These concerns at least occasionally move us to withhold knowledge from individuals if that knowledge would be especially harmful to the individual's well-being. To tell an individual, for example, that he has an untreatable and fatal genetic disorder may be all distress and no benefit. One might also want to restrict certain types of knowledge on the grounds that it can lead to actions destructive for whole societies and cultures. Robert Oppenheimer publicly lamented the discovery of the knowledge that released atomic energy for human use, including especially the development of nuclear weapons. Members of contraband groups know the deadly possibilities of certain knowledge. In parts of South Florida, stumbling upon a drug drop is often fatal. Those in the know do not want to know certain things. Many religions maintain privileged knowledge that can be known only by the select leadership and guard other types of knowledge that if known would imperil the soul of any knower.

Moral principles restrict the way knowledge is acquired. The human experiments conducted by the Nazis, for example, are universally condemned today as morally illicit no matter what knowledge they produced. Some spheres of knowledge are sealed off from public dissemination because they are privileged. Medical information on patients is generally maintained in the West as confidential by privacy shields, a protection deemed to be in the interests of both physician and patient. Other types of knowledge are restricted for reasons of state. All who have lived through the last two decades of the twentieth century are familiar with political institutions that routinely keep knowledge from their citizens as a method of governance. Daniel Moynihan, in tracking the secrets of the United States government during the Cold War, reminds us that the state uses secrecy laws to control populations by telling them what they can know. The sanctions for finding and disseminating information classified as secret do not today usually countenance banishment, but do include prison terms and the occasional death sentence. Those measuring proportionality in punishment might remember that God cast out Adam and Eve but did not kill them for their transgression of knowledge boundaries.

Of course what we don't know can also place us at risk. A literal interpretation of texts without the key variables can be both misleading and dangerous. Oedipus is told the legend that delineates his life: he is to kill his father and marry his mother. He understands the legend literally and promptly leaves home to escape his destiny. We know the rest. In his travels he meets, quarrels with, and kills a contentious old man at a crossing, later marrying the man's widow. Poor Oedipus. He did not know that he was adopted and had fled his foster parents. The man he killed was his biological father, the widow his mother. In another classical story, a man's servant encounters Death in the market square. The servant rushes home and asks his master for a fast horse to escape Death and then sets off for Samarra. The master goes down to the market and remonstrates with Death for frightening his servant. "I, too, was disturbed at seeing him here," Death replies, "for I have an appointment with him this very evening in Samarra." In both stories the protagonists interpret the narratives and events literally, as presented, *and without the requisite knowledge,* and then they flee to the destinies foretold. (If Oedipus had only known that he was adopted, the servant made aware of the coming evening encounter, or both had had instruction in destiny . . .) The language of the stories, the capacities of knowledge to stretch past the immediately literal to levels of knowing that permit more nuanced interpretation and multiple meanings, and the selective ignorance of the protagonists allow the plays on words and events that take the stories to their conclusions.

These two perspectives on perfect knowledge, the acquisitive ideal and forbiddance, are each elaborated and modified in complex ways throughout history. But a number of recent intellectual traditions have abandoned preoccupations with perfect and forbidden knowledge in favor of various models of limited knowledge offered without the real-life risks that textual ignorance can bring. Contemporary decision theories often develop standards of thinking in conditions of formal risk and uncertainty, where the rational person knows with probabilities but not certainties, and sometimes does not even know probabilities. The conditions of certainty revered in classical and modern theory are limited to narrow, perhaps experimental situations. The main reason for this referential shift seems to be that the wider world is understood today to be so complex and random that typical decisions must be modeled without any standard representing omniscience (with the consequence that one can be rational in one's decisions yet wrong on all reasonable criteria). Also, the assumptions informing virtually all of contemporary decision theory are that the human intellect is fundamentally limited, unable to grasp even imperfectly what God knows, and the search for high levels of knowledge has costs that can be avoided with lesser ambitions. So the standards for knowing are to be bounded by the limitations of knowing rather than unbounded by the aspirations to secure perfect information. Knowledge is denied because it is inaccessible or costly, not because it is forbidden.

One of the shaping features of reasoning in all secular circumstances may be the set of rules for excluding knowledge and sometimes even truth. It is commonplace today to limit knowledge to that which is relevant. All practices and professions admit information for consideration according to rules for securing and validating what is appropriate evidence. These rules delineate the range and type of information allowable for establishing proof or probability. The upshot is that practices and professions—law, science, teaching, engineering, for example—systematically exclude the irrelevant. Justifications for restricting information differ across these practices and professions, but the controlling thought is that rationality and moral integrity are best realized when the proceedings are confined to that which is relevant. One of the more publicly visible demonstrations of such restrictions occurs in courts of law. Only information that passes evidentiary tests drawn up from the acknowledged logic and purpose of legal trials is admitted. In science, a practice unusually preoccupied with method, there is a notorious adherence to strict rules for defining and admitting information. In all of these circumstances, information is consciously limited to help secure objectivity (meaning accurate and sound judgements) and to avoid bias and error.

These various types of limiting theories maintain that less is more, in several senses: a reduction in knowledge is more realistic and less costly, a basis for sound decisions, and a device for resolving disputes. This heightened sensitivity to what we do not know may or may not represent a fresh humility in epistemology, but it does invite some thought about the importance for human communities of imposed limits on knowledge, the types of justifications used to limit knowledge, and the instruments which are appropriate for negotiating the domains of the unknown that are inevitable byproducts or implications of some forms of limited knowledge.

2

One of the memorable features of talk about the supernatural is the unqualified confidence with which the principals (believers *and* skeptics) claim to know that alternative realities exist or do not exist. But for the impartial spectator in these discussions the question framed originally in ancient philosophy must be raised: How do we know that we know? And then there are the more modern, leading questions: What are the pathways and driving engines that take us toward acceptance or rejection of the supernatural? What explanations are appropriate for determining whether the supernatural is authentic, or bogus, and how do we acquire this knowledge from within human communities? And the question entertained again and again here, What are the implications of such knowledge for our identities and standing in the universe?

In the eighteenth and nineteenth centuries much effort was expended in the West to make science and religion compatible. Even the more radical of the early proponents of evolution (such as Erasmus Darwin, Charles Darwin's grandfather) were prepared to believe that the discovery of the underlying laws and structures of the universe simply revealed God's plan. Empirical inquiry (which Aquinas accepted as one way to prove the existence of God) was to reveal the design of the Creator: the better the science, the more accurate and detailed would be the empirical revelation of the grounds and subjects of religious beliefs. The problem that quickly occurred was that as science revealed the basic laws of nature, certain religious texts had to give way. The evolutionary doctrines of biology, for example, reject many of the events described in the Old Testament, for example the Flood. The required conclusion of evolution is that the Bible is false (at least in places) as an empirical transcription of history and nature, and where it is false as history and science it is best accepted as a text that provides a metaphorical account of the origin and development of the natural world.

But it is also important to know that, even with different outcomes, explanatory theories can be similar as we move across spiritual and scientific discourses. The most general levels of explanation yield few incompatibilities among *methodological* approaches to the natural and supernatural. Imagine a sequence of numbers governed by a simple rule: add two to any number in the set to get the following number.

2   4   6   8   10   12   14   16   18   20

Now select from this sequence, according to some rule of selection, a set of numbers that form another sequence, say

2   6   8   12   20

In the second sequence the combination rule of the initial sequence is masked. A different rule might describe a second such string of numbers, or the resulting string is random in the sense that it is so irregular that no rule is available to describe it (which seems to be the case here). But even if the second string is a random arrangement, the numbers are still members of the larger initial set, which is governed by a rule. The second sequence above is a set of random numbers explained by a higher order sequencing rule and a selection rule that can be disclosed with additional data and theory.

This move, from a random arrangement of limited data to an explanatory rule confirmed when the data are more complete and additional rules are revealed, is a standard pattern in scientific inquiry. One of the more famous of such explanations is found in the study of Brownian movement. In the early nineteenth century, botanist Robert Brown observed pollen particles suspended in water. The motion of the particles appeared erratic and was thought to be random. Later observations revealed that all particles suspended in fluid move in similar random fashion. The particle movement seemed to be, and was, independent of external influences, including the vibration of the container. Various qualitative models were introduced throughout the nineteenth century to explain such motion, but none was successful. In the early part of the twentieth century, Albert Einstein developed a set of equations that explained the movement as an instance of diffusion in the medium of suspension. These equations applied gas laws to all particles suspended in a liquid. The equations were later verified with more extensive observations of the patterns of movement.

Another form of explanation is also found in science. On occasion, perhaps even more frequently than the move from randomness to law-governed relationships, one set of laws will be replaced with another. Two of the most impressive changes in the history of science fit this pattern. Until roughly the sixteenth century, Ptolemaic astronomy dominated Western physics with its geocentric assumptions and elaborate system of epicycles to explain stellar observations. Copernicus, though still using epicycles, accepted a heliocentric view of the solar system. Kepler, with more exact observations, abandoned epicycles entirely and substituted ellipses for the circles that had been regarded as almost sacred forms of astronomical motion. Galileo introduced concepts of acceleration and inertia to further complete the modern account of motion. By the eighteenth century an entirely different set of laws had replaced Ptolemy's system.

A similar change in explanatory laws was introduced by Charles Darwin in the nineteenth century. The doctrine of evolution was discussed in generic form by biologists before Darwin. An anonymous author (later identified as Robert Chambers) introduced in 1844 a theory of evolution so ambitious as to include the astronomical universe and the mental history of humans. The stretch of this work was too speculative, and too distant from hard evidence, to be taken seriously by biologists (who talked about it with some interest nonetheless). But a later monograph by a respected biologist, Alfred Russell, outlined in 1855 a respectable and plausible framework for much of later evolutionary theory. The difference between these early efforts and Darwin's 1859 book, *On the Origin of Species,* was in part the evidentiary base. Darwin's long journey on the *Beagle,* especially the part of the voyage through the Galapagos Islands, gave him the opportunity to collect a wide range of data that led to the development and later support of his theories. His painstakingly detailed work on crustacean fossils, in particular barnacles, provided additional information on the workings of evolution.

Darwin also had the overriding benefit of being a genius. He was able to see and absorb theories from a wide range of disciplines, including geology and economics (in particular Malthus on population dynamics). The result in *Origin* was a combination of sophisticated theory and detailed evidence understood in new ways. Darwin introduced natural selection, a concept that required the dismissal of the immutability of species and the inheritance of acquired characteristics, and which made chance variation and adaptation the foundations of modern evolutionary biology. The book changed most of our basic understandings of human experience. In these types of explanatory shifts the events at issue are not random, but governed by laws dismissed as wrong or inadequate with the introduction of more powerful explanations. More data and, perhaps even more important, a different view of the same data, lead to the replacement of one set of laws with another.

Still a third pattern of explanation occurs. Sometimes a nomothetic explanation is jettisoned in favor of a random account of events. Among the contributions of quantum mechanics is the thought that micro events may not follow any laws, including the Newtonian and Einsteinian explanations successfully assigned to macro events. Recent work in chaos theory suggests that the structures and variables in nature may be random. Social theory has always entertained the existentialist and romantic prospect that human experience is meaningless, without explanation, at some fundamental level. Examinations of voting mechanisms have indicated that at least some forms of social practices may be random, not completely explained by the political rules used for centuries to make democracy both intelligible and attractive.

Note that only the third of these three patterns of explanation is inconsistent with a spiritual approach to human experience. Those who believe in realities beyond the conventional boundaries of human experience can and do support these beliefs with arguments that follow the general patterns of explanations one and two. These arguments maintain that (a) what appears random, chaotic, without meaning or purpose, is part of a larger design that cannot be seen in its entirety by humans. But from the perspective of a more cosmological range, where data are complete and explanatory models are more sophisticated, the random patterns of events give way to governing rules. The arguments also maintain that (b) what seems to be a reasonable and complete explanation of events in secular terms may be inadequate or wrong when more data are introduced or the data are looked at in a different way. A spiritual understanding of reality must assume that secular accounts are replaceable with spiritual accounts once a more complete understanding of events is in place. The one possibility not seriously considered in spiritual perspectives is that all covering laws are illusions, and that the underlying reality of human experience is random, chaotic, or meaningless.

The compatibilities of scientific and spiritual explanations do not mean that science supports a spiritual account of the world. The laws generated by scientific inquiry are different in both form and content from spiritual descriptions of reality. Scientific laws are falsifiable while spiritual laws tend to be maintained in the face of countervailing evidence. One of the intellectual consequences of arguments based on incomplete data must be that any proposed explanation or random pattern may be spurious when the complete picture is in place. The uncompromising efforts of science to retrieve all phenomena from the unknown and transfer them to the known, the privileging in science of doubt over faith, the resulting contrasts in scientific and spiritual accounts of reality produced by these priorities, and the natural binary split in domains of inquiry required by these two approaches—these are the incorrigible distinctions between scientific and spiritual understandings of experience. But one point remains in place. Spiritual points of view can use explanatory patterns consistent with science. The immediate consequence of this for both discourses is that even the most complete and satisfying scientific explanations cannot rule out a spiritual story of reality. The logic of scientific inquiry must always allow for the possibility that the data are incomplete, or the covering laws are wrong. These kinds of scientific limits eventually lead to the possibility of inquiries into alternative realities not anticipated by conventional science.

These inquiries, however, must settle on the *form* of knowledge presupposed in talk about the supernatural. Whether alternative realities exist or not, it is still productive to get right the type of knowledge we are talking about when we talk about these species of alternative realities. The model for this inquiry may well be drawn from the limitations outlined in a combination of acquisitive ideal and forbidden knowledge: ideal thresholds that, when crossed, bring sanctions in the form of irrevocable changes in how we understand experience. In this sense we recognize a distinction (not found in science) between secrets and mysteries. The supernatural does not seem to be a secret, a datum or theory to be uncovered by disclosure efforts. It rather has the appearance of a mystery, perhaps spiritual in nature, that may or may not yield to our inquiries. Our inquiries, in turn, may have to be shaped by a purpose analogous to practices like legal trials: we must know what we are seeking and why so as to identify the rules of evidence and inference that allow rational conclusions in human practices.

3

In exploring what and how we know, we can accept one thing without resistance: much of what we know is limited by our senses and intellect. No one can doubt this. If the observation is pressed it becomes stronger: perhaps *all* that we know is within the frames that are furnished by our biological endowments as modified by experience. If this stronger statement is true as a limiting condition, then even revelation from higher forms of life is filtered and accommodated by human categories of knowing. Human physical capacities are unexceptional. We see only so far along the color spectrum, for example. Ultraviolet light, outside the perceptual powers of our vision, can be seen by some other forms of biological life on Earth. The mental limits set by human neurology may also be no more than our limits, and they may be surpassed by life as we do *not* know it. John Barrow, in *Impossibility*, outlines types of limits. One of his distinctions, traceable to Kant, is between selective limits on knowing everything within some domain (the number of fish in Lake Michigan) and limits as boundaries which human knowing cannot cross (the mind of God). The first kind of limit is the source for justifications of bounded rationality:

that some domains are beyond our calculative powers, or are sufficiently dense with information that the acquisition costs exceed rational thresholds. The second kind of limit takes us a small but important distance to the edges of human thought and the role of the unknown in our thinking.

The more profound and interesting distinctions between scientific and spiritual ways of presenting human experience seem to emerge from the standing of the unknown in each of these two types of inquiry. Spiritual quests can be complex exercises in moral realism. But the interviews and arguments presented here also suggest that they can be direct and to the point. At the outset they aim to discover a natural order. The natural order in many religions is both fixed and external. It does not change even though opinions on its state or meaning may change, and it is not another convention but something outside of all human artifice. The methods in spiritual thinking used to gain access to a natural order are succinct. They typically consist of both critical reflection and intuitive experiences that allow individuals to see a reality beyond normal human experience. This privileged, or transcendent, perspective may not always be reached, so that failure to comprehend the full dimensions of the real must be entertained as a possible outcome of spiritual reasoning. But the acceptance of such a reality is not abandoned when that reality cannot be reached successfully. It exists for believers in the supernatural and it influences, in decisive ways, the meaning of human experience. Finally, the object of spiritual inquiries, an external reality, provides the understandings and moral principles by which to order human communities.

It is easy to see that spiritual inquiry, whatever else it does, denies the possibility of human understanding for least some important kinds of knowledge and treats this unknown dimension as an important consideration in reasoning. The contrasts of this view with a secular reliance on bounded rationality are impressive. Bounded versions of rationality acknowledge limitations in the human intellect that make it impossible for individuals to comprehend a complete range of information on alternatives. When these limitations are introduced to cost considerations, rationality requires that deliberations be bounded by the informational limits. These limits set the parameters for what individuals can consider. That which is outside the parameters is not relevant or accessible to rational discourse and, as Wittgenstein observed, is an area about which we must remain silent. The spiritual thinker, by contrast, can and must consider external knowledge as relevant and, on occasion, as more important in reasoning than internal knowledge. Rational limits are imposed not because of limitations on the human intellect, or from cost considerations, but rather on the acceptance of a substantive and controlling unknown. The contours of what is known, the limits and possibilities of knowledge, are shaped in spiritual communities by the unknown. On a spiritual view we reason with partial, though sometimes fairly complete, awareness of unknown forms that determine the meaning and value of human experience.

All thought allows for senses of the unknown in human experience. Some are casual. For example, there is the harmless way in which an inquiry may rest on unexamined premises. These premises may be knowable, but for any particular inquiry may be unknown due to the inattention of the inquirer. Or we often use the unknown (a definitely casual use of the term) to designate that which is accessible only to a gifted few, not available to others. Intuitive powers, found in both art and science, are among the discovery methods here, at least in the sense that knowing remains mysterious for the untalented or uninitiated. Other senses of the unknown are more serious. One is tacit knowledge, which may not be completely accessible but is still relevant to inquiry. Here one will find cultural knowledge, including the deep sets of expectations and ordering rules that produce the taken for granted, commonsense views of the world. Another sense of the unknown is represented by those deep principles in terms of which knowing occurs. Here might be found the neurological structures that are fugitive to reflections and perhaps not yet explained fully, but which make cognitive operations possible. These latter senses of the unknown mark a region which is outside the methods and theories of inquiry, and which must be accommodated in some way as inquiry in any field progresses.

A spiritual acceptance of the unknown is more than an effort to ground thought in terms that are outside the conceptual frameworks of discourse. If inductive reasoning has no non-arbitrary basis, then systems of belief require an anchor, a starting point that is itself outside the rules that retain and falsify beliefs. But such starting points are typically given only provisional status within scientific inquiry. They are constructs that allow a particular discourse to begin and can be dismissed if convenient to do so. The spiritual quest is more ambitious. Spiritual thinking depends on a permanent external framework that makes knowledge itself both intelligible and possible. This reality is not a convenient puzzle piece invented or endorsed simply as a means to begin discourse. The spiritual beliefs found in many religions typically accept the unknown as a token for realities beyond the scope of human knowledge. Human knowledge in a spiritual perspective is part of a more complete arrangement independent of subjective experience. From the acceptance of a reality independent of human beliefs, it follows that rational discourse *must* allow for the possibility that some important sources of knowledge are outside the powers of reason itself.

Modern science tries to manage the unknown with a variety of powerful descriptive and theoretical devices, including speculative hypotheses on the unknown, that *explain* phenomena. Spiritual approaches to experiences also attempt to make the unknown intelligible, but the acceptance of a higher sense of knowledge and being in spiritual communities includes three possibilities not addressed in scientific traditions. The first is that reality may only be knowable by intellectual perspectives outside human subjectivity and thus is beyond scientific methods of inquiry developed within human communities. (Religious discourses often accept such higher forms of life.) The second is that reality may be governed by design instead of the impersonal laws delineated in scientific inquiry. The third is that at least some part of this external knowledge or design may be grasped by means of intuitive experiences that cannot be replicated through conventional scientific methods. Any of these possibilities distinguishes spiritual inquiries from even the most aggressive scientific exploration of the unknown. But the most important difference from the scientific temperament is that some spiritual convictions allow an unknowable reality to define the status of human experience and influence rational discourse.

This sense of the unknown has profound implications for human reasoning and leads to radically different understandings of human cultures. It contrasts sharply with empirical approaches to reasoning. It is difficult to conceive of a suitable parallel or metaphor that illuminates this species of thinking. Though this is crude and not entirely correct, consider string theory in physics, which postulates additional dimensions that cannot be perceived but yet provide the basis for mathematical expressions that explain relationships in the perceptual world. If these dimensions were regarded as properties of reality, they would represent spiritual senses of the unknown. Or think of the cabalists of medieval Europe, who took for granted additional dimensions of reality that rendered sense experience intelligible. In these frameworks, the unknown profoundly affects the known and is the target of a full exercise of rational power, even as we realize that full access to this unknown and unknowable realm is not possible.

On these approaches to the unknown, spiritual attitudes and thought typically move beyond science, and sometimes abandon it completely. But note that intuitive or mystical approaches to reality can follow and complement what are regarded as limited modes of thinking trapped within the practices of scientific inquiry once the domains of inquiry are separated. Given the assumption in spiritual perspectives that the full cosmological picture is always inaccessible to human inquiry, it is not surprising that faith is introduced in spiritual accounts as a supplement to reason. *Permanent* limited access to an account of reality that provides meaning for human existence must incline one to seek help. The natural turn is toward the competence and goodwill of higher forms of life who can communicate indirectly the true and complete story of reality. Such dependence is anathema to science, which supports its laws by evidence fixed within human communities.

4

Do higher forms of life exist, and, if they do, can we reach them in such a way that they can provide the assistance required in spiritual thinking?

Consider the following thought experiment. Imagine forms of life with radically different neurologies. Say that the organs for gathering and processing "data" in these life forms are so different from ours that the world they perceive is entirely different in its content and form. This is not so difficult an imaginative stretch. We know that other forms of life here on Earth have different processing and synthesizing powers. The wasp, for example, has different experiences than humans do as a consequence of having radically different sensing and framing systems. Suppose we take such differences up to higher levels and even include different thinking structures. Suppose the imagined life forms just have completely different brains, and so different thoughts, including the concepts, principles, and rules that are used to think, perhaps even including those categories that define what thinking might mean. Can anyone going through this thought experiment doubt that experience is different for these life forms, and that the explanatory theories of this species would be radically different?

Now consider an extension of the thought experiment. In the phylogenetic scale used in biology to order life, no entry in the hierarchy knows the entry above it. We might even say that only the higher vertebrates know other forms of life in any way at all. But even among the vertebrates the limits are firm. If any of us in the human species strolls in the woods, there is no species (within our understandings of nature) that knows us as humans, by which I mean as reflective creatures. It is tempting to think that we are the highest entries on the phylogenetic scale. But if the limits on knowing are confined to the level of the entry and its subordinates, then we cannot know any life forms above us. Like the fly that cannot have a concept of the room where it is located, we may not have any concept of the larger settings and life forms that may succeed us on the scale. Staying with this logic means that higher life forms may exist here on Earth, but we cannot recognize them as higher life forms. We simply may not have the neurological resources to see the alternative realities that are part of our larger and (perhaps) infinitely more complicated ecology.

A tantalizing and controversial conjecture occurs when a threshold crossing into the supernatural is joined to the thought experiment that ranks life forms. Are we warranted in listing higher life forms as part of the full inventory of an external reality? A *yes* to the warrant is one of the assumptions in recent work on alien visitations and abductions. Here the life-form ranking is taken two steps beyond the thought experiment. One step is an acceptance of the existence of higher life forms. The other is an acceptance of the possibility of contact between higher life forms and human life, a contact initiated (as it must be) by the higher forms of life. The prospect is that we can exceed the limits of our epistemologies if we receive help from those who are outside our natures.

Contacts between alien and human life forms are described in a number of works. None of the described experiences seem to follow Western principles of liberty and informed consent. John E. Mack, in his book *Abduction*, describes the in-depth studies he has made of individuals who claim to have been abducted by aliens. The case studies are filled with the amazing details that make these stories so riveting. Like many accounts of the supernatural, the experiences follow a common model that allows for individual variation. Individuals are in their homes or cars, or out walking somewhere, when the experiences begin. An unexplained blue or white light fills the area. A buzzing or humming is heard. The individuals start feeling uneasy, uncomfortable. Sometimes they see a humanoid figure that looks like an apparition. Then they enter a state of paralysis during which they are transported across and through physical matter like rooms and walls to what the abductees describe as a spacecraft, often with additional odd figures in attendance.

Inside the vessel the individuals are subject to a variety of procedures conducted by the alien figures, who seem to be differentiated by a kind of hierarchy. Various drone-like aliens carry out a number of low-level tasks, and a species of gray humanoid figures, with a distinct leader, carries out the procedures on the abductees. Mack categorizes these procedures as physical and informational. The physical procedures begin with an undressing of the abductee and include an invasive examination of the entire body while the leader of the aliens visually scans the abductee (often from a distance of a few inches). Probes of the reproductive system also seem to take sperm samples from men and ova from women. Sometimes the abductee is physically altered. Some report various implantations: fertilized eggs into the women (which are later removed in subsequent abductions), and a variety of small devices that abductees regard as monitoring or tracking instruments. The individuals also report surgical procedures conducted inside their heads that they believe alter their nervous systems. Mack sees these invasive procedures as a type of genetic engineering that may be changing the human race.

The information procedures described by abductees support Mack's view. In this version of abduction the individual is shown certain scenarios about the future of the Earth. These presentations, which include images transmitted directly to the human's consciousness, delineate catastrophes: nuclear holocausts, lifeless landscapes, pollution and physical disasters like earthquakes and floods, sometimes including a vision of the Earth splitting in two. These sessions seem to be warnings of possible futures that will become real if human practices are not altered substantially. The informational sessions are often repeated over a lifetime for some individuals. At the end of both types of sessions, the abductee is returned to Earth to resume normal life. But the memories of the experience remain, sometimes concealed as dreams, and often emerging after years of repression. The pathological patterns, according to Mack, follow the form of a traumatic experience, with otherwise normal individuals trying to recover from an event that has altered their cognitive and emotional states of mind.

One of the intriguing features of the abduction reports is how difficult they are to either refute or confirm with independent evidence. There are almost no reports of the experiences from an uninvolved observer, and virtually no physical evidence to support the accounts. What we have is a set of compelling stories from rationally intact individuals who seem to have had an experiences that exceed the boundaries of what we take as the natural world. The best independent evidence of abduction would seem to be the tracking devices said to be left in the bodies of abductees. Like the surgeon leaving an instrument inside the body of a patient after an operation, an implanted device would be palpable proof of a surgical probe. Yet when such items are removed, they display no extraordinary features, no strange alien properties, and are usually consistent with manufacturing techniques and materials within human technologies. But this finding is not a falsification of the possible tracking properties of such devices. It cannot be beyond the powers of an advanced civilization to use ordinary and even biological material to make effective homing devices. The problem here is a classic one in the study of foreign cultures. One cannot restrict alien cultures with the technological insights of one's own civilization or expect that the insights of such cultures will be displayed on the terms of scientific criteria drawn entirely from one's indigenous technologies. If an entirely new phenomenon is being encountered then it is by definition not validated or comprehended by conventional means. We do not and cannot know the limits of a higher form of life, or what that form of life is all about, from our own limited technologies.

These limits dismiss many of the traditional reservations about alien visitations. The phenomena of such visitations may or may not be authentic (in any sense), but they are immune to the simple objection (expressed recently by Frederick Crews) that "you can't get here from there." It is true that the best science in human communities has identified upper limits on space travel set by the speed of light. The star nearest our sun is Alpha Centauri. It is three light years away, which means (as Crews notes) that at a speed of a million miles per hour it would take a spacecraft over six thousand years to make the round trip. Other stars, which may have the planetary systems not found around Centauri, would have even more prohibitive travel problems due to distance even when they are in our own galaxy. The galaxies themselves? Well, a local neighbor is the Triangulum galaxy, a mere three million light years from Earth. The size and distribution of matter in the universe seem to be a natural barrier to space travel among (possible) civilizations, imposing a unilateral lifestyle on intelligent life by virtue of the spatial insulations of our natural settings. But this judgement takes for granted that the limits identified in current human science are generalizable across all forms of life everywhere. Surely the experiences with the development of science here on Earth disabuses one of this view? Imagine the assurance with which scientists employing a geocentric view of the solar system pronounced limits on possible states of the universe now revealed as likely and even routine on a heliocentric view. We cannot deny the reality of a phenomenon simply with the possibilities delineated in any version of contemporary science. But then the question is, How are supernatural phenomena to be studied? What methods can we use to examine alternative realities?

The problem is that even with the requisite mental powers we may not be able to experience the far radical side of the unexpected because our inquiries are limited. Richard Swinburne maintains that we must know what an x is in order to experience it. ("Only someone who knew what a telephone was could seem to see a telephone.") On this line of argument we learn "what an experience of God would be like" by means of an understanding of what God is like. It is the understanding that would allow us to recognize God if we were to experience God. Swinburne's conditions are standard fare in cognitive psychology. Categories of knowing are required to have experiences. It follows that a thoroughly material human community is a very difficult place to make sense of spiritual experiences or alternative life forms because the background understandings in the community may be devoid of the necessary categories of knowledge.

Mack tells how he visited Thomas Kuhn, author of the household classic *The Structure of Scientific Revolutions,* as he began his studies of alien abductions. Kuhn noted that the Western scientific paradigm has assumed the standing of a theology, blocking alternative ways of understanding reality with a dense assortment of categories that trade on polarities such as real/unreal, exists/does not exist, objective/subjective, intrapsychic/external world. (To these polarities I would add self/other and mental/physical.) Kuhn advised Mack to try to avoid these dominating categories and see the experiences as they are presented, collecting raw data without relying on the language forms of our historical time and place. This advice, in effect an admonition to bracket one's cultural perspectives and allow the meanings of the experiences to emerge as they are compiled and collated, was the plan that Mack said he tried to follow in his studies.

Kuhn's advice is an initially attractive approach to the supernatural. If we can suspend our predilections, then it does seem that we have a better chance to see the unexpected, except that the unexpected is only revealed against the backdrop of the expected. A scientific anomaly occurs only when scientific normalities are understood. The supernatural is an experience that exceeds nature, and only if we have an understanding of nature can we say that an experience exceeds it. The contradiction is well known. We can have experiences only in terms of concepts, and these concepts are unavoidably influenced by a particular culture. But these concepts incline us toward exclusive ways of rendering experience intelligible. How can we suspend the categories to gain access to different experiences when we need some set of categories to negotiate our way through experiences?

Complicating the task of finding a way to understand the supernatural is the possibility suggested by the alien abduction stories: forms of life outside the boundaries of the natural world may be setting the terms of our understanding. It is easy to slip off the edge here by assuming that which we are trying to establish. But there is also a great distinction between understanding phenomena that do not have the powers of consciousness and those that do. The task of the archaeologist studying rock formations is framed primarily from the point of view of the archaeologist. The cultural anthropologist must attend to another dimension of meaning represented by the languages of the culture studied. This additional layer of meaning leads to methodological issues of translation across sometimes radically disparate forms of life, retrieving indigenous meanings without distortion and presenting the internal understandings of the life being studied to a community of scholars with different concepts and theories. Now suppose that the culture being studied is more complex than that of the anthropologist's culture and can effectively frame the terms of communication. What methods should the anthropologist employ to gain access and retrieve meanings?

The one clear beginning of a response to this question is that no algorithmic methods will succeed if we accept the fact of an active and intelligent alien life outside the conventional boundaries of nature. Rote applications of a method will not produce rote results unless there is a neutral substratum (a point accepted by Daniel Dennett and also Stephen Jay Gould, in a different discussion), meaning that if the subject of study can affect the methods of study then algorithms do not work. The methods of study would have to be interactive in some way, meaning that the study of the supernatural requires engaging it in a creative way if it contains life forms similar to those reported in the abduction literatures.

5

Again, let's start with what we know. First, the conceptual maps we use in explaining the universe must in some way be the direct or indirect result of evolution, yet there is no obvious reason to think that adaptive forces have produced neurological powers that can understand the universe. Such understandings may have negative survival values in the history of the planet Earth, with the result that the brain may be poorly equipped to understand the universe for good reasons of historical adaptation. Second, it is likely that many of our scientific abilities are side developments in the nonlinear fashion in which evolution surely proceeds. Natural selection combines with any number of other causal variables (like the laws of physics and random events) to produce traits in any complex species, and these traits are likely to include what Stephen Jay Gould calls "spandrels." In Gould's definition, these are "evolutionary features that do not arise as adaptations." Surely the intellectual abilities needed to master the abstractions of advanced physics and quantum mechanics are spandrels? Third, and as a consequence, science may not be the only or best way to approach the unknown. If some important neurological powers that have produced scientific methods are not connected to nature through the direct effects of natural selection, if they are sidebar products of the interaction of natural selection and other variables, then they may still have survival value but be inadequate in representing the complete scope of natural phenomena (which may include the supernatural). Some dimensions of science may be simple adjustments of multiple variables at the edges of adaptation, and as clumsy and restrictive in framing a robust version of nature as plea bargains are in depicting the full range of the criminal law. It is at least reasonable to think that the supernatural may be an extension of the natural that science cannot reach, and that it may yield to explanatory forms other than science, though one wants to think in combination with versions of science.

This methodological pluralism may be more acceptable on the recognition that a strictly material universe died a natural death long ago (though the philosophers who continue to defend materialism have not yet accepted the death certificate), which means that the move to pluralism in methods does not require abandoning respected doctrine. It is also old party material to point out that the materialism of common sense and scientific languages are quite different, so that (in the standard example) the porous nature of subatomic particles constituting a table is at variance with the solid table referenced in ordinary languages. It is just as safe to say that the physical objects in any language are considered entries in an inventory of material reality just because they occur with regularity in our sensory vistas. But they do not necessarily constitute a "real world" outside human seeing and knowing. They just have more stability than illusory or ethereal objects. The task has been and is to get our languages straight so that we can make sense of our experiences, and this exercise can be carried out without supposing that science is the privileged method for getting at an objective reality independent of our perceptions and understandings. It may be that the supernatural demands something in addition to science, since science, in trying to demystify the unknown with theories and laws that provide general explanations, must be limited on the terms of inquiry set for the supernatural.

Scientific inquiry is a remarkably effective instrument in providing an objective account of experience. It is the natural extension of that transition in thought from the individualism of the spoken word to the universality of the written language: objectivity as codified in the procedures of falsification recorded in written texts. But with this recorded objectivity that has yielded so much explanatory power has come a denigration of the unknown by categorization, since in science the unknown is a problem to be solved by absorbing it into objective accounts that fit comfortably with science. In all versions of mysticism the unknown is a condition of the universe, and testament to the dominance of what we do not know over the realms of the known and knowable. This striking difference between scientific and mystical approaches to the unknown can be traced to the contrasting roles of language in science and mysticism. The unity of the cosmos in mysticism cannot be successfully addressed with any instruments that partition experience. This truth immediately limits the use of the written language in reasoning about, and from within, mystical experiences. All languages organize and segment experiences, but written languages assign an objective standing to partitions. They codify life as an arrangement or sequence, which is contrary to the uncompromising holism of mysticism.

The only expression that might capture an encompassing unity is the spoken or written story, which occasionally ignores the boundaries of linear reasoning by suspending verities like time and space and replacing the ordinary partitions of language with holistic renditions of experience. Nondual philosophies often rely on stories to illustrate truth. The Zen Koan is a puzzling story given to novitiates. A concentration on the mystery of the Koan (a mystery not to be "solved") is one device to facilitate meditation and gain access to a higher state of being. The oblique and symbolic powers of stories can help individuals attain the proper state of mind to reach enlightenment and an eventual fusion with reality. Meditation on texts is to reveal that which is elusive to science. Like the forms in Plato's epistemology, the instruments of spiritual knowing may have to be absorbed, not seen and evaluated, and when used will not illuminate the objects of knowing so much as render them intelligible. An acceptance of the sacred and the mystical may be the first precondition for access to a reality that will not yield its secrets to the demanding needs of science to make everything known by making it visible.

Parables are especially apt illustrations of the ways that stories can summon and expand our intuitions while providing counterintuitive lessons from what the faithful believe is a reality that exceeds human understanding. In the parable of the Prodigal Son, the younger son of a man asks for his share of the family estate. The father divides his property and meets the request. The son departs for "a distant land" and there spends all of his money on "dissolute living." A famine breaks out, and the son finds that he cannot survive even as a servant to the propertied class. He decides to return home and offer himself to his father as a servant. But the father, seeing his son at a distance, rushes out and greets him with kisses and generous gifts of clothing and food. He orders his servants to prepare a feast in celebration of his returned son. The elder son, on hearing of his father's generosity, is angry. He remonstrates with his father on the grounds that he, the obedient son, has received no such celebration while his brother, "having gone through your property with loose women, you kill the fatted calf for him." The father replies with the story's moral and invitation: "My son, you are with me always, and everything I have is yours. But we had to celebrate and rejoice! This brother of yours was dead, and has come back to life. He was lost, and is found." As in all effective parables, the intuitions of the reader or audience are summoned to comprehend the story, but then shaped in new ways as the conclusion rearranges the conventional morals of the human community. To a religious sensibility the parable communicates an insight into a higher structure that is accessible only through certain narratives.

If we introduce the limits of human thought to a mystical sense of prayer and meditation, and to the use of texts that we regard as sacred, then the proper areas of reflection on the supernatural may well be the dilemmas and contradictions that remind us of areas beyond our comprehension. The types of discourses represented by narratives, allegories, parables—those instruments calibrated to interpret, to decipher, to render the mysterious intelligible without reducing it to human proportions—may be more appropriate for the unknown in human communities. There is a program of thought and action that emerges from these reflections. It starts with an acceptance of a higher, or at least more comprehensive, reality to which we have only partial access. From this acceptance five propositions follow.

One is an argument for faith in human experience. Belief without benefit of evidence is at the center of what it means to be human. The evidence we have to support the beliefs we must subscribe to in order to negotiate our way through experience is inadequate. We must believe without benefit of evidence, at least on occasion, because of intellectual limits. Second, the meaning of any human life, and human life in general, cannot be grasped in its entirety by those who are living. If we accept a larger universe beyond our comprehension, then it must follow that we cannot know what our tenure here, in the space-time domain that we know as human experience, means in any sense of a larger scheme of things. We may mean nothing in the cosmos (the radical existentialists may carry the day). Or we may live lives whose meanings, for example, are entirely a matter of providing solace for one minute to another human being. Or we may be God's favored children in which every minute of our lives is rich with significance. No one can know these things with anything approaching certainty. Third, there is at least a case to be made for following one's moral instincts. Doing the right thing on a private moral compass may be exactly that which fits the larger reality we cannot grasp. In an odd way both the moral anarchist and the moral intuitionist may be closer to the right strategy of life than the person armed with cognitive moral certainties.

Fourth, the logic of spiritual reasoning must be a deciphering inquiry, one that seeks the patterns or symbols within the accessible realm that might or might not reflect a more comprehensive reality. If limited knowing recognizes a domain of the supernatural, then one is authorized to seek connections that render human experience intelligible from an external perspective. Skills of interpretation and composition dominate the simple mathematical skills of aggregation. These skills are those which are not enclosed by the intellectual system at hand, but rather point to something other than the immediate undertaking. For example, adding integers or even calculating the solutions to sets of differential equations are operations that occur within systems of mathematics. But using mathematics to uncover or refer to patterns and structures outside mathematics is an exercise of connection and composition. This exercise is shaped by meditation on the limits of mathematics as exhibited in paradoxes and dilemmas. It is the type of inquiry that is characteristic of inquiries into realities beyond nature. It also meets the needs of those programs of reflection that Buddhism has always urged on us: acceptance (rather than grim efforts, as in magic or prayer, to alter reality in one's favor) and sustained meditation on the mysteries of experience itself.

Finally, rational discourse based on larger or more complete sources of knowledge that are essentially unknowable in their entirety to human forms of inquiry may not be amenable to the serial arrangements of *any* empirical models of reason. Reasoning on holistic terms might require the prior acceptance of a whole that is not completely accessible but yet structures the reality encountered by humans. To reason in such a program is not to move from one level to another in a series of steps. It is rather to *see* experience, perhaps reality, by means of intuitive principles not accommodated by serial thinking. Reasoning is holistic rather than sequential. The point to such an exercise is found deep within traditions of meditation: human consciousness is a process that is loosely organized and governed by random and elastic forces that must be brought under control if the full dimensions of reality are to be apprehended. This disciplinary program can hardly be contrary to any intellectual effort and is well within the contours of a more robust version of empirical science. It promises a union of spirit and matter elusive on the terms of a modern science crafted on simplistic materialism, and a recognition of practices that easily combine religious and secular purposes with an active participation in alternative realities. Like the logic of the electronic network, the form of thought is both instantaneous and universal and is alive to the possibility of holistic entities that are and are not the results of human cognition.

((Nine))

NATURAL INTELLIGIBILITIES

I

Only one blinded by faith can deny the destructive effects of spiritual beliefs in history. Religious wars, for example, are among the more malevolent events in human communities, and primitive beliefs in the supernatural can be dysfunctional in the extreme when science has illuminated another, advantageous way. But the spiritual has also been a positive force in human affairs. The beneficial side of beliefs in an unknown and unknowable reality are expressed in at least two practices. One is the provision of a foundation in human communities for a validation of oaths, and an effective guarantee that they will be honored. The other is explanatory. Accounts of the unknown fill the conceptual space left empty by the best objective theories of the universe, which are currently provided by science. Both of these elaborations meet utilitarian tests of adaptation. Human communities are more effective, more useful sites of life, if the reciprocities of truth telling and promise keeping are guaranteed with credible sanctions. On Hobbes's terms it then becomes rational to be moral: the losing alternatives manufactured by defections are nullified, and the sense of morality as rules of right living can be realized as benefits even by egoists. If threats of punishment from another dimension of reality can establish the conditions for these practices, then appropriate beliefs in alternative realities are utility fulfilling at high levels.

Resources that complete explanations are also useful. John Stuart Mill has provided the most compelling case for liberty in modern political philosophy. The main defense of liberty Mill offers is utilitarian and easily accepted: it is in the interests of all rational persons to have liberty as an enabling good, meaning that liberty typically is needed to secure other goods and also is a generally helpful principle in organizing a political society. But Mill also justifies liberty as a deontic good (a good in itself), which implies that it is a vital part of our makeup: we are free creatures by our nature, and, as a generalization of the myths assigned to gypsies, we must have a kind of general liberty in order to fulfill our identities. But then Mill does something unusually interesting. He folds liberty into truth. The main point to exercising liberty of expression is that free speech and open disputation are needed to find true statements. It seems that we are also truth-seeking creatures, and only as we are free can we successfully arrive at those statements and theories that can adequately make sense of our experiences.

It is always risky and usually wrong to explain anything by human nature given the great elasticities of identity across cultures and the well-known effects of environments on even the basic attributes of life. But it is surely safe to observe that human life everywhere has tried to make sense out of experience, that we are indeed truth-seeking creatures, but that these efforts have led to incomplete explanations throughout history when the explanations are bound by the terms of secular inquiry. It is also incontrovertible to observe that the supernatural has often functioned as a kind of bridge theory, connecting our limited knowledge about experience with variables drawn from what is thought to be an unseen world. These variables often require certain beliefs about the secular world in order to maintain beliefs about alternative realities. Beliefs in the supernatural may represent efforts by truth-seeking creatures to complete and fortify partial explanations about the universe in which we live. In this sense they are useful beliefs independent of whether they are true or not on the terms in which they are presented. Put simply, beliefs in supernatural realities fulfill basic human needs to make phenomena intelligible.

There are difficulties in encouraging beliefs just because they are useful in ordinary life. We know from studies of the placebo effect that false beliefs can heal. (The core requirement in the placebo effect is that the patient believe something that is false.) But the powers of belief demonstrated with placebos are limited in all discourses that seek or rely on truth (both religion and science, for example). Plato warned us that enlightenment can be painful, a point illustrated in the physical ascent (representing the turn from sensory experience to knowledge) in the Allegory of the Cave, where someone has to force the resisting cave dwellers up the path out of the cave to the luminous world of sunlight and "real" objects. Imagine, to illustrate the point in another way, that a man believes that his spouse is faithful when she is not. The false belief can be comforting (useful) in crafting a kind of bliss originating in ignorance, but we would still be inclined to say that the deceived man is an unfortunate creature. Better to know the truth, even when it is painful and possibly destructive, than to live a comfortable life of deception. Technically, and at the extremes, analogies with the placebo effect cut in the opposite direction in truth-functional discourses: a patient who benefits from the placebo would still be better off with true beliefs even if these beliefs prevented the restoration of health. Truth trumps the useful in truth-seeking ways of thinking.

But these are hard judgements. We may be inexplicably fortunate in having so many human discourses and terms that do not rely on truth to the exclusion of comfort (the capacity to hope, for example). And, in any case, beliefs in the supernatural may also be reasonable extensions of good and tried empirical theories of experience, and these extensions may be needed to accommodate our natures as the conscious creatures that we are. Both theory and human consciousness have certain features that make unlikely any complete and closed explanation for experience, and in particular seem to rule out closure for the depictions of the universe presented in physics. The signature mark of scientific theory is that it be falsifiable, which means that no theory can attain the certainty of a complete explanation (a theory of everything) because some event in the future may dismiss even the most fundamental truths about experience. Consciousness in turn seems to be or contain an open power that can chronically redefine any term in language and any account of experience. The stochastic qualities found in all renditions of any part of the universe require that even our best theories be partial and provisional. Speculations about the remainders in any account of things, the unexplained, the countertheory, are natural features of scientific inquiry. The only issue is what conditions have to be met for the speculations to be continuous with established accounts of experience.

The thresholds of continuity in even the best theories are remarkably low so long as the speculations are framed in terms of an intelligible universe. Perhaps the most impressive feature of "intelligible" is the broad and loose ways that materialism drifts through its intellectual landscapes. Here is an example. The standard model of the constituent parts of the universe currently refers to matter and forces. Matter consists at the most basic level of three types of fermions: quarks, antiquarks, and those particles resulting from a binding of quarks and antiquarks, mesons. There are four basic forces: the strong force (which holds together protons and neutrons), the weak force (which causes types of radioactivity), electromagnetic force (which binds atoms and molecules), and gravity (familiar to us as the force that holds together the structure of the universe). Various particles (gauge bosons, photons, gluons, gravitons) carry the forces among the particles of matter. In the last three decades this model has been challenged by physicists postulating infinitesimal one-dimensional strings vibrating in ten-dimensional space, and, more recently, branes, which are said to be surfaces that exist in multiple dimensions.

Are the vocabularies that express these basic units of the universe the terms of a material reality? Materialism is the doctrine that the universe can be completely explained by physical laws. The physical is generally defined as referring to body, as distinguished from the mind or spirit, or as pertaining to material things, or to matter and energy as these terms are used in the natural sciences. It does not take a linguist to recognize that these distinctions between the physical and the spiritual are largely empty in both the standard model and its rivals, that a good portion of the vocabularies of contemporary physics are as "spiritual" as any religious text, and that this is no disadvantage for explanatory theories of the universe. The properties of the universe seem to recoil from distinctions between material and spiritual, to veer quickly away from these polarities once the surface of ordinary life is left behind, and at the edges of the universe the exact composition of matter and force is not successfully captured by the dualities of body and mind (a point made in chapter 1).

What then marks off the explanatory powers of science? At the end of the day it seems that method rather than subject is decisive. The logic and practice of science require that, in some complex ways, propositions must be dismissed if evidence requires it. The historical transition from the authority of the sacred text to the dominance of a complex intertwining of empirical theory and evidence is the defining condition of modern science. Given this condition, the speculations that legitimately extend scientific programs must be capable in some acceptable circumstances of falsification. Then, having conceded this, the issues of continuity are turned in a different direction. Efforts to complete accounts of experience must be empirical propositions that are consistent with ongoing theory, not with doctrines of materialism. Empirical propositions, on any account, are statements about experience that can be falsified. Only if the universe is defined in purely material terms can such statements be restricted to Madonna's strictly material world. But we have seen that this definition of the universe will not support the phenomena known to exist in experience.

These are difficult thoughts. Some examples may help. String (or M) theory is a proposal that addresses both the standard model and the data that the model attempts to accommodate. The success or failure of string theory will turn on its retentive powers measured against rival theories in making experiences intelligible within the falsifying conditions of scientific inquiry. A perfectly idiosyncratic proposal, one outside all research programs or protocols, will not be an entry in this game of retention and dismissal. For example, a conjecture that angels are the forces that support cohesion among particles will not play. It adds nothing to any plausible explanation and is a proposition that cannot be falsified while maintaining the alternative conceptual system that yields meaning to the term "angel." But it is a non-starter because it is impossible to falsify, not because it is spiritual instead of physical. The full contents of the universe cannot be arbitrarily restricted to a material or physical base until statements test its scope. The traditional senses of the spiritual may yield as powerful a set of empirical statements *that can be falsified* as the set of statements that has been produced by material conceptions of the universe. The issue is not whether the content of such statements is admissible on material criteria, but simply whether the statements are falsifiable.

If we set materialism aside, then better questions can be asked in the completion game: Are any beliefs in the supernatural the kinds of falsifiable speculations that might complete accounts of the universe while remaining reasonably consistent with the best of these accounts? Can supernatural proposals plausibly extend any respectable versions of experience accepted in the natural sciences while remaining within the falsifying methods of science?

2

Near the end of chapter 3 I offered four tests to guide us in adjudicating claims on behalf of the supernatural. First, no experience can be dismissed just on the assertion that there is no evidence for its truth. Second, that a belief fails evidentiary and inference tests solely within particular human communities is not a decisive reason to reject it. Third, in what might be called a balance-of-plausibility test, it is illicit to rely on a poorer or less probable argument to refute a more plausible argument. Fourth, we must be at least provisionally skeptical of any conclusion that violates indisputable mathematical laws. I would argue that these tests have been practical maps in exploring the cases and theories presented in this work. I would also point out that using them inclines one toward *some* beliefs in the supernatural, rather than in the direction away from the supernatural that a materialist version of science suggests.

Many assertions for the supernatural are doubtful. Among these are claims for various types of psi in randomly selected populations. Individual claims are not exactly superb resources for evaluating ESP. But the skepticism of critics toward psi in general has been validated in many particular cases in and outside of the laboratory. Also, time, perhaps the primary good and dominating constraint of human experience, is a very useful background resource in the practical exercise of seeing the truth and falsity of claims in psychic discourses. I began this book with descriptions of visits I made to various psychics in a brief span of time. All made predictions, and the last psychic I visited gave me a formal reading exactly as she would have done with any other client. This last set of predictions was especially detailed and extended beyond me to my family. Since ten years have passed since these readings it is possible to evaluate their accuracy with more confidence than was possible at the time they were uttered. Predictions, after all, must be measured against the events they anticipate, however vague the projections might be. It is helpful that some of the predictions were sufficiently precise to allow a definite answer to whether, in retrospect, they were true or false.

1. My health is still good. The tentative observations on my stomach problems and weakness for alcohol have led to nothing. I am a non-addictive, high-energy person who has recently undergone arthroscopic surgery on both knees due to a lifelong engagement in sports and growing problems with arthritis. A surgical reconstruction of my right (baseball-throwing and tennis-serving) shoulder is the most recent medical intervention that I have experienced. (No psychic predicted the arthritis in my knees, right shoulder and lower back.)

2. I have not made any move to the western part of the United States ("California, maybe Arizona"), and that seems an increasingly unlikely possibility. I remain committed to the eastern coast of the United States, even more intensely as I have aged and grown to love our frequent visits to New York City. (I will hear no arguments on this—it is the greatest city in the history of the world.)

3. My father died in February of 1999 at the age of eighty-nine. No "elderly man, someone close to you" passed away in the fall after the summer 1989 predictions. My mother died in the fall, but in 1995. The best neurologists diagnosed her condition all along the

slope of her illness and death as Alzheimer's, not a metabolic disorder. Then there was the prediction about an elderly woman close to me having a serious health problem. Of course one thinks of one's ill parent on these occasions, but other friends also could somehow fit this bill more often than not.

4. My older daughter married at the age of twenty-six (hardly "late"). She did not go into a career in entertainment or the theater. She is an attorney in Manhattan (as is her husband). My younger daughter is indeed the moral voice of the family, and (I suppose) a humanitarian by nature. But she is not heading into any form of public health work. She is a PhD candidate in philosophy at the University of Michigan (ABD—all but dissertation) and, at the time of this writing, in her third year of study for a degree in law at New York University Law School. She has not disappointed "by marrying early" since she has not (yet?) married at all.

5. The observations about me are (I believe—but maybe I just don't get it yet) mixed. One psychic (in Key West) depicted me on several occasions in the reading as an impatient person with a tendency to get down on my work when it is not going well. Well, yes, but so too are many persons. Anyway, I don't have the time to respond to these descriptions (sorry for the burlesque joke). Another saw me as a writer. Finally, the prediction that I would die in my sleep is likely more probable for all of us than the other alternatives (death itself often the outcome of a kind of sleep?), but only time will bear this forecast out.

Any reasonable person inspecting these predictions would conclude that while some are promising, most have turned out to be spectacularly wrong in all important respects. If one is anxious to maintain any standing for the supernatural, the place to be is not (it seems) with most of the psychics I encountered, who offer their own brand of insights across space and time. Another place, not yet clearly defined but marked off with the humility imposed by our intellectual limitations, is the proper locus for reflections on things beyond nature.

Of course one might find the rare psychic who has true powers, the religious figure who is an authentic seer into the unknown, the right dream with the best and most accurate of foretellings. One can also conclude that whatever exists (if anything exists) outside the material world of the skeptic is too thinly connected to human experience to allow us to skip over the constraints of time and place that seem to mark our destiny. Observations like these help explain why the believer and the skeptic have remarkable survival powers in a complex world: There may be little in the way of compelling argument that can rule either perspective as completely illicit. But the most important thing to remember is that while both individuals are rational on the limiting conditions of human consciousness, neither seems to write the music of the universe.

3

Some propositions on the supernatural, however, *are* consistent with current science and its conjectures. These propositions all seem to derive from our inclinations to look past the boundaries of conventional realities and current visions to the domains of possible worlds. One thought seems particularly compelling in this gaze: there likely are other forms of life in the universe, and the dependence of reality on neurology indicates that there are also multiple alternative realities as a logical consequence of this admission. The clearest of all speculations is consistent with both the believer and the skeptic: human experience is but one entry in a larger theater of possibilities that exceed our powers of understanding.

There is a dissent from this expectation. The standard proposal for the possibility of other forms of "intelligent" life in the universe is based on the quite reasonable assumption that something like the formative conditions for life on Earth are surely replicated elsewhere in so vast a universe, and so the universe must be teeming with life (as and because the Earth is). But things may not be so simple. For life to develop even in identical conditions, there must be a law-like relationship between the antecedent conditions and the emergence of life forms. But there is much to suggest that the path on the Earth between at least higher forms of life and starting conditions is replete with stochastic events, meaning that the laws and conditions may not be exactly replicated anywhere. At least, the developmental patterns are not well enough understood for any conclusive theories on the possibilities, let alone the probabilities, of alternate life forms elsewhere. A pessimistic view of the possibility of intelligent life elsewhere seems to be supported in a study by Guillermo Gonzalez. Gonzalez maintains that the physical properties of our sun may be unique for the development of life on Earth. The sun's heat is very steady when compared to other stars; it contains high levels of the elements needed for the formation of rocky planets; and its unusual orbit near the center of the galaxy makes it unlikely that the solar system will encounter another star (with comets and asteroids that can damage planets). But there is also reason to believe in the existence of other forms of life. Paul Davies allows that "a blend of molecular Darwinism and laws of organizational complexity" may lead to an explanation of the evolution of higher life forms on Earth that may be generalizable to other parts of the universe. In an odd joining, information theory in union with physics and biology may support the possibility of life forms elsewhere.

If they exist, then what forms of organization might alternative, possibly higher, and perhaps spiritual civilizations have that are consistent with ongoing theory? Here we cannot know. But we can say that the most productive ways to answer this question are still found in the methods of science *broadly conceived,* not in the simple intuitions of the mystical savant nor in the controlled experiments of a restricted science. The intellectual largesse in an expansive vision of science is achievable with a thick set of theories, layered by the path from the interior explorations of the instruments that permit our intellectual life all the way to the exterior explanations of the events that constitute experience. This theoretical layering easily extends to those phenomena and speculations that traditionally have been designated as spiritual alternatives to a material universe. It is in fact a modest observation to say that the spiritual and secular can be comfortable companions in this type of inquiry.

Edward O. Wilson, in *Consilience: The Unity of Knowledge,* offers a narrative of scientific progress and convergence that ends with the dream of unity that tracks to the origins of science. He believes that "all tangible phenomena, from the birth of stars to the workings of social institutions, are based on material processes that are ultimately reducible, however long and tortuous the sequences, to the laws of physics." This conclusion follows Wilson's story trajectory from the Ionian scientists through the Enlightenment up to the present state of knowledge. Wilson is searching for consilience, which means "the proof that everything in the world is organized in terms of a small number of fundamental natural laws that comprise the principles underlying every branch of learning."

The complement to this program is the prototypical way in which mathematics adjudicates among competing scientific theories. The exercise begins with a helpful distinction between information content and message value. Any number of events, for example traffic patterns in a large city, can provide a great deal of information but little in the way of a message.

Objects falling in a vacuum within the Earth's gravitational field, however, represent a message of considerable value. This message is expressed in a single mathematical expression (the acceleration of descent equaling thirty-two feet per second, per second). One helpful way to rank order rival proposed explanations of the "same" phenomena is to examine the coded messages that competing theories deliver as explanations. In yet one more use of Occam's razor, the simplest and most elegant of the messages prevails. The ongoing character of this exercise is consistent with the possibility that the universe might be explained by currently encoded messages that so far we have been unable to decipher. Even the seemingly random and puzzling phenomena of quantum mechanics may be epiphenomena that will someday be explained by deeper algorithms that provide order where now we see only disorder. The complexity of the entire universe may yield to a few simple mathematical expressions once we understand its true nature.

But there are two closely related difficulties in establishing the ambitions of consilience. One is the profound disjunction between the natural and social sciences. When Socrates turned our attentions away from inquiries into the natural world to the inner terrain of the human soul, he was paying homage to the ways in which moral discourse cannot be completed with the studies initiated by the Ionian scientists. Long and distinguished traditions have recognized that a full explanation of the natural world will not provide complete instructions on what we ought to do. The simplest ground for these distinctions is that the social world presents an additional set of considerations not found in natural phenomena. An explanation of the natural world can be complete with concepts and theories drawn from the purview of the scientist. Explanations of the social world require at least some reference to the level of concepts and theories used by members of a culture in rendering their experiences intelligible. The fact of dual conceptual levels introduces the problems of translation and interpretation across the languages of observer and participant that are distinct to social inquiry, and the moral discourses that seem to exist only within the domains of these concepts. It is precisely this additional layer of concepts that inspires those well-known arguments that explanation in the natural and social sciences is, and must be, discontinuous.

The tiered arrangements of concepts in social inquiry turn consilience in a different direction. The main problems of continuity between the social and natural sciences are not solved by introducing, say, genetics or the effects of physical evolution to the social sciences. The issues are found rather in the need to join explanation and understanding, general theory and hermeneutics, and in doing so resolve the tension between objective and subjective perspectives that has been at the center of the human sciences since classical philosophy. On this understanding, consilience must find methods of explanation that are generalizable across the natural and social sciences on the recognition that different phenomena populate each area of inquiry.

The one area that can provide these methods is the domain of consciousness. The material of explanation is also the instrument of explanation. The implication of this fusion of substance and method is exactly what seems to be needed for the possibility of consilience: theories of consciousness can guide the Socratic reflections on the terrain of the soul into the domains of science without losing (as a consequence of the shift in the locus and techniques of inquiry) the perceiving moral agent. Explaining consciousness just *is* a depiction of the self in terms of science. Or, put another way, objective and self-reflective inquiries can be, at least in principle, the same in a successful theory of consciousness. The reason for this confluence is that accounts of consciousness do not require a distinction between an objective and a subjective world to produce generalizable explanations. The substance of reality must all be there in some form within consciousness.

The possibility of collapsing distinctions between the natural and supernatural also invites our attention, for also present in consciousness is the tendency to see experience with the categories of the supernatural. If we know one thing about human experience it is that we need some range of concepts that refer to additional realities in order to complete accounts of experience. A look into the nature and forms of conscious experience might explain this need and illuminate us on the standing of these metaphysical categories. Certainly the tests identified here for evaluating the supernatural would be shaped and consolidated by a theory of consciousness that provides generalizable laws and principles for all of human experience and assimilates these laws to the subjective experiences of human persons. On the terms of this possibility the search for consilience that is grounded in human consciousness might disclose a theory and understanding of "everything" that would surpass even the most ambitious hopes for unified human knowledge.

One must see, however, that the search cannot be conducted as an expedition seeking a privileged area of the brain where the neurological correlates of the supernatural are located. In a limited way that area has been (*very* roughly) indentified. The experiments conducted by Persinger and recent studies of shamanism (see chapter 7) have mapped certain sections of the brain that are correlated with mystical experiences. But the main problem of consciousness remains untouched with these mapping efforts. The second difficulty in realizing consilience is represented by V. S. Ramachandran and Sandra Blakeslee's observation that the "central mystery of the cosmos" is this: "Why are there always two parallel descriptions of the universe—the first person account ('I see red') and the third person account ('He says that he sees red when certain pathways in his brain encounter a wavelength of six hundred nanometers')?" First-person accounts are subjective, the products of the perceiving and thinking person, and represent the internal languages of human communities that house the fine discourses of understanding and interpretation. They constitute the inside of consciousness, the perspective of the subject. Third-person accounts are the dialogues of science, and the historical efforts to provide an account of the universe that is person-neutral, that is, objective. They sometimes express the outside of consciousness, the language we use to describe subjects without being able to enter their conscious states. These objective accounts have provided the most powerful explanations of reality that we have. Consciousness is the condition that generates *both* first and third person accounts. A true and complete consilience must unite these accounts in a single theory of consciousness. Locating areas of the brain correlated with experiences begs all of these issues and questions.

It is more than trivially interesting that the standard model for dismissing spiritual propositions is the first casualty in this special quest for consilience. The logical positivists of the early and mid twentieth century offered compelling arguments for the nonsensical standing of all spiritual expressions. On the austere program developed by A. J. Ayer the meaning of a statement is linked to its verification, and only two types of statements are verifiable: empirical (or synthetic) and analytic. Put simply, a statement is either true or false in terms of certain claims it makes on experience, or in terms of the meanings of the words used in the statement. For example, "Human life is finite," is true (so far) as a description of experience, and "The third planet from the sun is Earth" is true by definition. In the original positivist program value statements are not verifiable and so are meaningless. "Life is good," for example, is not truth-functional and is to be regarded as an expression of preference ("I like life"), a persuasive utterance ("You should like life also"), or both. The positivist program was also used to denigrate spiritual expressions, like "God exists," on the grounds that these utterances are typically framed so ambiguously that we cannot settle on the experiences that would falsify (or retain) them.

But the very sharpness of the distinctions that introduce the positivist program, and which contributed so much to the influence of positivism, blunt the richer distinctions provided by language. The proposition "God exists," for example, is by conventional standards a statement that attends to dimensions of reality at least partially outside human experience. But we can imagine multiple types of evidence and proof that attest to the existence of God, even as these data and arguments are contestable at the most fundamental levels. The adjudication of the truth or falsity of such statements cannot be carried out by a positivist system of classification that cannot itself be verified. A better approach would seem to be an exploration of the conditions in terms of which evidence and proof are recognized, and this exploration must finally be into our neurological natures. All indications are that the structure and logic of human thinking permit an ambiguity that tolerates experiences that cannot be shoe-horned into any tight system of verification. We might even say that the human impulse to explain experience in ultimate terms is real and compelling, that it leads to an examination of alternative realities, and that it can and does trump the simple positivist effort to collapse meaning into a narrow verification schema.

Explanations of the brain that currently occupy favored theory status, however, are not likely to complete a theory of consciousness that can accommodate the full range of human experience. The problem is that we are using the very instruments of experience to describe and explain the instruments of experience. In hyperbole this is analogous to Baron Munchausen's attempts to raise himself up by pulling on his bootstraps. But the theatrical analogy is not always the best source for insights into a problem. This may be better: a strange circle is formed by neurological explorations, since the truth of observations and explanations about the brain must be framed by the brain. Unless we can break out of the circle of limitations posed by our instruments of perceiving and knowing, successfully mapping the brain will be as restricted as any explanation of the full scope of reality.

These observations lead to another circle, one that is slightly creative: reflections on the products of science that use the narrative techniques of mysticism may be an unusually powerful set of intellectual tools to unravel the scope of human experience. We seem to need stories to keep our acts together, and the use of stories to fill and order the conclusions of science may the best, last chance to make sense of our persistent inclinations to see beyond the worlds that are presented to us. Perhaps only in that way can assertions for transcendence, which represent the efforts of human persons to see and understand areas beyond our limits, make sense even to the skeptic. We might even find a nexus between art and science, between the ancient animals that we are and the cognitive individuals that we also are and will be. This nexus is likely to be found in those areas where the grammar of narrative and generalizable explanations converge in understanding the human brain. It is also a small thing to hope that spiritual and scientific experiences may fuse in a single form of reality when we fully understand the kind of thinking that defines our identities. We may even turn finally to variations on older doctrines that tell us that transcendence is within each of us, and that the search for consilience can be successful only by establishing an understanding of who and what we are.

((NOTES))

I am grateful to four individuals who helped me find bibliographic data to complete the following notes: Scott Solomon (a doctoral student in political science at Syracuse University) and three individuals at the Rhine Research Center—Colleen Rae, Richard Broughton, and John Palmer—who helped locate those sources in parapsychology that seem never to be part of the holdings of secular university libraries.

One: DOMAINS OF CONSCIOUSNESS

Page 1   Even the rudimentary sensations listed here are complex. Some theories of consciousness speculate that sensory data are transmitted to the thalamus (a central brain structure) and then relayed to the cerebral cortex. There the data are somehow scanned and organized by a wave of nerve impulses transmitted from the thalamus. The now synchronized cells in the cerebral cortex send messages back to the thalamus. These messages constitute images. In some views consciousness just is this system of communication between the thalamus and the cerebral cortex. See Wendel Krieg, *Brain Mechanisms in Diachrome* (Evanston, IL: Brain Books, 1957). Summary in the *New York Times,* March 21, 1995, Science Times section. The notion of an abstraction would seem to be a product of this neurological activity, which is triggered and modulated by data that are secured through the sense organs and shaped by the framing powers of the brain. Or see the lists of more complex neural processes provided by Giulio Tononi and Gerald M. Edelman in "Consciousness and Complexity," *Science* 4:288 (December 1998), pp. 1846–51. These accounts try to define consciousness by explaining its neurological correlates.

Pages 2–3   Some of my thoughts here are inspired by Barbara Duden's presenta-

245

tion at the Conference of the Dutch Society for Philosophy and Medicine, *Medicine and Culture,* October 24–25, 1991, in Maastricht, the Netherlands.

Pages 3–4   In addition to various polls see the survey conducted by Andrew Greeley, *The Sociology of the Paranormal: A Reconnaissance* (Beverly Hills, CA: Sage Publications, 1975). Though the data are a bit old, there are some interesting observations and findings. Among my favorites are the use of sometimes legendary narratives as prefaces to the survey data (Jung's story of a visitation from a dead friend, for example) and the attempt to calibrate mystical experiences into time durations for survey responses.

Pages 5–6   The statement by the psychotherapist is from a taped interview on June 21, 1990. The tense play between usefulness and truth occurs throughout studies of beliefs in the supernatural. Jung regarded religion as a natural function, and its expression necessary for psychic health. The validity of religious beliefs is separate from this function, though (given Jung's epistemology) truth is itself expressed as a natural function. Others have seen religion as a coping device that can represent either mental stability or a pathology. John Spencer has tracked the number of Jehovah's Witnesses admitted for schizophrenia to West Australian Mental Health Service Psychiatric Hospitals and found the number to be three times as high as that for the general population. Still, the religious beliefs in question may be a coping device for mental disorders, or the mental disorders may be symptoms of these beliefs. Whatever the case, the truth of the beliefs is not settled by demonstrating how the beliefs function in human populations. See Carl Jung, *Psychology and Religion* (New Haven, CT: Yale University Press, 1938) and *Psychology and Western Religion* (Princeton, NJ: Princeton University Press, 1984), especially pp. 255–97; and John Spencer, "The Mental Health of Jehovah's Witnesses," *Watchtower Observer,* August 22, 1998. But see also the reports of the ongoing NIHR studies of religious beliefs (see below, note to pages 19–20).

Page 7   Karen Armstrong, *A History of God* (New York: Ballantine Books, 1993), introduction.

Page 8   Zeno of Elea, a fifth-century Greek philosopher, generated a number of paradoxes (the paradox of Achilles and the tortoise, for example) on a single puzzle: the thought that, since the distance between A and B can be subdivided into an infinite number of points, then moving from any point to another requires an infinite time—and so travel is impossible. John Robertson, my colleague in philosophy at Syracuse University, is the proximate source for the observation in the text on Zeno's paradoxes. The distal source is Nelson Goodman, *Fact, Fiction, and Forecast* (Cambridge, MA: Harvard University Press, 1983).

Pages 8–10   I have *consciously* used the following in writing this section on consciousness: Francis Crick and Christof Koch, "The Problem of Consciousness," *Scientific American,* September 1997, and "Consciousness and Neuroscience," an excerpt from *Cerebral Cortex* published on the Web at http://www.klab.caltech.edu/~koch/crick-koch-cc-97.html (as of August 21, 1999) and, if you prefer the conventional, in *Cerebral Cortex* 8 (1998), pp. 97–107; David Chalmers, *The Conscious Mind* (Oxford: Oxford University Press, 1996); John Searle, *The Rediscovery of the Mind* (Cambridge, MA: MIT Press, 1994); V. S. Ramachandran and Sandra Blakeslee, *Phantoms in the Brain* (New York: William Morrow, 1998), especially chapters 1, 9, and 12; Steven Pinker, *How the Mind Works* (New York: W. W. Norton, 1997); Christof Koch, "Towards the Neuronal Substrate of Visual Consciousness," in S. R. Hameroff, A. W. Kaszniak, and A. C. Scott, eds., *Towards a Science of Consciousness* (Cambridge, MA: MIT Press, 1996); Tononi and Edelman, "Consciousness and Complexity"; Daniel Dennett, *Consciousness Explained* (Boston: Little, Brown, 1991); Gerald Edelman, *Bright Air, Brilliant Fire: On the Matter of the Mind* (New York: Basic Books, 1992); Roger Penrose, *Shadows of the Mind: A Search for the Missing Science of Consciousness* (Oxford: Oxford University Press, 1994); Frank Jackson, "Epiphenomenal Qualia," *Philosophical Quarterly* 32 (1982), pp. 127–36, and "What Mary Didn't Know," *Journal of Philosophy* 83 (1986), pp. 291–96; Francis Crick, *The Astonishing Hypothesis: The Scientific Search for the Soul* (New York: Scribner's, 1994). I am also grateful to another colleague in philosophy, Robert Van Gulick, for helpful comments on this chapter.

Page 12   The phantom triangle is a common example of optical illusion. I have used one of the versions illustrating a discussion of illusory figures in Richard L. Gregory, ed. *The Oxford Companion to the Mind* (Oxford: Oxford University Press, 1987) pp. 344–47. The blind spot and the Cheshire Cat experiment are described (the latter illustrated with photographs) in Crick and Koch, "The Problem of Consciousness." Dennett, in *Consciousness Explained,* rejects the supposition that the brain fills in data in these experiences and argues that the brain instead ignores blind spots. But Dennett is eager on this point to deny a continuous self in order to discredit property dualism. The compensation exercises in cases like the phantom triangle and the blind spot do not, as least as I see them, relate to views on the nature of the self. But see Dennett, pp. 344–56.

Page 12 Jerome S. Bruner and Lee Postman, "On the Perception of Incongruity: A Paradigm" *Journal of Personality* 18 (1999), pp. 206–23.

Page 12 Amos Tversky and Daniel Kahneman, *Judgment under Uncertainty: Heuristics and Biases* (Cambridge: Cambridge University Press, 1982). For more on the distinctions between rational and psychological choices, see Robert Abelson and Ariel Levi, "Decision Making and Decision Theory," in Gardner Lindzey and Elliot Aronson, eds., *Handbook of Social Psychology* (New York: Random House, 1985). A different take on mental effects in viewing is found in those examinations of the psychology of perception found in studies of art, in particular here, E. H. Gombrich, *Art and Illusion: A Study in the Psychology of Pictorial Representation* (Princeton, NJ: Princeton University Press, 1969). In these studies the exploration of cultural settings often provides a deeper understanding of seeing than optical illusions and controlled experiments can possibly offer.

Page 13 Penrose's speculations on a quantum base for consciousness are in his *Shadows of the Mind.*

Page 13 The spectacle of rival explanatory theories that are consistent with the same data is a commonplace in science. The Duhem-Quine thesis, and indeed a good part of W. V. O. Quine's work, testify to the logical and empirical conditions in which this event occurs. See Quine, *Ontological Relativity and Other Essays* (New York: Columbia University Press, 1969), and *Word and Object* (Cambridge, MA: MIT Press, 1960).

Pages 14–15 The two-slit experiments and Schrödinger's cat join Heisenberg's indeterminacy principle in illustrating the strange world of quantum mechanics. "Tunneling" (as I—barely—understand it) produces time paradoxes with distance experiments: some things being able to go through an area and arrive before they leave. There is a wonderful precursor to these designs in *Through the Looking Glass,* where Lewis Carroll has a sketch of Alice moving through the mirror with a clock appearing quite in its normal form, and then on the next page there is Alice emerging on the other side of the mirror with the "same" clock now presenting what looks like a clown's face. Carroll seems to be saying that movement in space, at least across dimensions, can disturb time. See pages 111–12 in the Norton edition (New York, 1971), edited by Donald J. Gray.

Page 16   Herbert Benson, *Timeless Healing* (New York: Scribner, 1996).

Page 16   Herbert Simon, *Models of Bounded Rationality* (Cambridge, MA: MIT Press, 1982). The perspectival view of knowledge is the basis of sociology of knowledge claims.

Page 18   Einstein's brain apparently resided in pieces in a jar for forty years before these measurements were made. See the newspaper accounts in, for example, the *International Herald Tribune,* June 19–20, 1999. *People* magazine (no less) reports in its August 30, 1999, edition that retired pathologist Thomas Harvey, who performed the autopsy on Einstein in 1955, had preserved the brain. According to the story, Harvey initially showed Einstein's brain in 1996 to neuroscientist Sarah Witelson (discoverer of the expanded parietal lobes) by opening the trunk of his car and displaying an old cardboard box with jars that contained the blocks of neural tissue. See *People* 52:8, p. 126. One may definitely conclude that the practice of pathology extinguishes awe.

Pages 19–20   I am grateful to Mantosh Dewan for many of the examples I use here of mind-body effects. But see also the excursions in *Alternative Medicine: Expanding Medical Horizons,* A Report to the National Institutes of Health on Alternative Medical Systems and Practices in the United States (Washington, DC: Government Printing Office, 1992), pp. 3–43; and the summary of placebo studies in the *New York Times,* October 13, 1998, Science Times section. Also see the study reported in *JAMA* in which a sample of 112 patients with asthma or rheumatoid arthritis were randomly distributed into control and intervention groups. The intervention group (n=71) wrote about their stressful life experiences and experienced improvements in their "physical" health four months later that were not found in the control group (which received only medical treatment for their disease). "Effects of Writing about Stressful Experiences on Symptom Reduction in Patients with Asthma or Rheumatoid Arthritis," *JAMA* 281:14 (April 14, 1999), pp. 1304–9. The list of reports on religious beliefs (some of which may be true beliefs, and thus even further outside the defining parameters of the placebo effect than is even the writing exercise) is long and growing. The NIH offers these studies at this moment: church attenders have 50 percent fewer deaths from coronary arterial disease, 56 percent fewer deaths from emphysema, 74 percent fewer deaths from cirrhosis, and 53 percent fewer suicides; elderly heart patients are fourteen times less likely to die following surgery if they are both socially active and find strength or comfort in their religious faith; heart transplant patients who had strong faith had better physical and emotional well-being, fewer health worries, and better medical compliance; and so on through many other studies. (As of January 1999, one could view these studies at the NIHR Web site—www.nihr.org.) Then see the meta-study evaluating the methodologies used in placebo research: Department of Social and Preventative Medicine, University of Berne, Switzerland, "Adherence to Public Standards of Reporting: A Comparison of Placebo-controlled Trials Published in English or German," *JAMA* 280:3 (July 15, 1998), pp. 247–49.

Page 21   For example, the founder of therapeutic touch, Dolores Krieger, has consistently championed a science of controlled experiments to verify techniques that even practitioners regard as spiritual in nature and intent. (See the discussion in chapter 4.)

Two: PSYCHICS

Pages 23–27   Interview with Francine Bizzari on July 10, 1989.

Pages 27–30   Interview with Anne Maire Folger on July 9, 1989.

Pages 30–35   Interview with Nelson Guyette on November 20, 1992.

Pages 35–40   From an interview on March 18, 1989. See also James Randi, *The Faith Healers* (Buffalo, NY: Prometheus Books, 1987), for expansions of his skeptical beliefs on faith healing.

Pages 40–43   Reading on July 6, 1989.

Three: EXPERIMENTAL CONTROLS

Pages 49–51   James Randi, *Conjuring* (New York: St. Martin's, 1992); Migene González-Wippler, *Spells, Ceremonies, and Magic* (St. Paul, MN: Lewellyn, 1988); James G. Frazer, *The Golden Bough* (London: MacMillan, 1911–12); Leonard Zusne and Warren H. Jones, *Anomalistic Psychology: A Study of Extraordinary Phenomena of Behavior and Experience* (Hillsdale, NJ: Erlbaum, 1982) and *Anomalistic Psychology: A Study of Magical Thinking* (Hillsdale, NJ: Erlbaum, 1989).

Pages 49–50   González-Wippler, *Spells, Ceremonies, and Magic,* pp. 1–6.

Page 50   Attachment theory is currently in a state of flux. Michael Lewis has published research that challenges the importance of a secure attachment between baby and mother for self-adjustment later in life. Lewis ranks events like divorce, disease, and accidents as more important. See Lewis, *Altering Fate—Why the Past Does Not Predict the Future* (New York: Guilford Press, 1997). See also the emphasis on peer influence in Judith Rich Harris, *The Nurture Assumption* (New York: Free Press, 1998).

Pages 51–52   D'Arcy Thompson, *On Growth and Form* (Cambridge: Cambridge University Press, 1968); Ian Stewart, *Life's Other Secret* (London: Allen Lane, 1998).

Page 52   Bertrand Russell, *A History of Philosophy* (New York: Simon & Schuster, 1945), p. 215.

Pages 52–53   W. K. C. Guthrie, *The Greek Philosophers: From Thales to Aristotle* (New York: Harper & Row, 1960); Frederick Copleston, *A History of Philosophy,* Vol. 1 (Westminster, MD.: Newman Press, 1963).

Page 53   The sociologist's explanation would focus on the changes in conditions that might have occasioned nineteenth-century spiritualism, in particular the desperate wishes of women to communicate with their children who had died. Infant mortality rates were very high at the time of fashionable seances (and most of the mediums were women), and lower later, when seances fell from favor. I am providing the validity consideration: some practices could no longer be produced under the gaze of modern science no matter how much solace they may have provided for the practitioners.

Pages 54–61   I have intentionally used the "standard" narratives in the accounts of Home, Garrett, and Cayce in the text. This means that my sources are mainly books and articles by supporters of these psychics (including short pieces on the Internet). My goal here is to present the stories accepted by believers, not to engage the stories with the critical perspectives and newly discovered evidence that are obligatory in any good historical study. The datum for my own critical needs is what believers in the supernatural accept as a life of what I call a grand psychic, not what might or might not be the case in an impartial biography (if such exists).

Pages 54–55   Material on Home is scarce. I have scanned and selectively used accounts presented in Richard S. Broughton, *Parapsychology: The Controversial Science* (New York: Ballantine Books, 1991); Rosemary Ellen Guiley, *Harper's Encyclopedia of Mystical and Paranormal Experience* (New York: HarperCollins, 1991); Slater Brown, *The Heyday of Spiritualism* (New York: Hawthorn Books, 1970); Trevor H. Hall, *The Enigma of Daniel Home* (Buffalo, NY: Prometheus Books, 1984); and I. G. Edmunds,

D. D. Home: The Man Who Talked with Ghosts (Nashville: Thomas Nelson, 1978).

Pages 55–58   The material in the text on Garrett presents (as do the other sketches in this section) the dominant narrative events cited again and again in biographies of the subject. I have always regarded these standard and exceedingly sympathetic renditions as vital signs for the reputations of individuals in their own friendly communities. Garrett's own books help establish this vernacular reputation: *Adventures in the Supernormal: A Personal Memoir* (New York: Garrett Publications, 1949); *Telepathy: In search of a Lost Faculty* (New York: Creative Age, 1941); *Awareness* (New York: Creative Age, 1944); *The Sense and Nonsense of Prophecy* (New York: Berkeley, 1950); *Life is the Healer* (Philadelphia: Dorrance, 1957); *My Life as a Search for the Meaning of Mediumship* (London: Rider, 1949); and *Many Voices: The Autobiography of a Medium* (New York: G. P. Putnam's Sons, 1968). See also Allan Angoff, *Eileen Garrett and the World beyond the Senses* (New York: William Morrow, 1974); and Lawrence LeShan, *The Medium, the Mystic, and the Physicist: Toward a General Theory of the Paranormal* (New York: Viking Press, 1974). I am also grateful for Joanne D. S. McMahon's comments on this section, and I have read and found useful her monograph, *Eileen Garrett: A Woman Who Made a Difference* (New York: Parapsychology Foundation, 1994).

Pages 58–61   Again, I have relied on the accounts of believers: Thomas Sugrue, *There is a River: The Story of Edgar Cayce* (Virginia Beach, VA: A.R.E. Press, 1995); Reba Ann Karp, *Edgar Cayce: Encyclopedia of Healing* (New York: Warner Books, 1988); Mary Ellen Carter, *My Years With Edgar Cayce* (New York: Warner, 1974); W. H. Church, *Many Happy Returns: The Lives of Edgar Cayce* (San Francisco: Harper & Row, 1984); Rosemary Ellen Guiley, *Tales of Reincarnation* (New York: Pocket Books, 1989); Nicholas Regush, *The Aura* (New York: Berkeley, 1974); and Jess Stern, *Edgar Cayce: The Sleeping Prophet* (New York: Bantam Books, 1968).

Pages 61–70   In constructing the events in the Rhine narrative, I have relied on the autobiography by Louisa E. Rhine, *Something Hidden* (Jefferson, NC: McFarland, 1983), and various articles that seem to be taken from her book. See also Denis Brian, *The Enchanted Voyager: The Life of J. B. Rhine—An Authorized Biography* (Englewood Cliffs, NJ: Prentice-Hall, 1982) for anecdotal accounts, and Seymour Mauskopf and M. R. McVaugh, *The Elusive Science: Origin of Experimental Psychical Research* (Baltimore, MD: Johns Hopkins Press, 1980), for a history of the Rhine laboratory and psychical research in general. Rhine's research initiatives are summarized in J. B. Rhine (revised and enlarged by K. Ramakrishna Rao), *A Brief Introduction to Parapsychology* (College Station, NC: Foundation for Research on the Nature of Man, Parapsychology Press, 1991); Rhine, "History of Experimental Studies," in Benjamin B. Wolman, ed., *Handbook of Parapsychology* (Jefferson, NC: McFarland, 1986), pp. 25–47; Rhine, "Extrasensory Perception," in Wolman, *Handbook of Parapsychology*, pp. 163–74; J. G. Pratt, et al. (including Rhine), *Extrasensory Perception after Sixty Years* (New York: Henry Holt, 1940); and the two edited volumes by Rao: *The Basic Experiments in Parapsychology* (Jefferson, NC: McFarland, 1984), and *J. B. Rhine: On the Frontiers of Science* (Jefferson, NC: McFarland, 1982). The Wolman anthology is an excellent collection of the classic articles in parapsychology. Stephen E. Braude echoes the disappointment with the results of formal testing in *The Limits of Influence* (New York: Routledge & Kegan Paul, 1986). For the Hansel reference in the text: C. E. M. Hansel, *ESP and Parapsychology* (Buffalo, NY: Prometheus Books, 1966). See also, more generally, Robert Laurence Moore, *In Search of White Crows: Spiritualism, Parapsychology, and American Culture* (New York: Oxford University Press, 1977).

Page 65   For the RNG research: William Braud, Marilyn Schlitz, and Helmut Schmidt, "Remote Mental Influences of Animate and Inanimate Target Systems: A Method of Comparison and Preliminary Findings" Proceedings of Presented Papers: 32nd Annual Parapsychology Association Convention (San Diego, CA: 1989), pp. 12–25; H. Schmidt, "PK Effect on Pre-Recorded Targets," *Journal of the American Society for Psychical Research* 70 (July 1976); Stephen Braude, *ESP and Psychokinesis: A Philosophical Examination* (Philadelphia: Temple University Press, 1979); E. C. May, D. I. Radin, G. S. Hubbard, B. S. Humphrey, and J. M. Utts, "Psi Experiments with Random Number Generators: An Informational Model," *Proceedings of Presented Papers* Vol. 1, the Parapsychology Association 29th Annual Convention (1985), pp. 237–66; D. I. Radin and R. D. Nelson, "Evidence for Consciousness-related anomalies in Random Physical Systems," *Foundations of Physics* 19 (December 1989), pp. 1499–514 (for the meta-analysis of PK mentioned in the text).

Page 66   I have drawn on Mauskoff and McVaugh, *The Elusive Science,* pp. 259–61, for the B. F. Skinner material.

Page 66   For the psi research: K. Ramakrishna Rao and John Palmer, "The

Anomaly Called Psi: Recent Research and Criticism" *Behavioral and Brain Sciences* 10 (1987), pp. 539–51; C. Honorton and E. Schecter, "Ganzfeld Target Retrieval with an Automated Testing System: A Model for Initial Ganzfeld Success," in D. B. Weiner and R. D. Nelson, eds., *Research in Parapsychology* (Metuchen, NJ: Scarecrow Press, 1986), pp. 36–39; Richard S. Broughton, H. Kanthamani, and Anjum Khilji, "Assessing the PRL Success Model on an Independent Ganzfeld Data Base," in L. Henkel and J. Palmer, eds., *Research in Parapsychology* (Metuchen, NJ: Scarecrow Press, 1990), pp. 32–35.

Pages 66–69   For a critical view on these experiments: J. E. Alcock, "A Comprehensive Review of Major Empirical Studies in Parapsychology Involving Random Event Generators or Remote Viewing," in D. Druckman and J. E. Swets, eds., *Enhancing Human Performance: Issues, Theories, and Techniques*, Background Papers, Part 6 (Washington, DC: National Academy Press, 1988); R. Hyman, "A Critical Historical Overview of Parapsychology," in P. Kurtz, ed., *A Skeptic's Handbook on Parapsychology* (Buffalo, NY: Prometheus Books, 1985), pp. 1–96; Hyman, "The Ganzfeld Psi Experiment: A Critical Appraisal," *Journal of Parapsychology* 49 (1985), pp. 3–49. Then also see C. Honorton, "Meta-Analysis of Psi Ganzfeld Research: A Response to Hyman," *Journal of Parapsychology* 49 (1985), pp. 49–51 (for the meta-analysis of psi mentioned in the text); and the rest of the parapsychology section of the report prepared by the National Research Council of the National Academy of Sciences, *Enhancing Human Performance: Issues, Theories, and Techniques.*

Pages 69–70   Radin, *The Conscious Universe* (San Francisco, CA: Harper*Edge*, 1997). The meta-analyses I have cited are mainly in chapter 6. In his book Radin provides a remarkable quote from Carl Sagan that bears repeating: "At the time of this writing [the publication date on Sagan's book is 1996] there are three claims in the ESP field which, in my opinion, deserve serious study: (1) that by thought alone humans can (barely) affect random number generators in computers; (2) that people under mild sensory deprivation can receive thoughts or images "projected" at them; and (3) that young children sometimes report the details of a previous life, which upon checking turn out to be accurate and which they could not have known about in any other way than reincarnation" (page 3 in Radin, page 302 of Sagan's *The Demon-Haunted World* [New York: Random House, 1996]). The next three sentences (not quoted by Radin) reinforce Sagan's well-known skepticism: "I pick these three claims not because I think they're likely to be valid (I don't), but as examples of contentions that *might* be true. The last three have at least some, although still dubious, experimental support. Of course, I could be wrong." Of course, he could be right. But he was obviously intrigued, and almost on board.

Pages 70–78   For overviews: William R. Corliss, ed., *The Unfathomed Mind: A Handbook of Unusual Mental Phenomena* (Glen Arm, MD: The Sourcebook Project, 1982); J. Gaither Pratt, *ESP Research Today: A Study of Development in Parapsychology since 1960* (Methuchen, NJ: Scarecrow Press, 1973); Wolman, *Handbook of Parapsychology*; Sheila Ostrander and Lynn Schroeder, *Handbook of Psi Discoveries* (New York: Berkeley, 1975); Charles Tart, *States of Consciousness* (New York: E. P. Dutton, 1975); J. E. Alcock, *Parapsychology: Science or Magic?: A Psychological Perspective* (Oxford: Pergamon Press, 1981); H. M. Collins and T. J. Pinch, *Frames of Meaning: The Social Construction of Extraordinary Science* (London: Routledge & Kegan Paul, 1982); John A. Palmer, *An Evaluative Report on the Current Status of Parapsychology*, Contract DAJA 45-84-M-0405 (Alexandria, VA: U.S. Army Research Institute for Behavioral Sciences, 1985); and Zusne and Jones, *Anomalistic Psychology*, especially chapters 1, 2, 11, 12, 13, 14, and 15. The Zusne and Jones text is an excellent critical discussion of a wide range of claims and theories in what they label in their subtitle as "Extraordinary Phenomena of Behavior and Experience." I have learned much from their work and have allowed this part of the book to be influenced by their critical perspectives. Later I will try for a reasonable balance by critically evaluating skeptical scientific views on parapsychology. See also Broughton, *Parapsychology: The Controversial Science*.

Pages 72–73   Interview with Richard Broughton on April 30, 1999. Broughton reviews some general research into remote viewing in his *Parapsychology: The Controversial Science*, pp. 115–23. The government project Broughton mentions is described in Jim Schnabel, *Remote Viewers: The Secret History of America's Psychic Spies* (New York: Dell Books, 1997).

Page 73   Richard S. Broughton, "If You Want to Know How It Works, First Find Out What It's For," in D. H. Weiner and R. I. Morris, eds., *Research in Parapsychology 1987* (Metuchen, NJ: Scarecrow Press, 1988), pp. 187–202; H. Schmidt, "The Strange Properties of Psychokinesis," *Journal of Scientific Investigation* 1 (1980), pp. 103–18. Broughton has also written one of the two best overviews of parapsychology (the other is the Radin book cited above): *Parapsychology: The Controversial Science*. The reference book I have found most helpful is Guiley, *Harper's Encyclopedia of Mystical and Paranormal Experience.*

Pages 75–79 Whisenant, *On Borrowed Time* (Nashville, TN: World Bible Society, 1988). I have used Zusne and Jones, *Anomalistic Psychology,* especially chapters 1, 2, and 11, as a source for the observations and examples in the text on the role of the central nervous system in explaining psychic experiences in general and faith healing in particular and for the Mankind United story.

Pages 76–77 Randi tells the story of the Popoff exposé in *The Faith Healers,* pp. 139–81.

Pages 76–77 Fraud also is found in controlled conditions. The best single antidote for excessive faith in formal or controlled evidence for paranormal events remains the history of the Soal-Goldney experiments. These were cited as models for rigorous proof of precognition, and they were eventually exposed as fraudulent. See C. G. Soal and K. M. Goldney, "Experiments in Precognitive Telepathy" *Proceedings of the Society for Psychical Research* 47 (1943); B. Markwicke, "The Soal-Goldney Experiments with Basil Schackleton: New Evidence of Manipulation" *Proceedings of the Society for Psychical Research* 56 (1978); and the helpful summary by Christopher Scott, "Paranormal Phenomena: The Problem of Proof," in Gregory, *The Oxford Companion to the Mind,* pp. 579–81. Fraud in uncontrolled conditions apparently is not constrained by age (in either direction). Note the infamous photographs of fairies taken in 1917 by two English girls, ten and sixteen years old. Though easily transparent now, the Cottingley fairies were sensational at the time, inspiring luminaries like Conan Doyle to pronounce the photographs as a record of the spiritual world. One of the girls is said to have admitted later that they had simply stuck cutouts on hat pins for the photographic effects. See the review in the *New York Times* (February 1, 1998) of the exhibition at the Leslie Tonkonow Gallery in Chelsea of these and other so-called photographs of apparitions. After marveling at the gullibility of some who examined the photographs, it is refreshing to read the uncompromising critiques in James Randi, *Flim-Flam* (New York: Lippincott & Crowell, 1980), especially chapter 7; and Martin Gardner, *Science: Good, Bad, and Bogus* (Buffalo, NY: Prometheus Books, 1981).

Pages 77–78 For a reasonably complex view of science, and support for this part of the text, consult the following: Nelson Goodman, *Fact, Fiction, and Forecast;* Karl Popper, *The Logic of Scientific Discovery* (New York: Basic

Books, 1959) and *Conjectures and Refutations* (London: Routledge, 1969); W. V. O. Quine, "Two Dogmas of Empiricism," in *From a Logical Point of View* (Cambridge, MA: Harvard University Press, 1953), pp. 20–46, and *Word and Object;* Pierre Duhem, *The Aim and Structure of Physical Theory* (Princeton: Princeton University Press, 1964); Imre Lakatos, "Falsification and the Methodology of Scientific Research Programs," in Lakatos and Alan Musgrave, eds., *Criticism and the Growth of Knowledge* (Cambridge: Cambridge University Press, 1970); Paul Feyerabend, *Against Method* (London: Verso, 1993). See also the overviews in M. J. Mulkay, *Science and the Sociology of Knowledge* (Boston: G. Allen and Unwin, 1974) and Anthony O'Hear, *Karl Popper* (Boston: Routledge, 1980).

Pages 77–79   The best counter to skeptics in these areas is Stephen E. Braude's *The Limits of Influence.* Braude develops an interesting case for the use of nonexperimental evidence in assessing beliefs in psychic experiences, and so effectively combines enthusiasm for the paranormal with intellectual honesty that he sometimes demolishes the efforts of psychics and parapsychologists, as in his dismissal of retrocausality on the acceptance of cluster variables in causality. Braude is a required read in conjunction with the skeptical critiques in Zusne and Jones, *Anomalistic Psychology.* Each side is too extreme and quick to destroy the adversaries, but worth the effort in both books. The unremitting, search-and-destroy operations in these areas is found in the articles in *Skeptic* magazine. The magazine's publisher, Michael Shermer, is the author of a good compendium of skeptical views that also offers a modest range of explanations for beliefs in psychic phenomena, *Why People Believe Weird Things: Pseudoscience, Superstition and Other Confusions of Our Time* (San Francisco, CA: W. H. Freeman, 1997). Shermer also quotes Hume favorably on the balance-of-plausibility test I cite in chapter 4 of this text. A rewarding work is the revised autobiography of Susan Blackmore, which relates her failures to find experimental evidence for psi and provides a personal account of her experiences with the community of parapsychologists: *In Search of the Light: The Adventures of a Parapsychologist* (Amherst, NY: Prometheus Books, 1996).

Four: INTUITIVE SCIENCE

Page 80   Louisa Rhine, "Research Methods with Spontaneous Cases," in Wolman, *Handbook of Parapsychology.* I am thinking (among other developments) of biofeedback in my comment on causal paths for brain waves.

Pages 81–86   Interview with Will Provine on September 18, 1991.

Pages 84–85   See Thomas Kuhn, *The Structure of Scientific Revolutions* (Chicago: University of Chicago Press, 1962), and the enormous body of critical and interpretive literature that Kuhn's work has generated.

Page 87   O'Hear, *Karl Popper,* chapter 6 (and page 103 for the neutrino example). The Folkman story is told in the *New York Times,* December 9, 1997, Science Times section.

Pages 87–92   I have written this section from the notes I took during the two presentations Charles Gant made to my seminar in the spring terms of 1997 and 1998. Some census data on longevity show variations within Gant's data set, and the overall picture is somewhat different, though *roughly* within the same pattern. For example, if the data compare 1890 and 1995 *and* are broken down into white men and women, then the life span at birth for the men is 42.5 in 1890 and 72.5 in 1995, while the longevity at 40 is 29.37 additional years in 1890 and 28.76 additional years in 1995. The 1890 life span for the women at birth is 44.46 in 1890 and 79.4 in 1995, and a 40-year-old woman in 1890 could (statistically) expect to live another 28.76 years, another 41 years in 1995. See the chart "Expectation of Life" on page 846 of the *Information Please Almanac 1998* (Boston: Houghton Mifflin, 1997). These data represent more considerable differences in life expectancies across these time periods among women at the age of forty than Gant's data set does, but are still generally consistent with Gant's arguments that most of the differences in longevity from past to present are probably due to reductions in infant mortality and death among women in giving birth, not to the miracles of modern medicine. It would be helpful, however, to have an explanation for the impressive difference in life expectations among forty-year-old women from 1890 to 1995. The diet study that Gant suggests in the text is Robert Atkins, *New Diet Revolution* (New York: Avon Books, 1998). For more on Gant's views on diabetes and insulin, see his *Diabetes and Carbohydrate Addiction* (Syracuse, NY: MindMenders, 1998).

Pages 92–93   Therapeutic touch is just one of many entries in vernacular medicine today. The Office of Alternative Medicine at the National Institutes of Health, mandated by Congress in 1991 to support research into alternative medical practices, offers seven categories for vernacular medicine: alternative systems (acupuncture, Āyurveda, homeopathy), bioelectromagnetic (the manipulation of electromagnetic fields), diet, nutrition, lifestyle changes, herbal medicine, manual healing (massage, osteopathy, therapeutic touch), mind-body control (biofeedback, hypnotherapy, meditation), and pharmacological and biological treatments (the use of anti-oxidizing agents). The NIH office also stated (in 1994) that there is a "paucity of data" to establish whether alternative medicine is efficacious, safe, and/or beneficial. Yet a study by D. M. Eisenberg et al., "Unconventional Medicine in the United States—Prevalence, Costs, and Patterns of Use," published in the *New England Journal of Medicine* 328:1 (January 28, 1993), pp. 246–52, reported that Americans made approximately 425 million visits to providers of unconventional therapy in one year, 1990. We use alternative or complementary medicine but really do not know if it works or perhaps even how to determine if it works. But we are trying. See again the November 1998 issue of *JAMA,* which is devoted in its entirety to alternative medicine (including both theory and case studies). A follow-up study on use by Eisenberg et al., "Trends in Alternative Medicine Use in the United States, 1990–1997," published in this issue concludes that the use of alternative medicine increased substantially between 1990 and 1997, and this increase in "attributable primarily to an increase in the proportion of the population seeking alternative therapies, rather than increased visits per patient."

Pages 93–95   Linda Rosa, BSN, RN; Emily Rosa; Larry Sarner; Stephen Barrett, MD, "A Close Look at Therapeutic Touch," *JAMA* 279:13 (April 1, 1998), pp. 1005–10. Also see the numerous letters and comments on the Rosa study published under the title "An Even Closer Look at Therapeutic Touch," *JAMA* 280:22 (December 9, 1998), p. 1903.

Pages 95–102   Interview with Stuart Ledwith on March 19, 1998.

Pages 102–6   Interview with Ada on June 13, 1998, in London, England.

Pages 108–9   Shermer, in *Why People Believe Weird Things,* reports participating in an ESP experiment at the (Edgar Cayce) Association for Research and Enlightenment, where just such a mathematical mistake was made, and, even worse, the mistake was not understood by the organizers of the experiment when he pointed out the problem.

Pages 109–11   The metaphor of a web of beliefs, with a core and periphery, is drawn from W. V. O. Quine, *From a Logical Point of View* (Cambridge, MA: Harvard University Press, 1980).

Page 112 Descartes subscribed to substance dualism, a soul in the (human) body. Recent philosophy is content with property dualism, meaning that there are minds in bodies. Either version will do for psychic beliefs since the main requirement in these areas is that we are *both* nonmaterial (soul, mind, spirit) and material (body) in nature.

Pages 112–13 The definition and data on OBEs cited here are found in Susan Blackmore, *Beyond the Body: An Investigation of Out-of-Body Experiences* (Chicago: Academy Chicago Publishers, 1992), chapter 9.

Pages 113–16 Interview with Julie Gerrard on August 15, 1990.

Pages 116–18 Carlos S. Alvarado, "Research on Spontaneous Out-of-Body Experiences: A Review of Modern Developments, 1960–84," in B. Shapin and L. Coly, eds., *Current Trends in Psi Research* (New York: Parapsychology Foundation, 1986), pp. 140–67; "Trends in the Study of Out-of-Body Experiences: An Overview of Developments since the Nineteenth Century," *Journal of Scientific Exploration* 3 (1989), pp. 27–42; "Phenomenological Aspects of Out-of-Body Experiences: A Report of Three Studies," *Journal of the American Society for Psychical Research* 78 (1984), pp. 219–40; "ESP during Out-of-Body Experiences: A Review of Experimental Studies," *Journal of Parapsychology* 46 (1982), pp. 209–30; "Recent OBE Detection Studies: A Review," *Theta* 10:2 (1982), pp. 35–37; and "ESP and Out-of-Body Experiences: A Review of Spontaneous Studies," *Parapsychology Review* 14:4 (1983), pp. 11–13. Also see Janet Lee Mitchell, *Out-of-Body Experiences: A Handbook* (New York: Ballantine, 1981), Robert A. Monroe, *Far Journeys* (Garden City, NY: Doubleday, 1985), and D. Scott Rogo, ed., *Mind beyond the Body: The Mystery of ESP Projection* (New York: Penguin, 1978).

Pages 118–19 The experiment described here is presented in Karlis Osis and Donna McCormick, "Kinetic Effects at the Ostensible Location of an Out-of-Body Projection during Perceptual Testing," *The Journal of the American Society for Psychical Research* 74 (July 1980), pp. 319–29.

Pages 119–26 Interview with Alex Tanous on December 7, 1989. See also Tanous's autobiography (written with Harvey Ardman), *Beyond Coincidence,* for more theories and stories. All of the quotes in this section, however, are taken from the taped interview. To the obvious question—no, I have not checked the taped predictions of Lennon's murder and the shooting of then president Reagan, or the written accounts of Tanous's trans-country out-of-body experiences, for two reasons. First, just listening to tapes or reading reports without examining their veracity does not verify experiences, since error and fraud are always possible. (Even observing some of these events is no guarantee of their authenticity.) Second, remember, I am concerned in this part of the work with the fact that individuals *relate* such experiences, not whether the experiences are true or not. It seems to me that the interpretive key that unlocks Tanous's out-of-body experience is not a skeptical critique but an understanding of the controlling grammar of the story. Note, for example, the abrupt shift of perspective from Tanous to Elsworth when the author (Tanous) disappears from view.

Pages 127–32   I am using in the text here material from the following interviews I conducted for the Alex Tanous life project (a research project designed to collect taped interviews with those who had known Alex Tanous and were prepared to share their memories for research on this remarkable individual): Interviews with Alan Vaughan on August 8, 1997; Michael Grosso on August 11, 1997; Karlis Osis on February 10, 1997; Scott Jones on March 19 and August 1, 1997; David Johnson on April 12, 1997; and Elsworth de Merchant on November 4, 1998. The tapes of these interviews (and many others I conducted, and those secured by Polly Bennell, my co-researcher) are on file with the Alex Tanous Foundation, P.O. Box 3818, Portland, Maine 04104.

Page 133   As quoted in the special article devoted to science and religion in *Newsweek* (July 20, 1998). Russell is the founder of the Center for Theology and the Natural Sciences at the Graduate Theological Union in Berkeley.

Page 134   Sagan was of course one of the foremost critics of pseudoscience and promoters of rigorous science, and his opposition to faith healers and psychics is legendary.

Page 136   The panel report described in the text that calls for investigations of physical evidence for UFOs is published in the summer 1998 issue of *Society for Scientific Exploration*. The resistance to the existence of extraterrestrial life is on the other side of rational. Many physicists argue that the universe *must* be teeming with life if our biological principles have any validity at all. A recent book, Michael White's *Life Out There: The Truth of—and Search for—Extraterrestrial Life* (London: Little, Brown, 1998) rehashes the arguments made familiar by Carl Sagan, to the effect that the vastness of the universe makes the possibility of life somewhere in addition to Earth virtually a certainty, and offers the equation developed by Frank Drake, astronomer and SETI (Search for Extra Terrestrial Intelligence) researcher, that represents this very high probability. But, still, see the note here for pages 000 in chapter 9 for some nuances provided by Paul Davies. Of course the possibility that alternative life forms are interested in communicating with us (even if they do exist) is another matter.

Pages 137–40   Interview with Sally Feather on October 16, 1998.

Page 140   Interview with Dorothy Pope on September 9, 1998.

Pages 141–42   Louisa E. Rhine, *Something Hidden,* p. 2. I have relied on Mrs. Rhine's book in writing this section of my work.

Pages 141–42   The story of the ghost is on pages 198–99.

Pages 142–43   The letter quoted in the text is in the Timothy Leary Text Archives at the Duke University Parapsychology Laboratory.

Six: SPIRITUAL LANDSCAPES

Page 144   An early study by H. F. Saltmarsh found a preponderance of death coincidences in hallucinations, in "Report on Cases of Precognition," *Proceedings of the Society for Psychical Research* 42 (1934), pp. 49–103.

Pages 145–46   Raymond Moody, *Life after Life* (Atlanta, GA: Mockingbird, 1975); see also Moody, *The Light Beyond* (New York: Bantam, 1988); Kenneth Ring, *Life at Death: A Scientific Investigation of the Near-Death Experience* (New York: Coward, McGann & Geohegan, 1980); Michael Sabom, *Recollections of Death: A Medical Investigation* (New York: Harper & Row, 1982); Charles P. Flynn, *After the Beyond: Human Transformations and the Near-Death Experience* (Englewood Cliffs, NJ: Prentice-Hall, 1986); Elizabeth Kubler-Ross, *Living with Death and Dying* (New York: Touchstone, 1981); Ernst A. Rodin, "The Reality of Death Experiences: A Personal Perspective," *Journal of Nervous and Mental Disease* 168 (1980), pp. 259–63; and Susan Blackmore, *Dying to Live* (Buffalo, NY: Prometheus Books, 1993). The quote from Kellehear's book, *Experiences near Death* (New York: Oxford University Press, 1996), is on page 20. Though the clinical data on near-death experiences are recent, there are many accounts of the experiences throughout history. See the classic study of the experiences in medieval and modern eras by Carol Zaleski, *Otherworld Journeys* (New York: Oxford University Press, 1987). Also see her defense of the importance for Christianity of beliefs in near-death experiences: *The Life of the World to Come* (New York: Oxford University Press, 1996).

Pages 146–48 Interview with Helen Thornton on October 14, 1989. All quotes are from the interview.

Pages 148–49 Interview with William Sutter on October 14, 1989.

Pages 149–53 Interview with Frank Butler on October 17, 1989.

Pages 153–57 The recent history of efforts to define death can be tracked in the following contributions: Ad Hoc Committee of the Harvard Medical School to Examine the Definition of Brain Death, "A Definition of Irreversible Coma" *JAMA* 205:6 (August 1968), pp. 337–40; Hans Jonas, "Against the Stream: Comments on the Definition of Death," *Ethical Issues in Death and Dying* (New York: Prentice-Hall, 1996); Alexander Capron and Leon R. Kass, "A Statutory Definition of the Standards for Determining Human Death: An Appraisal and a Proposal," in Dennis J. Horan and David Mall, eds., *Death, Dying, and Euthanasia* (Frederick, MD: University Publications of America, 1980); Robert M. Veatch, "The Definition of Death: Ethical, Philosophical, and Policy Confusion," *Annals of the New York Academy of Science* 315 (November 17, 1978) and "The Impending Collapse of the Whole-Brain Definition of Death," *Hastings Center Report* 23: 4 (1993); Julius Korein, *Brain Death* (Washington, DC: President's Commission for the Study of Ethical Problems in Medicine and Biomedical and Behavioral Research, 1983); The New York State Task Force on Life and the Law, *The Determination of Death* (Albany, NY: The Task Force, 1989).

Pages 153–56 The best recent literature on these topics is: *When Death Is Sought* (Albany, NY: The New York Task Force on Life and the Law, 1994), and the Supplement to Report (April 1997); Hans Kung and Walter Jens, *Dying with Dignity* (New York: Continuum, 1995) Daniel Brock, "Death and Dying," first published in Robert Veatch, ed, *Medical Ethics* (Philadelphia, PA: Jones and Bartlett, 1998), and more recently as chapter 6 in Brock, *Life and Death* (Cambridge: Cambridge University Press, 1993); Sherwin Nuland, *How We Die: Reflections on Life's Final Chapter* (London: Vintage, 1997); Derek Humphry, *Final Exit* (Eugene, OR: Hemlock Society, 1990); Timothy Quill, *A Midwife through the Dying Process* (Baltimore, MD: Johns Hopkins University Press, 1996); and Ira Byock, *Dying Well* (New York: Riverhead Books, 1997).

Page 155 The point on human identity made at the end of the first full paragraph is drawn from the Jonas piece, "Against the Stream."

Pages 158–59   The survival of a soul or psyche was proposed by both Plato and Descartes. See Plato's *Alcibiades* and the *Phaedo,* and Descartes' *Discourses,* parts 4 and 5. A helpful collection of pieces on both the paranormal and survival after death (mainly skeptical in its orientation but including a wide variety of views) is Anthony Flew, ed., *Readings in the Philosophical Problems of Parapsychology* (Buffalo, NY: Prometheus Books, 1989).

Pages 159–60   LeShan, *The Medium, the Mystic, and the Physicist,* especially appendix C, "Human Survival of Biological Death," and chapter 6 for a chart of the differences between what LeShan calls "clairvoyant reality" and "sensory reality."

Pages 161–63   Karl L. R. Jansen, "Using Ketamine to Induce the Near-Death Experience: Mechanism of Action and Therapeutic Potential," *Ethnomedicine and the Study of Consciousness,* issue 4 (1995), pp. 55–81. Also on the Web as: http://www.lycaeum.org/drugs/synthetics/ketamine/Ketamine_near-death.html (as of January 1999).

Pages 164–66   Claire Sylvia, *A Change of Heart* (New York: Warner Books, 1998). Quotes in the text are on pp. 255 and 137, respectively.

Pages 166–71   Interview with Peter Walker on June 22, 1998.

Pages 171–74   I have relied in this section of the text on the version of *The Tibetan Book of the Dead* translated by Robert A. F. Thurman (New York: Thorsons, 1995), especially chapter 2. The story and quote from Pavarotti is from his book, *My Own Story* (Garden City, NJ: Doubleday, 1991).

Pages 173–74   C. G. Jung, *Psyche and Symbol* (Garden City, NY: Doubleday Anchor, 1958), pp. 283–301.

Seven: MYSTICAL EXPERIENCES: SELF AND REALITY

Pages 176–78   Three helpful books on mysticism are Robert Ellwood, *Mysticism and Religion* (Englewod Cliffs, NJ: Prentice-Hall, 1980); Richard H. Jones, *Science and Mysticism* (Lewisburgh, PA: Bucknell University Press, 1986); and (especially) Agehananda Bharati, *The Light at the Center* (Santa Barbara, CA: Ross-Erikson, 1976). I have also been enlightened (as always) by Walter Burkert's work, in this case *Ancient Mystery Cults* (Cambridge, MA: Harvard University Press, 1987), especially chapter 4.

Pages 178–79   Edward M. Hundert is very effective in summing up work from Descartes through Piaget (and even more recent cognitive psychology and neuroscience) that persuasively draws up such views of ordinary reality. See *Philosophy, Psychiatry, and Neuroscience* (Oxford: Clarendon, 1989).

Pages 179–80   The Bharati quote is from *The Light at the Center*, p. 39; the Finney section is from his *Memoirs* (New York: Fleming H. Revell, 1903), pp. 18–21; and the Ellwood quote is from his *Mysticism and Religion*, p. 12. All three mystical accounts are provided with helpful analyses by Ellwood in *Mysticism and Religion*.

Pages 180–81   Bharati's views are set forth in *The Light at the Center*. He still maintained them late in his life, as confirmed in my interview with him on September 15, 1989.

Pages 183–84   A helpful treatment of nondual philosophies is David Loy, *Nonduality: A Study in Comparative Philosophy* (New Haven: Yale University Press, 1988).

Page 184   Michael Persinger, "Religious and Mystical Experiences as Artifacts of Temporal Lobe Function: A General Hypothesis," (1983). See also his later study, *Neuropsychological Bases of God Beliefs* (New York: Praeger, 1987).

Pages 184–85   Peggy Ann Wright, "The Interconnectivity of Mind, Brain, and Behavior in Altered States of Consciousness: Focus on Shamanism," *Alternative Therapies* 1:3 (July 1995), pp. 50–56.

Pages 186–92   Interview with David Hoisington on August 21, 1997.

Pages 193–202   Interviews with John Delgrosso on February 16 and 23, 1998.

Pages 202–3   Evidence that prayer can affect attitude and thence healing abounds. A varied collection of studies: Jaap J. Beutler, Johannes T. M. Attevelt, Sybo A. Schouten, Joop A. J. Faber, Evert J. Dorhout Mees, Gijsbert G. Geijskes, "Paranormal Healing and Hypertension," *British Medical Journal* 296 (May 28, 1988), pp. 1491–94; Theresa L. Saudia, Marguerite R. Kinney, Kathleen C. Brown, and (Rev.) Leslie Young-Ward, "Health Locus of Control and Helpfulness of Prayer," *Critical Care* 20:1 (January 1991), pp. 60–63, for a study of the relationship between health locus of control and helpfulness of prayer as a direct-action coping mechanism in patients before having cardiac surgery (no relationship, and prayer is an effective coping mechanism); Elisabeth McSherry et al., "Spiritual Resources in Older Hospitalized Men," *Social Compass* 34:4 (1987), pp. 515–17; Joan D. Koss, "Expectations and Outcomes for Patients Given Mental Health Care or Spiritualist Healing in Puerto Rico," *American Journal of*

Psychiatry 144:1 (January 1987), pp. 56–61; and, of course, Herbert Benson, *Timeless Healing* (New York: Scribner, 1996), especially the chart on page 175 summarizing data from another required read: D. A. Matthews, D. B. Larson, and C. P. Barry, *The Faith Factor: An Annotated Bibliography of Clinical Research on Spiritual Subjects,* Vol. 1 (Radner, PA: John Templeton Foundation, 1994); and finally, the consolidations in Dale Matthews, *The Faith Factor: Proof of the Healing Powers of Prayer* (New York: Viking, 1998).

Page 203   Randolph C. Byrd, "Positive Therapeutic Effects: Intercessory Prayer in a Coronary Care Unit Population," *Southern Medical Journal* 81:7 (July 1988), pp. 826–29.

Page 203   C. R. B. Joyce and R. M. C. Welldon, "The Objective Efficacy of Prayer: A Double-Blind Clinical Trial," *Journal of Chronic Diseases* 18 (1965), pp. 367–77.

Pages 204–6   Interview with Sally Aderton on April 7, 1998.

Eight: ON KNOWING AND NOT KNOWING

Page 207   Steven Hawking, *A Brief History of Time* (New York: Bantam, 1988).

Page 207   I am using the Douay Bible for my quotes from Genesis, in this case the edition published in 1941 by the John Murphy Company (Baltimore, MD). (Yes, it is a family Bible.)

Page 208   On forbidden knowledge: Roger Shattuck, *Forbidden Knowledge: From Prometheus to Pornography* (New York: St. Martin's, 1996); and, on a different note, the discussion of moral limits in Nicholas Rescher, *Forbidden Knowledge and Other Essays in the Philosophy of Cognition, Episteme 13* (Norwell, MA: D. Reidel, 1987), especially chapter 1 (which I have drawn from) and chapter 4.

Page 208   Daniel Patrick Moynihan, *Secrecy: The American Experience* (New Haven, CT: Yale University Press, 1998).

Pages 209–10   Simon, *Models of Bounded Rationality.*

Pages 212–13   A wonderful treatment of these theoretical changes is in Janet Browne's biography of Darwin, *Voyaging* (Princeton: Princeton University Press, 1995).

Pages 213–14   This third pattern of explanation is represented in the arguments and overviews in William Riker, *Liberalism against Populism* (San Francisco,

CA: W. H. Freeman, 1982). Also, note (and be grateful) that I am not addressing a number of dense issues in scientific explanations, in particular whether nomological or various contextual forms of explanation are more appropriate in inquiry. The starting entries in this discussion are of course the older literatures: Carl Hempel, *Philosophy of Natural Science* (Englewood Cliffs, NJ: Prentice-Hall, 1966); Ernest Nagel, *The Structure of Science* (New York: Harcourt, Brace & World, 1961); Peter Winch, *The Idea of a Social Science* (London: Routledge & Kegan Paul, 1958).

Pages 215–16   Barrow's book, *Impossibility: The Limits of Science and the Science of Limits* (Oxford: Oxford University Press, 1998) is a wide-ranging discussion of, well, limits. The Kant reference is on page 69.

Page 216   Wittgenstein of course did not consider informational costs in establishing rational limits. His concerns were with the limits of language. In *Philosophical Investigations* (Oxford: Oxford University Press, 1958) he famously reflects on how rules are followed until a foundation is reached that simply must be accepted. I will spare the reader the familiar phrases about bedrock and spades (pp. 84–85). But the point is worth stressing again. Reason must allow for areas in which nothing more can be said. Reflection, or critical inquiry, is spared an infinite regress of reason by convention. Practices simply are, and no rational answer can justify them on conventional understandings of reason.

Page 217   The most innocuous sense of the unknown must be unexamined premises, though even here metaphysical considerations can intrude. Economics textbooks chronically warn novitiates that correlations between business cycles and sunspots, no matter how strong, are not accepted as causal because contiguity cannot be established on our unexamined understandings of reality. The methodological unknown is that which we take for granted, though we may examine it, as a way of moving ahead with what are considered genuine research agendas. The second sense of the unknown is developed by Michael Polanyi simply as tacit knowledge, assumptions at surface and deep levels that allow us to go about our intelligent business. One might also include (in an expanded sense of this category) the noncognitive knowledge explored in Alfred Schutz's philosophies. This version of the unknown, like the unconscious in psychotherapy, must be retrieved if it is to be known, an exercise that is often laborious and usually not entirely successful. The third sense of the unknown mentioned in the text is illustrated by the mystique attached to Richard Feynman, a physicist whose biography by James Gleick is entitled *Genius* (New York: Vintage

Books, 1993). Feynman is said to have done much of his work with intuitive reflections unavailable to other physicists. Though "civics science" suggests that scientific results must be capable of replication by all other scientists, Feynman's genius testifies to the truly mysterious generation of seminal knowledge. Some individuals seem to have access to discovery techniques and combination rules that are simply fugitive to all others, and while we can falsify results, the details of genesis may remain forever unknown. The fourth sense of the unknown may be attached to the neurological structures that are slowly being identified in the work done in neurology, artificial intelligence, and inquiries into consciousness. But the structures may not produce consistent theories of mind *or* body since they are the condition and not the object of knowing. Like the paradoxes that occur as a system aspires to both completeness and consistency, the subjective frames we must assign to objective accounts of the mental seem to halt reductionist efforts. Self-reflective paradoxes may keep some conditions of inquiry outside the scope of the known.

Page 217   R. M. Hare in "Can Theological Statements Be Tested Empirically?" introduces the notion of "bliks" (roughly, assumptions that cannot be tested by observation) as conditions for having explanations. Bliks are both unprovable and vital to segregating systems of belief. My point is that in at least classical realism the bliks are conditions that must be *true* for any genuine exercise of reason. Worth reading on these thoughts is the entire symposium in which the Hare article appears, *New Essays in Philosophical Theology,* ed. Anthony Flew and Alasdair MacIntyre (New York: Macmillan, 1955).

Pages 218–19   Some of these observations are compatible with classical realism and can be tracked in Leo Strauss, *Natural Right and History* (Chicago: University of Chicago Press, 1953). For example, Strauss understands classical political philosophy as admitting that "the distinction between nature and convention is fundamental." Nature, its discovery "the work of philosophy" and source of truth, is available to human beings through a kind of transcendence, "the quest for the natural or best political order." Then, in one of the most intriguing passages in the book, Strauss describes the Socratic sense of philosophy in this way: "[P]hilosophy is knowledge that one does not know; that is to say, it is knowledge of what one does not know, or awareness of the fundamental problems and, therewith, of the fundamental alternatives regarding their solution that are coeval with human thought." This understanding requires philosophy to address the natural, as opposed to the conventional, and seek understanding of the whole, that framework which makes knowledge possible: "All understanding presupposes a fundamental awareness of the whole: prior to any perception of particular things, the human soul must have had a vision of the ideas, a vision of the articulated whole." But such awareness may be fugitive, for "[t]here is no guarantee that the quest for adequate articulation will ever . . . go beyond the stage of discussion or disputation." Philosophers, like all of us, may be frustrated in efforts to comprehend the natural order that may inform all knowledge. The quotes above are on these (succeeding) pages in *Natural Right and History:* 11, 81, 15, 32, and 125.

Page 218   String theory has been revived and renamed. Now called M theory, it seems currently to be the leading candidate to unify quantum mechanics and general relativity. See the summary in the *New York Times,* September 22, 1998, Science Times section.

Pages 220–23   John E. Mack, *Abduction* (New York: Simon & Schuster, 1994).

Page 223   There are less benign accounts of alien abductions than Mack offers. See David M. Jacobs, *The Threat* (New York: Simon & Schuster, 1998). Also, for what I keep thinking is the fringe (the outer limits?), see the high octane presentations of Whitley Strieber as he describes his own abductions in *Communion* (New York: Avon, 1987), and his overviews in *Confirmation: The Hard Evidence of Aliens among Us* (New York: St. Martin's, 1998). Like psychic practices, however, the presence of extravagant claims should not undermine the possibilities of small but vital truths in the literatures. The quote from Crews (which he sets off in quotes in his own piece for a kind of emphasis) is in his critical review of some recent books on aliens, "The Mindsnatchers," *New York Review of Books,* June 25, 1998, pp. 14–19. For a postmodern take on alien abduction consult Jodi Dean's *Aliens in America* (Ithaca, NY: Cornell University Press, 1998).

Page 223   Richard Swinburne, *Is There a God?* (Oxford: Oxford University Press, 1996), pp. 130–37.

Page 223   Mack, *Abduction,* p. 20.

Page 224   Huston Smith makes the point more poignantly: "Science can only reveal what is inferior to us." By science he means experimental science, and by inferior he means the range of phenomena within our perceptual and cognitive powers. He argues that if higher beings exist, they are beyond the grasp of controlled experiments: "They know more than we do, and will walk into our experiments if they choose to; otherwise not." In Smith,

Essays on World Religions, ed. by M. Darrol Bryant (New York: Paragon House, 1992), p. 200.

Page 225   With these remarks on evolution I align with Stephen Jay Gould against the ultra-Darwinists (as he calls them), who see natural selection as the single and only explanation for the way life is at any given historical moment. Gould is surely on the side of the right and the good in this dispute since it is inconceivable that a single explanatory principle like natural selection can explain its own side effects as it operates in nature, especially since that principle is influenced reciprocally by the biological laws governing organisms and, more generally perhaps, by the laws of physics, as well as by the more immediate effects of contingent events (accidents like an asteroid striking the Earth) that may distort selective pressures. I keep thinking of putative instantiations of models in the social sciences, like the pure market, and how they are inevitably compromised by the effects of extraneous and random variables. Why should natural selection be insulated from variables that corrupt primary explanatory theories? See Daniel Dennett for an ultra view of natural selection, *Darwin's Dangerous Idea: Evolution and the Meanings of Life* (New York: Simon & Schuster, 1995); Gould's two essays in the *New York Review of Books,* "Darwinian Fundamentalism," and "Evolution: The Pleasures of Pluralism," (respectively, June 12 and 26, 1997); and the obligatory exchange of notes in the August 14, 1997, issue. For a thoughtful defense of the primacy of natural selection based on the principle of convergence (that environmental conditions constrain adaptations toward a set of similar workable traits), see Conway Morris, *The Crucible of Creation* (Oxford: Oxford University Press, 1998). Another interesting discussion is in chapter 9 of Ramachandran and Blakeslee, *Phantoms in the Brain.*

Nine: NATURAL INTELLIGIBILITIES

Page 230   Walter Burkert, *Creation of the Sacred* (Cambridge, MA: Harvard University Press, 1996), pp. 169–76, for a discussion of the importance of religion in the validation of oaths.

Pages 230–31   John Stuart Mill, *On Liberty,* ed. David Spitz (New York: Norton, 1975).

Pages 237–38   See Davies, *The Fifth Miracle: The Search for the Origin and Meaning of Life* (New York: Simon & Schuster, 1999), especially chapter 10, for an imaginative discussion of these matters. The Gonzalez study is reported in various publications, including the *London Sunday Times,* July 4, 1999.

Page 238   Edward O. Wilson, *Consilience: The Unity of Knowledge* (New York: Knopf, 1998).

Pages 238–39   Paul Davies, *The Mind of God* (New York: Simon & Schuster, 1992), especially chapter 5 for what I am saying here in the text. Charles Bennett is the source for the distinction between information content and message value, in "Dissipation, Information, Computational Complexity, and the Definition of Organization," in *Emerging Syntheses in Science,* ed. D. Pines (Boston: Addison-Wesley, 1987). Davies provides the central quote from Bennett on page 137 of *The Mind of God.*

Page 239   Literatures on whether there is continuity between the natural and social sciences can fill one's shopping bag with truly delectable items (and my taste for the older works is unabated). The traditional arguments for discontinuity are in Peter Winch, *The Idea of a Social Science.* Also Winch, "Understanding a Primitive Society," *American Philosophical Quarterly* 1 (October 1964), 307–24. The continuity thesis is delineated in wonderful terms by Ernest Nagel, *The Structure of Science.* For the deductive nomological explanations revered in positivist philosophy of science, Carl Hempel and Paul Oppenheim, "The Covering Law Analysis of Scientific Explanation," *Philosophy of Science* 15 (1948), 135–74. See also the collection of pieces in Maurice Natanson, ed., *The Philosophy of the Social Sciences* (New York: Random House, 1963). Ironically, the philosophy and practice of science is itself a kind of story. See Joseph Rouse, "The Narrative Reconstruction of Science," *Inquiry* 33 (June 1990), 179–96.

Page 241   Ramachandran and Blakeslee, *Phantoms in the Brain,* p. 229. I am less enthused about the author's imaginative suggestion that these accounts can be folded into each other by (hypothetically) fusing brain tissue through a cable that connects separate and individual neurologies. The hypothetical cable collapses differences among individuals, but does not fuse first and third person accounts. It simply creates a kind of collective self, a joined first-person account. But see the listing of types of self later in the chapter. This inventory of different senses of the self is simply excellent, and important for literatures that typically rely on a single sense of the self.

Pages 241–42   A. J. Ayer, *Language, Truth, and Logic* (New York: Oxford University Press, 1950).

((INDEX))

carbon-based neurons, 10
card reading, 25
Carrington, Hereward, 57
Carroll, Lewis, 248
Catholicism, 31
Cayce, Edgar, psychic case example, 58–61, 251
Cayce Foundation, 59, 60
cell memory theory, 164–65
ceteris paribus, 122
Chalmers, David, 9–10
Chambers, Robert, 213
channeling, 3, 56–57, 205
chaos theory, 213–14
Charlie Rose television show, 134
Cheshire Cat experiment, 11, 246–47
Chews, Frederick, 222
Children's Hospital in Boston, 87
Christianity: miracles of, 50; resurrection belief in, 144
Chronicle, 142
clairaudiance, 25, 57
clairvoyance, 3, 25, 27–30, 57; controlled experimentation of, 64; in dreams, 188–89; *vs.* ESP, 69; symbolic images and, 29; *vs.* telepathy, 122. *See also* mediums
classical realism, 268
Cleanthes, 52
codes: ancient philosophers and, 51; magic control of nature and, 50; science explanation of nature and, 51, 53
cognitive development, infant, 50
cognitive limits, 14–19
collective consciousness, 124, 206
College of Wooster, 138
common sense, 108
consciousness: cognitive limitations and, 14–18; definition of, 8–9; knowledge as artifact of culture and, 16, 248; mind/body causal chains and, 19–20, 21–22, 249–50; neurological coping devices and, 11–12; neurological correlates of, 9, 13–14, 19, 254; organizational invariance concept and, 10; physical perception and, 10–11; redefinition capabilities of, 232; in shamanism, 185; subjective experiential nature of, 9–10; subtle consciousness and, 173; therapeutic powers of beliefs and, 20, 249–50; usefulness and truth and, 246. *See also* domains of consciousness; mystical experiences

Conscious Universe (Radin), 69
Consilience: The Unity of Knowledge (Wilson), 238
contiguity, 134–35
Copernicus, 52, 212
Copleston, Frederick, 175
Copperfield, David, 53
Cornell University, 81–86
Cottingley fairies, 255
Crandon, Margery, 62
Crick, Francis, 11, 247
"crossing over" concept, 176, 181. *See also* boundary crossings
crystal ball reading, 25

Darwin, Charles: data dependence upon theory and, 135; natural selection, evolution concepts of, 81, 83, 211, 212–13; ultra-Darwinism and, 270
Davis, Paul, 238
death, 160; archetype concept (Jung) and, 160; biological holism theory and, 164, 165: brain death criteria for, 154–56; Buddhist beliefs regarding, 171–74; Christianity resurrection belief and, 144; cognitive activities and, 153–54; ease of, 149, 175; existence after, 144; holistic view of reality and, 159–60; human identity criteria and, 155, 159; imminent death state and, 156; indisputable feature of, 157; irreversible coma criteria and, 156–57; linguistic categories of, 154; *vs.* living biological functions, 153–54; materialist view on, 158; mind-body dualism and, 164, 175; mysteriousness of, 157; patient best interests and, 156–57; permanent vegetative state criteria and, 156; physiological changes of, 153; reincarnation and, 169–70; sensory reality and, higher level of, 160–61; soul as divine representation and, 158–59, 253; spiritual state of mind and, 175; terminally ill state and, 156; tests for, controversiality of, 154–55; universality of, 144. *See also* mediums; near-death experiences
Delgrosso, John, healing case example of, 192–202
de Merchant, Elsworth, 124–25, 129–30
Descartes, 52, 179, 260, 264
devils, belief in, 3
disease, emotional basis of, 78
Divine plans, predestination, 30

domains of consciousness: alternative realities possibility and, 13, 17; anthropic principle of, 17–18; binocular rivalry, 11; consciousness defined and, 8–9; consilience and, search for, 238–43, 271; definition of, 8, 9; depressed *vs.* nondepressed individuals, 6; doubt, and science, 2; first *vs.* third person accounts and, 241; illusions and, 6; logical positivism and, 241–42; mathematics and, unified system of, 15–16; mysteriousness of, 8–9; psychic experience statistics and, 3–4; sensory and abstract instruments of, 1; vision relying on knowing and, 2–3. *See also* consciousness

Doyle, Sir Arthur Conan, 62, 256

Drake, Frank, 261

dreams: clairvoyant, 188–89; contacts with the dead in, 168

Duke University, 63, 137, 138–39, 142

eating disorders, 78

ectoplasmic activity, 64

Edgar Cayce Institute, 24

EEG tests, of brain death, 154

Einstein, Albert, 212, 249

Ellwood, Robert, 180–81

embryogenesis, 83

empathy, 176; in counseling, 190–91; in healing, 191–92; mystical experiences and, 186

end-of-the-world predictions, 75

epiphenomena, 30

ESP. *See* extrasensory perception

ethical life, Buddhist death preparation and, 171–72

euthanasia, 156

experimental controls, 47–79. *See also* magic

Extra-Sensory Perception (Rhine), 139

extrasensory perception (ESP), 3, 34, 35, 139; *vs.* clairvoyance, 69; conditions of, 29–30; controlled studies of, 61, 64, 65–66, 67–68, 71, 138; as evolutionary survival trait, 71; as existing powers extension, 109; Carl Sagan on, 253–54. *See also* clairvoyance

extraterrestrial intelligence, 34–35, 136

faith healing, 25; emotional basis of, 78; fraud in, 76–77

Feather, Sally, 137–40

Feynman, Richard, 268

Finney, Charles, 179–81, 182

Fodor, Nandor, 57

Folger, Anne Marie, 27–30

Folkman, Dr. Judah, 87

Fordham University, 122

fortunetellers, 76

Foucault, Michel, 134

Foundation for Research on the Nature of Man, 57

free speech, 231

Galapagos Islands, 135

Galileo, 52, 212

Gallup Poll, 3, 145

Gant, Charles: disease and, external causes of, 88; —, homeostatic imbalances and, 88, 90–92; —, internal body changes and, 88; —, mortality rate statistics and, 89–90, 258; —, nutrition focus and, 90–91; nutrition, 90–92; orthomolecular medicine of, 88–92, 107; Western medicine and, 88–89

Gardner, Martin, 67

Garrett, Eileen, psychic case example, 55–58, 61, 139, 251, 252

Ganzfeld procedure, of sensory deprivation, 65–66

Geller, Uri, 64

Gerrard, Julie, out-of-body experience case example, 113–16

ghosts, 25, 30, 32, 141

God: belief in, explanation of, 85; design of *vs.* natural selection, 83; empirical evidence of, lack of, 84; eternal timelessness and, 204; forbidden knowledge and, 207–8; objective meaninglessness of, 7; perfect knowledge of, 207; quantum mechanics and, 133; religion *vs.* science and, 211; self and objects existence and, 179

God-in-the-gaps argument, 83, 85

Gödel, Kurt, 15–16

Gödel's theorem, 15–16

Goebbels, Joseph, 33

Gonzales-Whippler, 49–50

Gonzalez, Guillermo, 237–38

Gould, Stephen Jay, 225, 270

Greece: body and mind non-distinctions in, 52; culture, 52; philosophers, 51; scientists, 52

Guyette, Nelson, 30–35

hallucinations, about death, 144, 148–49

Hansel, C. E. M., 67

Hare, R. M., 268
Harvey, Thomas, 249
healing, 26–27, 59–61; advanced empathy and, 191–92; John Delgrosso case example of, 192–202; prayer and, 202–4, 265; through therapeutic touch, 104–6, 107
Heisenberg, Werner, 14
Herkoff, Peter, 28, 32, 33, 34
Hilbert, David, 15, 16
History of God, A (Armstrong), 7
Hoisington, David, mysticism case example of, 186–92
holistic healing, 112
holistic reasoning, 229
Holy Ghost, experience of, 179–80
Home, Daniel D., psychic case example, 54–55, 73, 251
homeopathy, 60
Homer, 52
Human Genome Project, 9
Hume, David, 108, 179
Huxley, Julius, 83
hypnosis, 36, 57, 70

images, symbolic, 29
imminent death state, 156
Impossibility (Barrow), 215
India, 26
Institute for Parapsychology, 63
intelligence. *See* natural intelligibilities
intuition: knowing sensitive psychic state and, 204–5; parables and, 227; the unknown and, 217, 268. *See also* intuitive science
intuitive science: alternative medicine and, 258–59; beliefs embedded in systems of knowing and, 109–11; evaluation of, 108–9; familiar *vs.* strange, balanced by, 87; observation and reason as tools, 81–82; orthomolecular medicine and, 88–92; therapeutic touch discipline and, 92–106. *See also* Gant, Charles; Provine, Will; therapeutic touch (TT)
irreversible coma, death criteria of, 156–57

James Randi Educational Foundation, 94
Jansen, Karl, 161–63
Jay, Ricky, 48, 53
Jehovah's Witnesses, 246
Johns Hopkins University, 57
Jones, Scott, 128
Journal of Parapsychology, 140, 142

Journal of the American Medical Association, 93–94
Jung, Carl, 173–74; empathy concepts of, 176; religion as a coping device and, 246

Kellehear, Allan, 146
Kepler, 212
ketamine experimentation, NDE and, 161–63
kinetic effect, 118
kinetic power, 54–55
Klopper, Peter, 142–43
knowing sensitive case example, 204–6
knowledge: acquisition of, moral principles of, 208; as artifact of culture, 16, 248; bounded rationality limits and, 215–16, 267; changes in explanatory laws and, 212–13; chaos theory and, 213–14, 267; contemporary decision theories of, 209–10; dangerous lack of, 208–9; evolutionary theory and, 212–13; forbidden knowledge and, 207–8; form of knowledge and, 215; God's perfect knowledge and, 207; higher life forms and, 219–20; —, alien contact experiences and, 220–22, 269; —, alternative ways of understanding and, 223–24, 237–43; —, study subjects affecting study methods and, 224; how do we know what we know and, 210–11; limitations of knowing and, 209–10, 215–19; limits of language and, 267; natural order and, 269; natural selection theory and, 213; natural *vs.* social science and, 239–40; from randomness to law-governed relationships and, 211–12; rules for excluding, 210; science and religion compatibility and, 211; scientific *vs.* spiritual understanding of reality and, 214–19; Socratic philosophy and, 268–69; unknown and, importance of, 217–19, 267–68; vision relying on, 2–3; Western dualisms and, 223. *See also* unknown
Koch, Christof, 11, 247
Krieger, Dolores, 92–93, 93–95, 250
Kuhn, Thomas, 223

Lakatos, Imre, 87
Las Meninas (Velázquez), 2
Ledwith, Stuart, 112; and relaxation therapy, 98; therapeutic touch practice of, 95–102, 107
Lennon, John, 120

near-death experiences (NDEs), 85–86: anomaly of, 168; brain activity and, 161–62; certitude of survivors of, 6; controlled research regarding, 162–63; *vs.* death experience, 158; dimensional alternatives and, 158; existence after death, proof of, 157–58; Gallup Poll regarding, 145; ketamine experimentation and, 161–63; mind-body dualism and, 163, 164; mystical experience and, 177; null case example of, 149–53; as out-of-body experience, 113; psycho-social aspects of, 146; sensory reality and, higher level of, 160–61; skeptics of, 85–86; statistics regarding, 145–46; survivors of, 6; William Sutter case example of, 148–49; Claire Sylvia case example of, 164–65, 166; technical possibility of, 145; Helen Thornton case example of, 146–48; uniformity of, 145–46, 162
neurological resources, experience, 13
neurological structures, 10
neurons, 11
New Frontiers of the Mind (Skinner), 66
noncognitive knowledge, 267

OBEs. *See* out-of-body experiences (OBEs)
Occam's razor, 239
Oedipus, 209
On Liberty (Mill), 81
On the Origin of Species (Darwin), 81, 213
Oppenheimer, Robert, 208
optical illusions, 11, 247–48
organ transplantation, 156, 164–65
orthomolecular medicine, 88–92
Osis, Karlis, 127–28, 131
Osis/McCormick study, 126, 127–28
out-of-body experiences (OBEs), 39–40, 120; empirical explanation of, 78; empirical research on, 118; explanations of, 116–17; frequency data on, 113, 116–17; Julie Gerrard case example, 113–16; interpretation of, 117–18, 119; mind and body dualism and, 112–13, 116; mind-body separations and, 117–18; personal case of, 187; *vs.* remote viewing, 69; Alex Tanous case example of, 119–25, 127–28; as a travel experience, 116–17; types of, 112–13; verification of, 77

palmistry, 188
parables, 227

paranormal. *See* magic; mediums; mystical experiences; parapsychology; psychic powers; psychic power techniques
parapsychology: controlled experimentation on, 62–70, 138–43; McDougall as founder of, 61, 138
Parapsychology Foundation, 58
Parapsychology Laboratory, Duke University, 63
past life reading, 25
Pauli, Wolfgang, 87
Pearce, Hubert, 67–68
Pearce-Pratt experiments, 67
Penrose, Roger, 13
permanent vegetative state, 156
Persinger, Michael, 184
phantom limb experience, 165
phantom triangle, 12, 13, 247–48
phenomenon, natural, 30
physical side of perception, 10–11
physiology, 11
PK (psychokinesis): controlled studies of, 61, 64–65, 69; as evolutionary survival trait, 71
placebo effect, 20, 21, 78, 107, 192, 231, 232, 249–50
Plato, 52, 253; enlightenment methods of, 226; knowledge acquisition and, 208; painfulness of enlightenment and, 231; paradox of Epimenides and, 15; *Republic,* 4–5
Plutarch, 52
Polanyi, Michael, 267
poltergeist activity, 57, 64
Pomme, 134
Pope, Dorothy, 140–41
Popoff, Peter, 76–77
positivism, 241–42
Pratt, J. G., 68
prayer: empirical studies of, 202–3; eternal reality through, 204; expectations from, 203–4; as magic within religion, 203; mind affecting body in, 202; as mystical experience, 202–4, 265; positive healing attitude and, 202; subject-object dualism and, 204
precognition, 61, 77, 110, 255
property dualism, 9
property dualism concept, 259
protean molecules, 9
Provine, Will: alternative realities concept and, 84; background of, 82; belief in God explanation of, 85; biology, conflicts of, 82, 84;

cumulative *vs.* noncumulative feature of science and, 84–85; empirical evidence *vs.* faith and, 82–83; God's existence and, 83–84; and modern biology, 132; natural selection, evolution focus of, 83, 84; near-death experiences and, 85–86; observation and reason as tools, 81–82

psi (psychic ability), 37–38, 58, 61, 80, 128, 235

psychic ability (psi), 37–38, 58, 61, 80, 128, 235

psychic powers: aura reading, 25, 26, 58, 102, 193 (*see also* magic; supernatural); author's sessions with, 40–46, 234–36; card reading, 25; channeling, 3, 56–57, 205; clairaudiance, 25, 57; clairvoyance, 25, 27–30, 57, 142–43; critic of, 35–40; crystal ball reading, 25; faith healing, 25; ghost hunting, 25, 30, 32, 141; healing, 26–27, 58–61; hypnosis, 57; kinetic power, 54–55; past life reading, 25; psychometry, 25; telekinesis, 29, 30. *See also* psychic powers, controlled research on

psychic powers, controlled research on, 61–70, 79, 235; alternative reality possibility of, 73–74, 237–43; empirical explanations and, 78; as evolutionary survival traits, 71; expansive nature of, 74; eyewitness bias and, 75; faith healing and, 76–77; falsification requirement and, 74–76; fraud evidence and, 76–77, 255; as human abilities, 72–73; predictions, results of, 235–36; reverse causality and, 77, 257; spontaneity requirement of, 74

psychic power techniques: alpha waves, 41; holy ashes, 26–27; table tapping, 55, 56; vibrations, 28

psychics: abilities, 46; author's sessions with, 40–46, 234–36; Francine Bizzari, 23–27; Edgar Cayce, 58–61, 251; controlled experiments on, 119–20; evaluation of events, 108–9, 133; Anne Marie Folger, 27–30; Eileen Garrett, 55–57, 61, 139, 251, 252; Nelson Guyette, 30–35; Daniel Home, 54–55, 251; life readings, 23; James Randi, critic of, 35–40; supernatural powers of, 54–55. *See also* magic; psychic powers; psychic powers, controlled research on; supernatural

psychokinesis (PK), 123; controlled studies of, 61, 64–65, 69; as evolutionary survival trait, 71

psychometrics, 188

psychometry, 25

psychotherapists, 5

Ptolemaic astronomy, 212

Pythagoras, 51, 52

Quackwatch, 95

quantum mechanics, 14–15, 115, 132–33, 248

Quinlan, Karen Ann, 153, 159

Radin, Dean, 69

Ramachandran, V. S., 241

Randi, James, 35–40, 67, 75–77

Randi (magician), 64

random number generation (RNG), 65

Reagan, Ronald, 121

reality: absolute (Zen), 179; objects *vs.* subjects in, 178

reincarnation, 168, 169–70

relaxation therapy, 98

religion: as a coping device, 246, 249–50; magic and, 49–50; prayer as magic within, 203–4; religious cultures and, 3; religious wars and, 230; science compatible with, 211. *See also specific religion*

remote viewing, 69

Republic (Plato), 4–5

Rhine, J. B., 57–58, 61–70

Rhine, Louisa, 61–70, 80, 141

Rhine laboratory, 70, 71–72, 137–43

Rhine Research Center, 58, 72, 139

RNG (random number generation), 65

Roosevelt Hospital, 57

Rosa, Emily, 94, 107

Rosa, Linda, 94–95

Rose, Charlie, 134

Russell, Alfred, 213

Russell, Robert John, 133

Sagan, Carl, 134, 253–54, 261

Salem witch trials, 6

Sarner, Larry, 94–95

Saturday Review of Literature, 66

Schmeidler, Gertrude, 68

Schmidt, Helmut, 54

Schutz, Alfred, 267

science: ancient philosophers and, 51; background expectation affects and, 135; contemporary physics and, 232–33; continuity concept and, 134–35; data dependence upon theory in, 135–37;